RETAIL THERAPY:
MOOD-ALLEVIATIVE SHOPPING
BEHAVIOR AMONG WOMEN

Chandandeep Kaur

ACKNOWLEDGEMENT

The present research would not have been successfully completed without the direct or indirect support and encouragement of many people, to whom I feel indebted. Today is the time to acknowledge their help. Before that, I would like to thank Almighty for giving me the opportunity, strength and ability to undertake and complete my research work. I would also like to thank University Grants Commission (UGC) for providing financial support to researchers to comfortably carry out research.

Teachers and mentors have been regarded as the true advisors who show correct path and instill a love for learning among their students. Here, words would fall short to thank my supervisor, Dr. Jasveen Kaur (Head of the Department, University Business School, Guru Nanak Dev University, Amritsar), for her dedicated guidance and analytical insights towards my work. Her intellectual discussions have always been brainstorming and have encouraged critical reasoning.

I am grateful to some of the other academicians as well, who have directly or indirectly supported me during my doctoral journey. To name a few- Dr. Piyush Kumar Sinha (Professor, Indian Institute of Management, Ahmedabad); Dr. Subhadip Roy (Associate Professor, Indian Institute of Management, Ahmedabad); Dr. Sandeep Kapur (Comptroller, Punjab Agriculture University, Ludhiana and Professor, Department of Business Management, Punjab Agriculture University), Dr. Neeraj Kaushik (Associate Professor and Head, Department of Business Administration, National Institute of Technology, Kurukshetra); and Dr. Baljinder Kaur (Assistant Professor, Lyallpur Khalsa College, Jalandhar).

I would also, in general, like to thank all the faculty members and the administrative staff of the University Business School, Guru Nanak Dev University, Amritsar and to the library staff of Bhai Gurdas Library of Guru Nanak Dev University, Amritsar, for being cooperative and kind enough to extend any kind of help needed on their part. In addition, I would also like to acknowledge the support of various external libraries including that of Punjab Technical University Jalandhar, Indian Institute of Management Ahmedabad, Management Development Institute Gurgaon etc.

My sincere thanks to Dr. Kim K. P. Johnson (Professor Emerita, Department of Design, Housing and Apparel, University of Minnesota), co-author of the retail therapy scale used in the present research. Through countless e-mail communications, Dr. Johnson has selflessly supported and helped me in clarifying on various issues related to the concept of retail therapy.

I also appreciate the cooperation extended by different colleges, government/ non-government offices etc. to allow me for collecting data from their employees and also the patience of all the study respondents in filling out the questionnaires.

My acknowledgement would be incomplete if I only thank my academic supporters. It has been the whole-hearted support and motivation from my family and friends that encouraged me to carry out the research work enthusiastically. I firstly wish to pay my heartfelt thanks to my parents, S. Harbhajan Singh and Late Mrs. Ravinder Pal Kaur, who always emphasized on the importance of studies and extended high emotional support. Losing my mother during the tenure of Ph.D. has been the greatest loss. But her life-lessons and blessings have always remained with me and motivated me to complete my work passionately.

I wish to sincerely thank my In-laws, S. Manjeet Singh and Mrs. Manjeet Kaur, for taking care of my needs throughout the PhD tenure and also happily and altruistically raising my son. I would especially like to thank my mother in-law for managing the home and family in my absence, while never letting me feel any guilt for the same.

My whole-hearted love and thanks to my husband, S. Gagandeep Singh, who has been my greatest strength and support throughout my tenure and who selflessly allowed me to stay away from home and complete this full-time degree. It has been his continuous pushing that never let my morale go down.

I would like to extend my gratitude to my sister, Gagandeep Kaur, for being my close friend and extending emotional support whenever and wherever required. At the same time, I would also like to thank my brother, sister-in-law and brother-in-law for their moral support during the research journey.

Biggest thanks to my son, Manraj Singh, who showed the greatest level of patience and adjustment in my absence. His sacrifice has been the greatest source of power for me to work hard and complete my work. His unconditional love for me has been my strength throughout the years put in for Ph.D. I, in fact, dedicate this thesis to my son.

At last, I would extend my gratitude to all my friends and colleagues who have been a continuous source of encouragement for me and have morally supported me during the tenure. Closest ones among them being Gurleen Kaur, Dr. Harpreet Kaur, Dr. Nidhi Bhagat, Priya Mehndiratta, Dr. Jaspreet Kaur, Kanwalroop Kaur, Rupinder Kaur, Ishleen Kaur Kohli, Dr. Balpreet Kaur and Dr. Kiranjot Kaur. I especially thank my dear friends Dr. Baljit Kaur, Dr. Abha Bhalla, Navneet Kaur and Dr. Mandeep Kaur Ghuman for their academic support as well.

Chandandeep Kaur

TABLE OF CONTENTS

LIST OF TABLES

LIST OF FIGURES

ABBREVIATIONS

CCB	:	Compensatory Consumption Behavior
IBT	:	Impulse Buying Tendency
TSM	:	Therapeutic Shopping Motivation
TSV-P	:	Therapeutic Shopping Value- Positive Reinforcement
TSV-N	:	Therapeutic Shopping Value- Negative Mood Reduction
TSO	:	Therapeutic Shopping Outcomes
SEM	:	Structural Equation Modeling
IPIP	:	International Personality Item Pool
EFA	:	Exploratory Factor Analysis
CFA	:	Confirmatory Factor Analysis
MLE	:	Maximum Likelihood Estimation
GFI	:	Goodness-of-Fit Index
AGFI	:	Adjusted Goodness-of-Fit Index
RMSEA	:	Root Mean Square Error of Approximation
SRMR	:	Standardized Root Mean Residual
CFI	:	Comparative Fit Index
CR	:	Composite Reliability
AVE	:	Average Variance Extracted
MSV	:	Marginal Shared Variance
ASV	:	Average Shared Variance
LB	:	Lower Bound
UB	:	Upper Bound
AMOS	:	Analysis of Moment Structures
AGFI	:	Adjusted Goodness of Fit Index
TLI	:	Tucker-Lewis Index
SPSS	:	Statistical Package for the Social Sciences

INTRODUCTION

CHAPTER-1

INTRODUCTION

'Retail Therapy' refers to the act of going on a shopping spree to alleviate negative mood (Kang, 2009). It is a consumption behavior that is engaged in to cope with stress or depression, caused by some negative event that a person is either unwilling to or unable to tackle directly (Woodruffe, 2001). Consequently, she (/he) uses shopping or buying as an indirect means to reduce the tension and feel relaxed (Woodruffe, 2001). Shopping activity works as a coping mechanism that generates happiness in short-run (Hama, 2001; Kang, 2009; Atalay & Meloy, 2011), and enhances psychological well-being in the long-run (Kang & Johnson, 2011). Different types of therapeutic benefits offered by shopping include- distraction, escape, indulgence, relaxation, sensory stimulation, social connection etc. (Luomala, 2002; Lee, 2013).

As per the existing literature and based on the survey reports of various expert agencies' websites (e.g. ebates.com, dendyneville.co.uk, addictionexperts.co.uk, creditkarma.com, etc.), it has been found that the usage of shopping for therapeutic reasons is more common in western countries like U.S. and U.K. This is mainly because of the developed retail market in these countries, which offers wider product choice to shoppers as well as gives them an entertaining and pleasurable shopping environment (McVeigh, 2000). However, the adoption of retail therapy in less developed or developing countries, has so far, not been much acknowledged. The research in this field has also been limited in these countries. The present study has been an effort in this direction. It has advanced the knowledge regarding usage of retail therapy among shoppers in India, which is a country with a different kind of retail environment and cultural background as compared to the developed countries.

Another important observation, based on the previous literature, has been that women engage more in retail therapy as compared to men (Luomala, 2002, D'Souza, 2012). They feel an emotional connection with shopping and believe that shopping can help them in overcoming any kind of stress that they experience in their day-to-day life (Luomala, 2002; Arnold & Reynolds, 2003; Noble, 2006; Kang & Ahn, 2014).

1

Following this, the present research has also been focused on women shoppers only. The study begins with a general understanding of the usage of shopping as a coping mechanism by the Indian women and then further determines different factors that encourage the adoption of such behavior. The specific focus has been on one's personal characteristics that can help predict indulgence in retail therapy. Apart from this, the therapy shopping trip behavior of those women, who actually engage in retail therapy, has also been examined.

The present chapter covers general overview about the meaning of retail therapy, its prevalence and adoption in different countries, rationale for studying it in Indian context and all the related stuff that helps in enhancing conceptual clarification of this shopping behavior. The chapter has been organized in different sections. Section 1.1 explains the concept of retail therapy. Section 1.2 clarifies on the linkages of retail therapy with other related types of shopping behaviors. Section 1.3 explains the prevalence of retail therapy in different countries. Section 1.4 and 1.5 highlight the importance of retail therapy from the perspective of women and from retailers' and marketers' perspective, respectively. Section 1.6 presents the relevance of studying retail therapy in Indian context. This is followed by Section 1.7 that lists out the different objectives of the present research. Finally, the chapter-wise organization of the thesis has been shown in Section 1.8.

1.1 CONCEPT OF RETAIL THERAPY

Within the existing literature, the concept of retail therapy has mainly been explained through two approaches- the 'Compensatory Consumption Approach' and 'Mood-Alleviative Approach'.

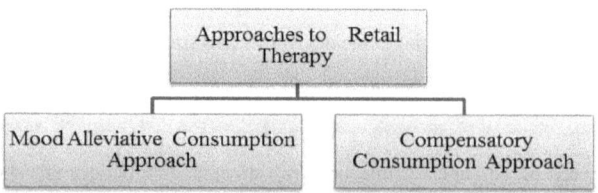

Fig 1.1: Approaches to Retail Therapy (based on previous literature)

2

Both the approaches to retail therapy have been explained in detail as under:

1.1.1 Compensatory Consumption Approach:

As compensatory consumption, retail therapy refers to the use of shopping as compensation for some 'lack' or 'psychological deficiency' in life, that cannot be satisfied with primary fulfillment. Accordingly, shopping is used as a substitute to that 'lack' (Woodruffe, 1997; Woodruffe, 2001; Yurchisin et al., 2006; Yurchisin et al. 2008). In words of Woodruffe (2001),

"Compensatory behavior is engaged in by individuals in response to a need or a 'lack' which they are unable or unwilling to satisfy directly so they seek and use an alternative means of fulfillment. When this alternative need satisfaction takes the form of consumption activity, this is termed compensatory consumption."

Compensatory consumption may be motivated by two different types of factors i.e. 1) internal, and 2) external factors. The internal factors are mostly related to 'self' e.g. self-discrepancy, self-anxiety, lack of self-esteem etc. (Woodruffe, 2001; Mandel et al., 217). On the other hand, external factors include relationship issues and situational factors (Woodruffe, 2001). Further, all these factors may either be 1) episodic (e.g. poor performance at an exam, a boring day, fight with someone etc.), or 2) ongoing (e.g. continuous poor relations with partner, issues related to one's physical appearance like short height, being skinny etc.). Compensatory consumption is not necessarily motivated by temporary negative mood, but may also be motivated by deeper psychological issues (Woodruffe, 2001; Yurchisin et al., 2008; Mandel et al., 2017).

1.1.2 Mood-Alleviative Consumption Approach:

From the mood-alleviative perspective, retail therapy refers to the "consumption behavior, including shopping and buying, that individuals engage in to improve their negative mood" (Kang, 2009). Retail therapy is used as a fix for negative mood caused by reasons like- feeling lonely or bored, quarrel with someone, a bad day at work etc. (Luomala, 2002; Kang, 2009). It may be resorted to for gaining sense of control, seeking hedonic or utilitarian benefits, social interaction, distraction, relaxation etc. (Luomala, 2002; Kang & Johnson, 2011; Rick et al., 2014; Lee, 2013).

3

Compensatory consumption is, in fact, a wider term that includes mood-alleviative shopping also (Kang, 2009). As such, within the existing literature, the mood-alleviative perspective has been more commonly used to define retail therapy as compared to the compensatory consumption approach (e.g. Luomala, 2002; Kang & Johnson, 2010; Atalay & Meloy, 2011; Rick et al., 2014; Cifci & Ekinci, 2018). Accordingly, for the present research also, the term 'retail therapy' has been used to mean 'mood-alleviative shopping' only, and not 'compensatory consumption/ shopping'.

In order to better understand as to how retail therapy works towards mood-alleviation; it is first important to understand its basic elements including- mood and its types, role of mood in consumer behavior, managing of mood through shopping, and the relation of mood-management with coping. These aspects have been explained as under:

➢ **Meaning and types of mood:** Mood is an affective state, which is transient, generalized and not directed to a particular target object (Gardner, 1985; Schwarz & Clore, 1988). It is a relatively long-lasting feeling state. Usually, people experience a particular mood without exactly knowing its source or cause (Gendolla et al., 2007). It has strong motivational power, which can affect a person's thoughts as well as behavior (Isen, 2001; Schwarz, 1990).

According to Luomala (2001), mood states can be of three basic types- (i) positive, (ii) neutral and (iii) negative. The negative mood can further be of three types- (a) Irritation (annoyance, hostility, agitation and frustration), (b) Stress (anxiety, distress, nervousness, uneasiness, worry and restlessness) and (c) Dejection (depression, sadness, misery, unhappiness, woe etc.). Irritation is a milder version of anger; stress belongs to the family of fear; while dejection relates to sadness (Luomala, 2001). People usually get irritated due to actions of others or due to circumstances i.e. they do not consider themselves to be responsible for the negative state of affairs (Luomala, 2001).

Stress, on the other hand, is experienced when there is some kind of uncertainty or complexity in the situation, and the person concerned has fear of losing control on it

4

(Luomala, 2001). Stress has been found to affect every person in every facet of life (Farrell et al., 2017); only its reasons and sources may be different e.g. younger generation may have more of school related stress issues, middle aged experience work-related issues more and older generation experiences more of health-related issues (Chen et al., 2017). The third type of negative mood i.e. Dejection, is the strongest amongst the three. The person experiencing dejection or depression usually feels paralyzed by the situation and shows more of passive behavior (Luomala, 2001).

➢ **Role of mood in consumer behavior:** Mood state of a person has been found to have a strong impact on their shopping decisions and behavior (Babin & Darden, 1996). It has been observed that in-store positive mood leads to increased spending on the part of the shoppers. It positively affects approach behavior, satisfaction and even re-purchase intention (Osman et al., 2014). Negative mood, on the other hand, has been found to negatively affect the satisfaction level with a retailer (Babin & Darden, 1996).

Within the consumer behavior research, the role of mood has usually been studied either as 'an intervening situational variable' and or as 'an object of control' (luomala, 1998). Most of the traditional research on mood has been limited to studying of mood as an intervening situational variable. Researchers have found that the in-store factors like music, design and display etc. first affect the mood and emotions of the shoppers, which in turn affect their actual behavior (Luomala, 1998; Turley & Milliman, 2000; Chang et al., 2011).

Apart from examining mood as an intervening situational variable, mood has also been studied as an object of control, wherein its self-regulatory power has been examined (Luomala, 1998). According to this perspective, mood acts as a motivator behind shopping. People consciously engage in shopping activity to get themselves relieved from negative mood. Sometimes, they even do so for maintaining or enhancing positive mood (Kang, 2009; Lee, 2013).

➢ **Mood-management and coping:** 'Mood management' refers to a conscious effort to regulate one's mood with the intention of achieving its desired level/state (Chen & Pham, 2019). In general, people have been found to be inherently motivated to

5

preserve and enhance positive mood (/maximizing pleasure) and alleviate negative mood (/minimizing pain) (Cornwell et al., 2014; Taquet et al., 2015). Following this principle, they try to engage themselves in activities that can help in maintaining this balance (Penley et al., 2002; Chen et al., 2017).

The concept of 'Coping' is also very closely related to mood-management in the sense that it is mainly focused on conscious efforts to reduce stress and improve mood (Chen & Pham, 2019). People may try to manage/cope with stress and other negative moods either by managing the problem at hand (problem-focused coping) or by using any indirect ways to overcome the negative mood caused by the problem (emotion-focused coping) (Lazarus & Folkman, 1984; Chen et al., 2017). Some of the emotion-focused strategies may include- watching television, going out for a movie, meeting friends, consuming hedonic food items, cognitively reappraising the situation, seeking social support, helping others etc. (Miedziun & Czabała, 2015; Chen et al., 2017).

➢ **Role of shopping in mood-management:** Shopping activity (i.e. retail therapy) has been regarded as one of the important mood-management techniques that have the ability of providing immediate relief to the person concerned (Woodruffe, 2001; Zheng & Peng, 2014). It is an emotion-focused coping strategy that helps in escaping from the stressful situation and regain control (Hama, 2001; Burke, 2018). It works on the dynamic mood theory, wherein people try to reduce the discrepancy between their current and desired mood state (Andrade, 2005). They indulge in shopping expecting that their current negative mood would change and they would feel better. As such, lonely individuals seek social connection through shopping; bored shoppers seek sensory stimulation; stressed out shoppers seek distraction through shopping etc. (Luomala, 2002; D'Souza, 2012; Lee, 2013).

1.2 LINKAGES OF RETAIL THERAPY TO OTHER RELATED SHOPPING BEHAVIOR TYPES

The term retail therapy has, many a times, being confused with various other types of emotional shopping behaviors. First amongst them is compensatory consumption, which has already been explained in section 1.1. The following sections

6

explain the linkages of retail therapy to other related shopping behaviors including compulsive buying, impulse buying, self-gifting, hedonic shopping etc. This has helped in presenting the distinctness of retail therapy and conceptualizing it in a better way.

1.2.1   Retail Therapy and Compulsive Buying:

Compulsive buying is a behavioral disorder wherein an individual goes on making continuous purchases regardless of the financial, social or other consequences (Ergin, 2010). It is followed by an increased discomfort and impatience to spend more and more money on material items (Black, 2007). Compulsive buying has been regarded as a maladaptive shopping behavior with many ill consequences. In the field of Psychiatry, it has been regarded as one of the diseases and an impulse control disorder, where the patients believe that buying for something would alleviate negative mood. Thus, they keep on indulging in shopping again and again (Workman & Paper, 2010). This repetitive behavior gives only temporary relief and leads to detrimental effects in long-run e.g. disturbed financial condition, disturbed inter-personal relations, increased dissatisfaction from oneself etc. (Joji & Raveendran, 2007; Workman & Paper, 2010).

Some of the known characteristics of compulsive buyers include- anxiety (those at the higher side of the continuum mostly indulge in shopping to combat anxiety, while those at the lower side do so for reasons such as boredom); perfectionism (they have higher levels of expectations for personal achievements); lack of self-esteem; fantasy and day-dreaming; lack of impulse control; probability of other compulsive disorders; lack of self-confidence; seeking social approval; lack of internal locus of control; depression experience; use of more avoidance coping strategies; denial; materialism; disturbed family background such as- compulsive disorder amongst any of the other family members, childhood ignorance etc. (Nair, 2004).

Retail therapy is not a part of the definition of compulsive buying. However, a major connection between the two is that both are motivated by negative mood. As such, many researchers have used the items related to retail therapy while designing compulsive buying scale (See Kang, 2009). However, both the shopping types are evidently different from each other. Some of the differentiating points include- 1) Retail therapy usually has positive outcomes that are also retained for a sufficiently long time;

7

whereas, compulsive buying is usually accompanied by immediate high positive emotions, but highly negative emotions in long-run (Workman & Paper, 2010); 2) Compulsive shoppers usually possess one or more additional compulsive habits e.g. compulsive gambling, compulsive eating, etc.; whereas, this is not so in case of retail therapy (Workman & Paper, 2010); 3) Compulsive buying has been regarded as one of the psychological disorders (Ergin, 2010), whereas retail therapy has been found to be a normal shopping behavior (Lee, 2013); 4) Buying for something is an essential part of compulsive shopping, whereas it is not a necessary condition in retail therapy. Rather, therapy shoppers may even feel happy after window shopping (Kang, 2009; Kaur & Kaur, 2016); 5) The products bought during compulsive buying usually lose importance immediately after purchase and the act is followed by guilt; whereas in retail therapy, the products bought usually carry good feelings and when they are used in future, they remind the shoppers of the pleasurable shopping experience (Kang, 2009).

1.2.2 Retail Therapy and Self-Gifting:

Self-gifting, in simple terms, refers to buying a product as a gift for oneself (Mortimer et al., 2015). Since, the product indicates a gift; it carries a special value for the shopper. Self-gifts mainly possess three types of characteristics i.e. Exchange, Communication and Specialness (Mick & DeMoss, 1990). The 'exchange' feature indicates that a goal is exchanged for a self-gift e.g. gifting oneself for achieving a set target. The second feature i.e. 'communication' indicates that the person concerned himself acts as the sender as well as receiver of the symbolic message communicated through a self-gift. The last feature i.e. 'specialness' refers to the role of self-gift as an emotional nutrient that helps in mood-management (Mick & DeMoss, 1990).

People may engage in self-gifting followed by different reasons like hedonic, reward, celebratory, therapeutic etc. (Mortimer et al., 2015). They may buy gifts for themselves when they have achieved something (e.g. a business target) and want to celebrate this achievement, or on particular occasions e.g. birthday or Christmas etc. At times, self-gifts may also be bought to resolve any self-discrepancy issues i.e. filling a gap between what one actually is and what she(/he) desires to be (Kleine et al., 1995). Similarly, self-gifts may also be bought for therapeutic reasons such as buying smart clothes to overcome lack of confidence, rewarding oneself with an expensive gift for sacrifices made over a period of time etc. (Mortimer et al., 2015). It has been observed that, many a times, therapy shoppers like to buy self-gifts to pamper themselves and feel relaxed (Mick et al., 1992; Luomala, 1998; Atalay & Meloy, 2011; Mortimer et al., 2015). Thus, retail therapy and self-gifting are closely related to each other.

1.2.3   Retail Therapy and Recreational/ Hedonic Shopping:

Hedonic shopping is related to the multi-sensory and emotive aspects of shopping experience. It is focused on emotional quality of products and the shopping experience as a whole (Voss et al., 2003). Hedonic shoppers usually find pleasure in browsing in stores and getting knowledge of new fashion trends (Buttner et al., 2013). They are attracted towards sensory elements present in retail atmosphere. They are less concerned with the price/quality of a product and are more influenced by its packaging and display (Babin et al., 1994; Arnold & Reynolds, 2003; Buttner et al., 2013).

Many of these features of hedonic shopping are also present in retail therapy, thus creating a common link between the two shopping behaviors (Kang, 2009). Both hedonic and therapy shoppers try to explore the fun side of shopping and are attracted to the emotional elements in the retail environment. Arnold and Reynolds (2003) identified six dimensions of hedonic shopping motivations i.e., adventure, social, gratification, idea, role, and value shopping. Out of these, the gratification motivation represents retail therapy. Kang (2009) also stated that retail therapy belongs to the family of hedonic shopping and that hedonic shoppers seek therapeutic benefits from shopping.

1.2.4   Retail Therapy and Impulse Buying:

Impulse buying refers to shopping without thinking. According to Rook (1987), "Impulse buying occurs when a consumer experiences a sudden, often persistent urge to buy something immediately. The impulse to buy is hedonically complex and stimulates emotional conflict. Also, impulse buying is prone to occur with diminished regard for its consequences". The most important element in impulse buying is that it is a spontaneous buying decision. As such, impulsive buyers think about immediate gratification only and are less concerned about the delayed consequences of the purchase (Baumeister, 2002; Gasiorowska, 2011).

According to Gasiorowska (2011), impulse buying may be led by many factors including the individual traits, situational factors and moderating factors. The individual factors may include impulse buying tendency, optimum level of stimulation, temporal orientation, gender, money attitude, recreational shopping tendency etc. The situational factors may be- emotions at the time of buying, atmospherics, in-store stimuli, comfort and easiness of shopping etc. The moderating factors may be- level of self-control, direct access to money, type of money used e.g. credit/debit/cash/online, normative evaluation (i.e. what is right or wrong as per societal norms) etc.

Negative mood-alleviation has been observed to be one the motivations behind impulse buying (Baumeister, 2002; Kang, 2009). It has been found that sad and stressed out shoppers usually engage in impulse buying because their focus is more on mood-alleviation. As a result, they lose focus on impulse control and start purchasing items without giving much attention to the outcomes of such purchase (Atalay & Meloy, 2011). At times, people even intentionally behave impulsively if they believe that this would lead to a mood-lift (Baumeister, 2002). Impulse buying usually gives an immediate high to the shoppers, although many of them might regret their decision afterwards (D'Souza, 2012).

The above discussion reflects that retail therapy is a distinct concept, though it shares many common features with other types of emotional shopping behaviors. In fact, impulse buying, hedonic shopping, self-gifting etc. seem to be the tools and tactics used during retail therapy to help in mood-alleviation.

1.3   PREVALENCE OF RETAIL THERAPY

The tendency of using shopping for therapeutic reasons is more common in western countries. The concept mainly originated from U.S. The Chicago Tribune mentioned the term in 1980's, stating that people go to stores to improve their mood (Reyhle, Jan. 8, 2014). In 2013, Ebates.com carried out a survey of 1000 people in U.S., in which it was found that more than half of them indulged in shopping for mood-alleviative reasons (64 percent among them being women). A survey by Yarrow (2013), in Times Magazine, also showed that about 52 percent of the Americans indulged in retail therapy, where more than 62 percent shopped for cheering themselves up.

In a later survey of 2000 Americans, by Paul (2017), it was found that, in a year, more than one fifth of the products were purchased for therapy reasons, for which an average amount of $1652 was spent. In another survey by creditkarma.com (2017), it was found that more than half of the U.S. respondents were caught in the cycle of stress spending. 48 percent of them shopped following some financial stress, 38 percent shopped due to emotional issues like anxiety, depression etc., whereas, 31 percent did so to overcome negative feelings due to family stress. It was, however, found that majority of the people (83%) regret their purchases afterwards.

Apart from U.S., retail therapy is also common in other countries e.g. the Greenpeace study (2016) about the shopping behavior of people in China, Hong Kong, Taiwan, Italy and Germany, found that 31 percent of the Chinese and 14 percent of the Germans shop when they are feeling bored or lonely. It was found that people in these countries are following the lifestyle of Americans, but the results are not positive. About 51 percent of the clothing purchased goes unworn and most of the people, who shop for therapy, regret their purchase within 24 hours. Since, China has the world's largest e-commerce market; the concept of e-tail therapy has also gained huge popularity there. In fact, in China, retail therapy has become so popular that it has been entitled as a national pastime (agencychina.com, March, 6, 2018).

A survey by dendyneville.co.uk (Jan, 16, 2018) found that about four-tenth of the people in U.K. use shopping activity for cheering themselves up. In fact, many of the people in U.K. are also showing compulsive symptoms affecting up to 10 percent of the population (addictionexperts.co.uk). A report by Tran (2019) showed that people in U.K. are following similar shopping pattern as that of those in North America. About 80 percent of their shopping is done on impulse and 4 out of 10 do so in the name of retail therapy. In Britain also, retail therapy has become the most pleasurable leisure activity. The reason is mainly attributed to the modernization of the retailing sector, which has offered beautiful and attractive shopping options to the shoppers (McVeigh, 2000).

As far as usage of retail therapy in India is concerned, the term 'therapy' is, now days, quite commonly used in magazine articles or promotional advertisements etc. e.g.

in year 2019, lifestyleasia.com published an article listing out seven best stores in India where people can enjoy both retail therapy and food. Similarly, an article in the retail section of 'The Economic Times' newspaper (dated October 13, 2019), described how online and offline stores in India are promoting retail therapy by building up experiential zones in their stores. An article in Hindustan Times (dated September 2, 2019) also criticized retail therapy. It mentioned that, although, retail therapy can help in alleviating sad mood, but can also lead to negative consequences in the form of reduced savings, increased debt etc. To sum up, usage of the term retail therapy is becoming common in India also and it seems people are adopting this practice.

1.4 ROLE OF RETAIL THERAPY IN WOMEN'S LIVES

Previous research has highlighted that women are more inclined towards the emotional features of shopping. They engage in shopping not only for utilitarian reasons; rather also to get a break from their overscheduled lives or to deal with boredom or loneliness (Woodruffe, 1996; Underhill, 1999; Luomala, 2002; Arnold & Reynolds, 2003). Shopping gives them energy and a feeling of control (Woodruffe, 1997). The studies like 'Why women go shopping when they're fed up and other stories' (Woodruffe, 1997); 'Consumer shopping behaviour and the role of women in shopping- A literature review' (Kumaravel, 2017); 'Enhancing older females' psychological well-being through social shopping.......' (Kang & Ahn, 2014); 'Indian women and compensatory consumption......' (Singh, 2017) etc. are all the examples where the emotional role played by shopping in women's lives has been clearly stated. It is not that men do not go for therapy shopping, but the therapeutic values derived from shopping have been found to be more strong and effective in case of women (Dittmar & Drury, 2000; Noble, 2006).

1.5 IMPORTANCE OF RETAIL THERAPY FROM RETAILERS' AND MARKETERS' VIEW-POINT

The act of therapy shopping is not only beneficial for the shoppers; rather it also carries special importance for the retailers and marketers as well (Lee, 2013). This is mainly because of the unique behavioral characteristics exhibited by the therapy shoppers e.g. frequently visiting shopping places; making more impulse purchases when in sad mood; buying more self-gifts; spending more time in browsing and trying on different items etc. (Kang, 2009; D'Souza, 2012). Also, it has been found that, many of the therapy shoppers are store loyal. They like to visit the same retail stores every time they are in a down mood (Kang, 2009). Thus, if retailers can exactly know as to what makes these shoppers happy; they can work on those issues and increase the chances of retaining therapy shoppers in the long-run. In this regard, previous literature has highlighted that some of the retail elements can be emphasized upon to help therapy shoppers in mood-alleviation e.g. courteous behavior of the employees, attractive displays, offers and discounts, store ambience etc. (D'Souza, 2012; Lee, 2013; Surendran & Vardhan, 2014).

1.6 RELEVANCE OF STUDYING RETAIL THERAPY IN INDIAN CONTEXT

Carrying out a research on retail therapy in Indian context has been found to be relevant mainly because of two reasons i.e. uniqueness of the Indian retail market as compared to the western countries and different lifestyle and culture of Indian women. These reasons have been explained in the following sub-sections:

1.6.1 The Indian Retail Market:

According to the previous literature, establishment of modern retail formats offering huge variety and discounts to the shoppers, has been regarded as one of the major reasons for adoption and popularity of retail therapy in western countries (Gillan, 2019; Lee, 2013). As such, the Indian retail market has also undergone some major transformations over past few years. Earlier, there used to be only unorganized market with small shops being managed single-handedly by their owners. However, with time, the market developed a lot and witnessed tremendous changes in its structure and functioning (Kaur & Kaur, 2013; India Brand Equity Foundation's retail report, 2017). Especially, after the economic reforms for liberalization and globalization, the Indian retail sector has been left open for the entry of private players, corporate players and international players (Bansal & Yadav, 2008). Today's Indian retail market comprises of modern formats like departmental stores, specialty stores, hypermarkets, supermarkets, malls and so on (Sinha & Uniyal, 2005; Tanwar et al., 2011). Indian consumers have also shown overwhelming acceptance to these formats (Kaur, 2013). Further, entry of foreign players created an altogether new kind of retail environment while offering huge discounts, faster billing system, creative loyalty programs, and an added entertainment element to shopping (Ghosh et al., 2010; Srivastava et al., 2012). This, however, also posed some challenges to the existing Indian retailers and reminded them of focusing on the 7 P's of marketing for their successful survival (Kaur, 2014). Such up-gradation has led to a sea change in the shopping style and behavior of the shoppers too. They are now not only concerned with fulfilling their product needs; rather they have also started seeking more entertainment and emotional value (Kaur & Kaur, 2013; Kiran & Jhamb, 2011).

The uniqueness of the Indian retail market lies in the fact that, despite all the developments, the traditional market still dominates over the modern organized market (India Brand Equity Foundation's retail report, 2017). Many people still choose to go to local bazaars for shopping. Apart from this, in India, shopping is more of a familial activity. A large proportion of people like to shop with families and visit malls to spend their family leisure time and feel relaxed (D'Souza, 2012). These features of Indian retail market make it quite different from that of the western countries, where the retail markets are much modern and developed. Accordingly, it seems to be meaningful to study the adoption of retail therapy in context of shoppers from the Indian market.

1.6.2 The Culture, Lifestyle and Status of Indian Women:

The lifestyle and status of women in India is much different from that of women in western countries. Comparatively, Indian women enjoy less independence. Although, country laws might support them; they usually lack support from their families and society (Srinivasan, 2013). Even when large number of Indian women are earning on their own, many of them still depend upon others for their life decisions (whether financial or non-financial). Further, the condition has been found to be more disadvantageous for housewives, who get very less financial independence and also bear more societal pressures and restrictions (Solanki et al., 2019). They mostly get less time for themselves and devote more time to their families (D'Souza, 2012). Primarily, they are responsible for managing the house, but enjoy very less freedom to move out or

14

take major decisions related to their personal requirements e.g. decisions related to their health care, visiting parents, buying expensive items like jewelry, going to market without permission etc. (Kishor & Gupta, 2004).

In most of the middle class families, men usually give only limited money to their wives, while at the same time, expecting them to rationally manage the monthly household expenses (Bains, 2010, 'The Tribune'). Due to all these factors, many of the Indian women go through depression and anxiety disorders. Over and above, they (especially housewives) also get very few coping options to deal with their problems. They love to shop, but they lack independence in that also. Even there are many of the women in India who feel that they have to justify their purchases to other family members (Sheth & Vittal, 2007).

It follows from the above discussion that, as compared to the modern western women; Indian women might be enjoying less independence in making use of shopping for mood-alleviative reasons. Further, if they do so, their lifestyle and culture is most likely to be reflected in their shopping behavior.

Taking into consideration the above mentioned points, it is expected that some new insights can be found by carrying out retail therapy research in India. Some of the research questions that the present study has tried to answer, include- How Indian women handle stress or deal with negative mood situations? What type of coping/mood-alleviative activities they use? Whether and to what extent they use shopping for mood-alleviation? What is their belief about shopping as a therapeutic activity? What outcomes they experience after shopping for therapeutic reasons? How they behave during a typical retail therapy trip etc.

1.7 OBJECTIVES OF THE RESEARCH STUDY

The objectives of the present research have been:

1. To explore different types of coping strategies/activities adopted by Indian women to overcome negative mood (with special focus on determining the usage of shopping for coping).

15

2.   To analyze the retail therapy behavior of women in India. Within that, to analyze the-

➤ Therapeutic shopping motivations

➤ Therapeutic shopping values, and

➤ Therapeutic shopping outcomes.

3.   To assess the influential impact of personal characteristics on retail therapy behavior of women in India. Within that, to assess the impact of-

➤ Demographic characteristics

➤ Big-five personality traits

➤ Chronic shopping orientation, and

➤ Impulse buying tendency.

4.   To analyze the retail therapy trip behavior of women therapy shoppers in India. Within that, to analyze-

➤ The shopping decisions undertaken by Indian women during a retail therapy trip (e.g. decisions relating to retail format, products, payment mode, person accompanying, time and money etc.), and

➤ The role of shopping process elements in mood-alleviation (including the role of retail attributes).

1.8   ORGANIZATION OF THE THESIS

The research work of the present study has been organized into eight chapters. Chapter-1 i.e. the present chapter has given a detailed account of the concept of retail therapy, its connection to other related types of shopping behaviors, its prevalence in various countries, its importance in life of women and for the retailers and marketers and finally the reasons and rationale for studying this concept in the Indian context.

Chapter-2 presents the review of the previous literature. The review has been organized in different sections with each section representing literature for each of the objectives of the research. It covers the previous studies related to coping strategies used by people to deal with negative mood and also the usage of shopping activity as a coping strategy. Further, the literature related to the concept, motivations, therapeutic values and outcomes of retail therapy has been explained. This has been followed by the review related to the role of personal factors in retail therapy behavior. Finally, the previous research related to the shopping behavior exhibited by the therapy shoppers has been given. At the end of the chapter, different research gaps identified in the literature and the rationale for the present study has been presented.

Chapter-3 is related to the research methodology followed in the present research. It gives a detailed account of the objectives and scope of the study, the research design, details about the preliminary, pilot and final study data collection techniques and sample, details of the survey instrument used for the research, the reliability and validity measurements used, and finally the statistical techniques used to achieve the objectives of the research.

Chapter-4 covers the first objective of the research i.e. 'To explore different types of coping strategies/activities adopted by Indian women to overcome negative mood (with special focus on determining the usage of shopping for coping)'. It shows the data analysis results for the frequency of experiencing negative mood by women in India, different types of coping strategies used by them, usage of shopping as a coping strategy and the relation between frequency of experiencing negative mood and the frequency of using shopping for mood-alleviation.

Chapter-5 presents the data analysis results for the second objective of the research i.e. 'To analyze the retail therapy behavior of women in India'. It firstly shows the scale validation results for the retail therapy scale used in the study (developed by Kang, 2009). This has been done using exploratory and confirmatory factor analysis. This is followed by descriptive analysis for all the scale items along with the number of women agreeing or disagreeing to each of the items.

Chapter-6 covers the third objective of the research i.e. 'To examine the influential impact of personal characteristics on retail therapy behavior of women in India'. The chapter gives all the data analysis results for testing the impact of demographic variables, Big-five personality traits, shopping orientation and impulse buying tendency on retail therapy behavior. The data in this chapter has been analyzed using different techniques including- correlation analysis, independent sample t-test, one-way Anova, exploratory factor analysis, confirmatory factor analysis and path analysis.

Chapter-7 presents the data analysis results for the last objective of the research i.e. 'To analyze the retail therapy trip behavior of women therapy shoppers in India'. It answers different questions such as- the products bought by therapy shoppers for mood-alleviation; the shopping formats they like to visit; the payment mode they like to use; frequency of buying impulsively; time and money spend; the role that shopping environment plays in uplifting their mood etc. The analysis is followed by a comparison of the findings of the present study with that of the previous studies.

Chapter-8 shows the summary of the present research work. It also lists out different implications for the stakeholders including the customers, retailers/marketers and implications for consumer behavior literature. This is followed by giving an account of the limiting factors in the present study and directions for future research.

For the purpose of clarity and convenience, references related to works cited in every chapter have been given along with that chapter itself. Other studies that had helped in one or the other way in carrying out the present research, but not being cited as such, have been covered at the end of all the chapters, in the bibliography. The appendix I and II contain the questionnaire used for the data collection for the study and also the coding details for the scale items.

REFERENCES

1. Agarwal, M. (2019). *Retail therapy: A little good, lot of bad.* Hindustan Times (September 2, 2019), available at https://www.hindustantimes.com/business-news/ retail-therapy-a-little-good-lot-of-bad/story-YmsDQOhrhJSdOKq1KFWFjL.html.

2. agencychina.com (2018). Why China? China's shopping addiction (part 3/3) (March 6, 2018). Available at https://agencychina.com/blog/why-china-chinas-shopping-addiction-part3-3/.

3. Andrade, E. B. (2005). Behavioral consequences of affect: Combining evaluative and regulatory mechanisms. *Journal of Consumer Research*, 32(3), 355-362.

4. Arnold, M. J. & Reynolds, K. E. (2003). Hedonic shopping motivations. *Journal of Retailing,* 79(2), 77-95.

5. Atalay, A. S. & Meloy, M. G. (2011). When the going gets tough, the tough go shopping- An examination of self-gifting behaviour. *Advances in Consumer Research,* 33, 259-260.

6. Babin, B. J. & Darden, W. R. (1996). Good and bad shopping vibes: Spending and patronage satisfaction. *Journal of Business Research*, 35(3), 201–206.

7. Babin, B. J., Darden, W. R. & Griffin, M. (1994). Work and/or fun: Measuring hedonic and utilitarian shopping value. *Journal of Consumer Research*, 20(4), 644-656.

8. Bains, H. K. (2010). Cost of living quite high in Ludhiana (April 17, 2010). Available at https://www.tribuneindia.com/2010/20100417/edit.htm.

9. Bansal & Yadav (2008). An analytical study on mall shopping- Attitude and perception among young adults. *Synthesis*, 5(2).

10. Baumeister, R. F. (2002). Yielding to temptation: Self-control failure, impulsive purchasing, and consumer behavior. *Journal of Consumer Research*, 28(4), 670–676.

11. Black, D. W. (2007). A review of compulsive buying disorder. *World Psychiatry*, 6(1), 14–18.

12. Burke, K. (2018). The neuroscience behind retail therapy. *All Regis University Theses*. 864. https://epublications.regis.edu/theses/864

13. Buttner, O., Florack, A. & Goritz, A. S. (2013). Shopping orientation as a stable consumer disposition and its influence on consumers' evaluations of retailer communication. *European Journal of Marketing,* 48(5/6), 1026-1045.

14. Chang, H. J., Eckman, M. & Yan, R. N. (2011). Application of the stimulus-organism-response model to the retail environment: The role of hedonic motivation in impulse buying behavior. *The International Review of Retail, Distribution and Consumer Research*, 21(3), 233-249.

15. Chen, C. Y. & Pham, M. T. (2019). Affect regulation and consumer behavior. *Consumer Psychology Review*, 2, 114-144.

16. Chen, C. Y., Lee, L., & Yap, A. J. (2017). Control deprivation motivates acquisition of utilitarian products. *Journal of Consumer Research*, 43(6), 1031-1047.

17. Cifci, S. & Ekinci, Y. (2018). Undesirable effects of retail therapy on consumer emotions and consumer-based brand equity (CBBE). Paper presented at the *Management International Conference, Bled, Slovenia*, 30 May- 2 June, 2018, 169-176.

18. Cornwell, J. F., Franks, B. & Higgins, E. T. (2014). Truth, control, and value motivations: The "what," "how," and "why" of approach and avoidance. *Frontiers in Systems Neuroscience*, 8, 194.

19. creditkarma.com (2017). *Survey: More than half of U.S. respondents caught in cycle of stress spending* (November 16, 2017). Available at https://www.creditkarma.com/studies/i/stress-spending-study/.

20. D'Souza, D. (2012). *Retail therapy: A study in the Indian context to understand compensatory consumption and its implications on consumer's psyche*, Dissertation in partial fulfillment of the requirements for the Post Graduate Programme for Communications Management Diploma.

21. dendyneville.co.uk (2018). *UK consumers spending significant amounts on 'impulse buys', survey reveals* (January 16, 2018), available at https://www.dendyneville.co.uk/news/business-news/archive/article/2018/January/uk-consumers-spending-significant-amounts-on-impulse-buys-survey-reveals.

22. Dittmar, H. & Drury, J. (2000). Self-image – is it in the bag? A qualitative comparison between "ordinary" and "excessive" consumers. *Journal of Economic Psychology*, 21(2), 109–142.

23. Duttagupta, I. (2019). *Online and offline brands offering retail therapy now have a new category: experiential zones.* The Economic Times, October13, 2019.

24. Ebates.com (2013). Available at http://www.businesswire.com/news/home/20130402005600/en/Ebates-Survey-51.8-Americans-Engage-Retail-Therapy%E2%80%94.

25. Ergin, ElifAkagun (2010). Compulsive buying behavior tendencies: The case of Turkish consumers. *African Journal of Business Management*, 4(3), 333-338.

26. Farrell, A., Simpson, J., Carlson, E., Englund, M. & Sung, S. (2017). The impact of stress at different life stages on physical health and the buffering effects of maternal sensitivity. *Health Psychology*. 36(1).

27. Gardner, M. P. (1985). Mood states and consumer behavior: A critical review. *Journal of Consumer Research*, 281-300.

28. Gasiorowska, A. (2011). Gender as a moderator of temperamental causes of impulse buying tendency. *Journal of Customer Behaviour*, 10, 119-142.

29. Gendolla, G. H., Brinkmann, K. & Richter, M. (2007). *Mood, motivation, and performance: An integrative theory, research, and applications.* In Mood and Human Performance: Conceptual, Measurement, and Applied Issues. (Ed) Andrew M. Lane, 35-61.

30. Ghosh, P., Tripathi, V. & Kumar, A. (2010). Customer expectations of store attributes: A study of organized retail outlets in India. *Journal of Retail & Leisure Property*, 9(1), 75-87.

21

31. Gillan, J. (2019). *The changing psychology of shopping: Three trends set to shape retail.* The Drum (January 23, 2019). Available at https://www.thedrum.com/opinion/2019/01/23/the-changing-psychology-shopping-three-trends-set-shape-retail.

32. Greenpeace (2016). Available at https://theculturetrip.com/asia/china/articles/are-chinese-shoppers-using-retail-therapy-as-an-antidepressant/.

33. Hama, Y. (2001). Shopping as a coping behavior for stress. *Japanese Psychological Research, Special Issue- Consumer Behavior,* 43(4), 218-224.

34. https://www.addictionexperts.co.uk/shopping.html.

35. *India Brand Equity Foundation Retail Report (2017).* Available at https://www.ibef.org/ archives/industry/indian-retail-industry-analysis-reports/indian-retail-industry-analysis-january-2017.

36. Isen, A. M. (2001). An influence of positive affect on decision making in complex situations: Theoretical issues with practical implications. *Journal of Consumer Psychology,* 11(2), 75-85.

37. Joji, Alex N. & Raveendran, P.T. (2007). Compulsive buying behavior in Indian consumers and its impact on credit default- An emerging paradigm. *International Marketing Conference on Marketing & Society.*

38. Kang, J. & Ahn, M. (2014). Enhancing older females' psychological well-being through social shopping, social coping, and informal social activities. *Family and Consumer Sciences Research Journal*, 42(4), 341-357.

39. Kang, M. (2009). *Retail therapy: A qualitative investigation and scale development.* Doctoral dissertation, University of Minnesota.

40. Kang, M. & Johnson, K. K. P. (2010). Let's shop! Exploring the experiences of therapy shoppers. *Journal of Global Fashion Marketing,* 1(2), 71-79.

41. Kang, M. & Johnson, K. K. P. (2011). Retail therapy: Scale development. *Clothing and Textiles Research Journal,* 29 (1), 3-19.

42. Kaur, J. (2013). Customers perception towards global retailers influencing the Indian organized retailing. *The Indian Journal of Commerce*, Quarterly publication of the Indian Commerce Association, 66(3), 41-50.

43. Kaur, J. (2014). Role of FDI in restructuring retailing sector in India: Is it a blessing or curse- Opinion---retailers and customers. *International Conference on Management –"Changing Face of Modern Retail: The New Economic Order", GDGU-ICON, 2014*, 128-139. GD Goenka University, Gurgaon & Excel India Publishers, New Delhi.

44. Kaur, J. & Kaur, C. (2013). *The Indian retailing sector- Recent trends and future prospects.* Seminar proceedings "Building Competitiveness in Indian Manufacturing Sector", GNA Institute of Management and Technology, Phagwara, Punjab, India, ISBN: 978-81-921766-2-8, 185-191.

45. Kaur, J. & Kaur, C. (2016). *How they buy? –Analyzing the shopping behaviour of retail therapy shoppers.* Paper presented at International conference on Marketing, Technology and Society, at Indian Institute of Management, Kozhikode (Kelara), on September 29- October 1, 2016.

46. Kiran, R. & Jhamb, D. (2011). A strategic framework for consumer preferences towards emerging retail formats. *Journal of Emerging Knowledge on Emerging Markets,* 3(1), 437-453.

47. Kishor, S. & Gupta, K. (2004). Women's empowerment in India and its states: Evidence from the NFHS. *Economic and Political Weekly*, 39, 694-712.

48. Kleine, S., Kleine, R. & Allen, C. (1995). How is a possession 'me' or 'not me'? Characterizing types and an antecedent of material possession attachment. *Journal of Consumer Research*, 22, 327-43.

49. Kumaravel, R. (2017). Consumer shopping behaviour and the role of women in shopping- A literature review. *Research Journal of Social Science and Management,* 7, 50.

50. Lazarus, R. S. & Folkman, S. (1984). *Stress, appraisal, and coping.* Springer. New York. 40-48.

51. Lee, L. (2013). The emotional shopper: Assessing the effectiveness of retail therapy. *Foundations and Trends in Marketing,* 8(2), 69-145.

52. lifestyleasia.com (2019). *Eat, shop, love: 7 beautiful store where you can indulge in both retail therapy & food.* Lifestyle Asia (April 30, 2019). Available at https://www. lifestyleasia.com/ind/culture/architecture/the-most-beautiful-stores-in-indian-to-shop-and-eat-at/.

53. Luomala, H. T. (1998). Self-regulation of negative moods in a consumption context. Irritation-, stress-, and dejection-alleviative self-gift behaviours in focus. *Vaasa: Universitas Wasaensis.*

54. Luomala, H. T. (1998). A mood-alleviative perspective on self-gift behaviors: Stimulating consumer behavior theory development. *Journal of Marketing Management,* 14, 109–132.

55. Luomala, H. T. (2001). Consumption as therapy: A phenomenological inquiry into mood-alleviative consumer behaviors. *ACR Asia-Pacific Advances in Consumer Research,* 4.

56. Luomala, H. T. (2002). An empirical analysis of the practices and therapeutic power of mood-alleviative consumption in Finland. *Psychology & Marketing,* 19(10), 813-836.

57. Mandel, N., Rucker, D. D., Levav, J. & Galinsky, A. D. (2017). The compensatory consumer behaviour model: How self-discrepancies drive consumer behaviour. *Journal of Consumer Psychology,* 27(1), 133-146.

58. Mick, D. G. & DeMoss, M. (1990). Self-gifts: Phenomenological insights from four contexts. *Journal of Consumer Research,* 17(3), 322-32.

59. Mick, D. G., DeMoss, M. & Corinne, F. (1992). A projective study of motivations and meanings of self-gifts: Implications for retail management. *Journal of Retailing,* 68(2), 122-144.

60. Miedziun, P. & Czabała, J. C. (2015). Stress management techniques. *Archives of Psychiatry and Psychotherapy,* 4, 23–30.

61. Mortimer, G., Bougoure, U. S. & Fazal-E-Hasan, S. (2015). Development and validation of the self-gifting consumer behaviour scale: The self-gifting consumer behaviour scale. *Journal of Consumer Behaviour*, 14(3), 165–179.

62. Nair, K. (2004). *Compensatory consumption among modern Indian women: A phenomenological exploration*, Submitted in partial fulfillment of post-graduate diploma in communications, Mudra Institute of Communications, Ahmedabad.

63. Noble, S., Griffith, D. & Adjei, M. (2006). Drivers of local merchant loyalty: Understanding the influence of gender on shopping motives. *Journal of Retailing*, 82, 177–188.

64. Osman, S., Ong, F. S., Othman, M. N. & Khong, K. W. (2014). The mediating effect of mood on in-store behaviour among Muslim shoppers. *Journal of Islamic Marketing,* 5(2), 178-197.

65. Paul, S. (2017). *Americans spend $1,652 per year on retail therapy* (December 6, 2017), available at https://nypost.com/2017/12/06/americans-spend-1652-per-year-on-retail-therapy/.

66. Penley, J., Tomaka, J. & Wiebe, J. (2002). The association of coping to physical and psychological health outcomes: A meta-analytic review. *Journal of Behavioral Medicine,* 25(6), 551-603.

67. Reyhle, N. (2014). *The history of retail shopping: A millennium of change.* Retail Minded.com (January, 2014).

68. Rick, S. I., Pereira, B. & Burson, K. A. (2014). The benefits of retail therapy: Making purchase decisions reduces residual sadness. *Journal of Consumer Psychology*, 24(3), 373-380.

69. Rook (1987). The buying impulse. *The Journal of Consumer Research*, 14(2), 189-199.

70. Schwarz, N. & Clore, G. (1988). *How do I feel about it? Informative functions of affective states.* In book: Affect, Cognition, and Social Behavior, Publisher: Hogrefe, Editors: K. Fiedler, J.P. Forgas, 44-62.

71. Schwarz, N. (1990). *Feelings as information: Informational and motivational functions of affective states.* In E. T. Higgins & R. Sorrentino (Eds.), Handbook of Motivation and Comition: Foundations of social behavior, 2, 527-561. New York: Guilford Press.

72. Sheth, K. K. & Vital, l. (2007). *India: Shopping with the family.* The McKinsey Quarterly, 74-5.

73. Singh, S. (2017). Indian women and compensatory consumption: A confirmatory factor analysis approach. *International Journal of Engineering Technology Science and Research (IJETSR)*, 4(9), 19-31.

74. Sinha, P. K. & Uniyal, D. P. (2005). Using observational research for behavioral segmentation of shoppers. *Journal of Retailing and Consumer Services*, 12(1), 35-48.

75. Solanki, H. K., Kaur, A., Das, M., Awasthi, S. & Jain, S. (2019). Coping mechanism used by homemakers in Kumaon region (Uttarakhand, India) to deal with stress in their day-to-day life. *Journal of Family Medicine and Primary Care*, 1138-1144.

76. Srinivasan, M. (2013). *Differences on women rights and choice between the US, India and the-Middle-East,* available at https://www.esamskriti.com/e/National-Affairs/Current-Affairs/Differences-on-women-colon-s-rights-and-choice-between-the-US,-India-and-the-Middle-East-1.aspx.

77. Srivastava, C., Sternquist, B. & Mahi, H. (2012). Organized retailing in India-Upstream channel structure and management. *Journal of Business and Industrial Marketing*, 27(3), 176-195.

78. Surendran, J. & Vardhan, R. (2014). Retail therapy: Understanding the phenomenon to improve customer experience. Available at http://tejas.iimb. ac.in/articles/Tejas_ December%20Edition_Article%204.pdf

79. Tanwar, S., Kaushik, N. & Kaushik, V. K. (2011). Retail malls: New mantra for success. *Sri Krishna International Research & Educational Consortium*, 2, 103-113.

80. Taquet, M., Qouidbach, J., Alexandre, Y., Desseillesf, M. & Gross, J. J. (2016). Hedonism and the choice of everyday activities. *PNAS*, 113(35), 9769-9773.

81. Tran, W. (2019). *Retail therapy and the power of the impulse buy* (April 2, 2019). Available at https://www.dacgroup.com/en-gb/blog/retail-therapy-and-the-power-of-the-impulse-buy/.

82. Turley, L. W. & Milliman, R. E. (2000). Atmospheric effects on shopping behavior: A review of the experiential evidence. *Journal of Business Research,* 49, 193-211.

83. Underhill, P. (1999). *Why we buy: The Science of Shopping.* New York: Simon & Shuster.

84. Voss, K. E., Spangenberg, E. R. & Grohmann, B. (2003). Measuring the hedonic and utilitarian dimensions of consumer attitude. *Journal of Marketing Research,* 40 (3), 310-320.

85. Woodruffe, H. (1996). Methodological issues in consumer research: Towards a feminist perspective. *Marketing Intelligence & Planning*, 14, 13-18.

86. Woodruffe, H. (1997). Compensatory consumption: Why women go shopping when they're fed up and other stories. *Marketing Intelligence & Planning*, 15(7), 325-334.

87. Woodruffe, H. (2001). *Retail therapy: An investigation of compensatory consumption and shopping behavior*, Thesis submitted to Lancaster University for the Degree of Doctor of Philosophy (Phd).

88. Workman, L. & Paper, D. (2010). Compulsive buying: A theoretical framework. *The Journal of Business Inquiry,* 9(1), 89-126.

89. Yarrow, K. (2013). *Is retail therapy for real? 5 ways shopping is actually good for you.* Business.time.com (April 16, 2013).

90. Yurchisin, J., Yan, R. N., Watchravesringkan, K. & Chen, C. (2006). Why retail therapy? A preliminary investigation of the role of liminality, self-esteem, negative emotions, and proximity of clothing to self in the compensatory consumption of apparel products. *Psychology*, 60(6), 895-910.

27

91. Yurchisin, J., Yan, R., Watchravesringkan, K. & Chen, C. (2008). Investigating the role of life status changes and negative emotions in compensatory consumption among college students. *College Student Journal,* 42(3), 860-868.

92. Zheng, X. Y. & Peng, S. Q. (2014). Consumption as psychological compensation: A review of compensatory consumption. *Advances in Psychological Science*, 22, 1-8.

REVIEW OF LITERATURE

CHAPTER-2

REVIEW OF LITERATURE

The previous chapter (Chapter-1) has given a general introduction about the concept of retail therapy, its relation to other emotional shopping types, its role in women's lives, world-over prevalence of retail therapy, and also the importance of studying this phenomenon in Indian context. The present chapter gives a detailed account of the existing literature on retail therapy and all the related concepts used within the present research. The review has been presented in different sections, while each section presenting the literature related to each of the objectives of the study. Section 2.1 shows the literature covering the first objective of the research i.e. 'To explore different types of coping strategies/activities adopted by Indian women to overcome negative mood (with special focus on determining the usage of shopping for coping)'. It gives an account of what the previous literature says about the concept of coping with negative mood and different strategies used for it. It also explains how shopping activity is used as a coping strategy.

This is followed by Section 2.2 that covers literature related to the second objective of the research i.e. 'To analyze the retail therapy behavior of women in India'. It first gives an account of the studies explaining the concept of retail therapy (from compensatory consumption view-point as well mood-alleviative view-point). Further, it details out the observations of different researchers with regard to the negative mood situations leading to retail therapy, the therapeutic values that people derive from shopping and also the consequences of retail therapy. All the studies related to retail therapy have also been presented in tabular form in Table 2.2.

Section 2.3 is related to the third objective i.e. 'To assess the influential impact of personal characteristics on retail therapy behavior of women in India'. Since, retail therapy is an emotional shopping type; indulgence in it is highly expected to be affected by personal characteristics of an individual. Accordingly, Section 2.3 covers studies that have already examined the role of some of these factors in retail therapy, along with the research gaps mentioning the variables that seem to be important, but have not yet been

29

covered by the previous researchers. This is followed by detailed explanation of all these identified variables and their expected relationship with retail therapy based on directly or indirectly available literature.

The next section i.e. Section 2.4 covers the last objective of the present research i.e. 'To analyze the retail therapy trip behavior of women therapy shoppers in India'. This section particularly focuses on the literature related to the shopping behavior of the shoppers when they go for therapy shopping. It explains the observations of the previous researchers regarding the decisions taken by therapy shoppers e.g. choice of retail formats, product choice, payment modes used, time and money spend etc. It also gives an account of the studies that have examined the role of shopping environment in giving therapy to the shoppers.

The last section of this chapter i.e. Section 2.5 details out the different research gaps identified based on the review of the studies related to retail therapy and rationale of the study based on these gaps. This is finally followed by conclusion of the chapter.

2.1 REVIEW RELATED TO COPING AND USE OF SHOPPING AS A COPING STRATEGY

2.1.1 Meaning and Definition of Coping:

The term 'coping' refers to the specific behavioral or psychological efforts taken to combat stress (Lazarus & Folkman, 1984). It is a conscious defense mechanism that is used to overcome negative emotions and regain control (Schweitzer, 2001). Folkman et al. (1986) defined coping as "the person's cognitive and behavioral efforts to manage the internal and external demands in the person-environment transaction".

Luomala (2001) observed that people experience stress when they perceive that a situation is threatening and they lack resources to deal with it. They try to cope with such stress by either modifying the source of stress or by increasing their available resources to deal with it (Lazarus & Folkman, 1984). Whether or not their actions are successful depends upon the particular type of situation they are facing and the particular type of strategies that they adopt to overcome it (Chen et al., 2017). The following sections give a brief account of the commonly used coping strategies and about how shopping activity is also used for coping with negative mood.

30

2.1.2   Coping Styles/Strategies:

The existing research mainly talks of two broad categories of coping strategies including 'problem focused' (i.e. dealing directly with the problem) and 'emotion focused' coping strategies (using indirect means to reduce anxiety) (Lazarus & Folkman, 1984). Chen et al. (2017) classified the emotion-focused strategies as-positive emotion-focused and negative emotion-focused strategies. Similarly, Schnider et al. (2007) classified the emotion-focused coping strategies into 'active' or 'avoidant' strategies. The active emotion-focused strategies such as acceptance, humor, emotional support etc. have been found to be adaptive strategies that lead to reduction of stress and improve well-being. On the other hand, the avoidant strategies such as distraction, self-blame etc. have been found to lead to negative consequences (Ryan, 2013).

As far as the effectiveness of these strategies is concerned, it has been found that using problem-focused strategies may be more beneficial in the long run (Penley et al., 2002), rather than using emotion-focused strategies that might lead to negative consequences such as depression and anxiety (Baker & Berenbaum, 2007). However, sometimes the problem at hand may be such that nothing can be done about it or trying to solve it may rather produce counter-productive outcomes (Lazarus, 1993). In some other cases, the problem might be related to non-material needs like love or care etc., which are difficult to express and compensate directly. In such cases, an indirect approach (i.e. managing the emotions rather than the problem) may work better (Woodruffe, 2001). Chen et al. (2017) observed that not all the emotion-focused strategies are mal-adaptive, e.g. strengthening ties to others, providing emotional support; helping others, exercising, suppressing impulse etc. have been found to be positively related to positive affect and well-being.

Apart from the broader classification of coping strategies into problem-focused and emotion-focused, researchers have also identified some other types e.g. Thayer et al. (1994) divided the self-regulatory strategies into six categories: 1) active mood management, 2) seeking pleasurable activities and distraction, 3) passive mood management, 4) social support, ventilation, and gratification, 5) direct tension reduction, and 6) withdrawal-avoidance. Similarly, Garnefski et al. (2001) identified different types of coping styles as- social, behavioral or physiological; conscious or

31

unconscious; cognitive or behavioral etc. Social coping may involve accessing inter-personal support etc.; physiological coping may be through increase in the pulse rate or shortness of breath; behavioral coping may involve screaming or crying etc. The researchers further observed that coping with stress may even be done unconsciously without the knowledge and control of the person doing it. Also, it is not necessary that a person has to actually take an action for coping; rather the act may be cognitive as well. Garnefski et al. (2001) found that some of the conscious cognitive coping strategies may include- self-blame, blaming others, acceptance, rumination, positive refocusing, refocus on planning, positive reappraisal etc.

Miedziun and Czabała (2015) categorized the stress-management techniques into different classes including- physical activity (walking, exercise, travelling and physical work etc.); replacement gratification (listening to music, hobbies, artistic activities, reading, meeting friends etc.); distancing (sleeping, joking about the situation, forgetting or neglecting stress factors, escape etc.); escaping the difficulty (substance abuse, comfort food, religious practices, risky behavior etc.); solving problems (planning, analyzing and taking action); support (seeking support from family or even outside); adjusting tension and emotions (meditation, deep breathing, muscle relaxation, self-affirmation etc.); and lack of activity-helplessness (resigning and passive waiting). In their study, the survey results for 100 people showed that out of these techniques, the most often used ones were- problem solving, replacement gratification and distancing.

Chen and Pham (2019) observed that the coping strategies may be behavioral or mental. Behavioral strategies include- avoidance and withdrawal (e.g. avoiding the person concerned or trying to be alone or avoiding complex decisions); and engaging in pleasurable activities (e.g. engaging in hobbies, listening to music, shopping and self-gifting, watching television, movies, use of social media and smart phones). Mental coping, on the other hand, involves selective exposure to positive information (e.g. recalling only positive news); self-generation of positive thoughts (e.g. planning vacation, recalling of happy old memories); and cognitive reappraisal (e.g. reappraising the stress creating situation as beneficial and non-threatening or in fact as a learning opportunity).

Different types of categorizations of coping strategies, made by the previous researchers, have been presented in summarized form in Table 2.1.

32

Table 2.1: Coping Styles and Strategies

COPING STRATEGIES/STYLES		GIVEN BY	DETAILS
Problem-focused (Lazarus and Folkman, 1984)	Cognitive	Golpelwar (2014)	Direct action to resolve or improve the problematic situation
	Action-oriented		
Emotion-focused (Lazarus and Folkman, 1984)	Active	Schnider et al. (2007)	Using indirect means to reduce anxiety or to manage emotions arising from stressful situation
	Avoidant		
Engaged		Tobin et al. (1989)	Active problem solving, cognitive restructuring, increased social contact, increased emotional expression etc.
Disengaged			Problem avoidance, wishful thinking, self-criticism and social withdrawal
Active mood management		Thayer et al. (1994)	Relaxation techniques, exercise, evaluating feelings etc.
Seeking pleasurable activities and distraction			Involving in enjoyable activities
Passive mood management			Watching TV, eating something, taking a rest or a nap, shopping
Social support, ventilation, and gratification			Talk to or call someone, meeting someone, crying, eating
Direct tension reduction			Consuming drugs, alcohol or coffee, having sex
Withdrawal-avoidance			Being alone, avoiding others, crying etc.
Social, behavioral or physiological		See Garnefski et al. (2001)	Social- inter-personal relations Behavioral- crying, screaming, shouting etc. Physiological- rapid pulse, increased breathing, perspiration

COPING STRATEGIES/STYLES	GIVEN BY	DETAILS
Cognitive	Garnefski et al. (2001)	Positive reappraisal, rumination, self-blame, acceptance
Physical activity		Walking, exercise, travelling and physical work etc.
Replacement gratification		Listening to music, hobbies, artistic activities, reading, meeting friends etc.
Distancing	Miedziun & Czabała (2015)	Sleeping, joking about the situation, forgetting or neglecting stress factors, escape etc.
Escaping the difficulty		Substance abuse, comfort food, religious practices, risky behaviour etc.
Solving problems		Planning, analyzing and taking action
Support		Seeking support from family or even outside
Adjusting tension and emotions		Meditation, deep breathing, muscle relaxation, self-affirmation etc.
Lack of activity-helplessness		Resigning and passive waiting
Adaptive	Ryan (2013)	Strengthening ties to others, providing emotional support, helping others, exercising, suppressing impulse, acceptance, humor etc.
Mal-adaptive		Distraction, self-blame, impulsive behavior etc.
Behavioral	Chen & Pham (2019)	Avoiding others, engaging in hobbies, shopping, using social media etc.
Mental		Recalling positive news, planning for a vacation etc.

Source: Author's elaboration based on review of literature

2.1.3 Coping Strategies used by Women:

Since, the present research study is focused on women, thus it becomes imperative to understand as to what type of coping strategies are mostly used by them. Research has shown that women show more of the depressive and anxiety symptoms as compared to men (Keita, 2007). Also, they make more use of emotion-focused coping, while men mostly use problem-focused coping methods (Mezulis et al., 2002; Matud, 2004). Matud (2004) examined gender differences with regard to stress and coping. Based on the results of the data analyzed for 2,816 respondents (more than 50% being women), it was found that women experience more chronic stress and also minor daily stressors. Further, they use more of the emotion-focused coping strategies. Kelly et al. (2008) also found that women usually seek more emotional support as compared to men. In a survey by CALM (The Campaign Against Living Miserably) (2016), it was found that more of the severely depressed women are likely to 'talk to someone' (67%). Further, according to Liddon et al. (2017), under stressful situations, women are more likely to talk to their friends, comfort eat (i.e. consuming hedonic food items), take prescription medicine, chat on internet, rely on self-awareness of their emotions and also to consult a doctor or psychotherapist for help.

As far as the coping strategies used by Indian women are concerned, Hussain (2018) observed that the most commonly used coping strategies include- social interactions, adopting religious practice, watching television, indulging in hobbies, physical exercise, listening to music, shopping, meeting friends, traveling, eating, etc. Some other ways include- crying, sleeping, using social media, medication, smoking and consuming alcohol, social service, availing salon services, etc. Similarly, Solanki et al. (2019) found that the most commonly used coping mechanisms by Indian women include- watching television (TV), getting busy in some work, praying, spending time while discussing about their kids behavior, walking, getting massage, planning for solving problem, sleeping, indulging in hobbies such as reading, listening to music, singing, and cooking etc., self-medication, doing nothing, having some 'me' time etc. About 30 per cent women in that study had mentioned that they watch television for coping with stress and this was especially found to be true in case of aged women.

2.1.4 Role of Shopping Activity as a Coping Strategy:

Since long, shopping has been observed to be a source of distraction and diversion (Thayer et al., 1994; Kacen, 1994/1998; Luomala, 1998/2002; Arnold & Reynolds, 2009; Kemp & Kopp, 2011; Rick et al., 2014 etc.). It has been regarded as a passive-mood management strategy (Thayer et al., 1994). Although, there are number of researchers who have presented the negative side of mood-alleviative shopping in the form of impulsive or compulsive buying (e.g. Faber & Vohs, 2004; Silvera et al., 2008; Workman & Paper, 2010); there are still others who believe that shopping is rather an adaptive coping strategy (Burke, 2018; Hama, 2001), offering a number of therapeutic benefits that lead to psychological well-being (Luomala, 2002; Kang & Johnson, 2011).

Emphasizing on the positive role of shopping in stress management, Burke (2018) observed that though, shopping is not a medicine that can cure everyone; however, the act of shopping can be therapeutic at least for those who actually perceive it to be so. Such people get motivated to use shopping for mood-alleviation not merely because of the satisfaction they get from spending money, rather because shopping is also socially rewarding. Shopping as 'retail therapy' may also sometimes, involve the use of impulse buying or self-gifting etc. for immediate gratification (Baumeister, 2002; Atalay & Meloy, 2011; D'Souza, 2012; Barden, 2015). However, buying for something is not always necessary; rather therapy shoppers may even feel good by window-shopping or by the overall shopping experience (Kang, 2009). The upcoming section i.e. section 2.2 further details out the reasons for importance of shopping as therapeutic activity and also the consequences of using shopping for coping with negative mood.

2.2 REVIEW RELATED TO RETAIL THERAPY BEHAVIOR (CONCEPT, MOTIVATIONS, THERAPEUTIC VALUES AND OUTCOMES)

2.2.1 The Concept of Retail Therapy:

As mentioned in the previous chapter (chapter-1) also, the term retail therapy has usually been explained through two approaches- compensatory consumption approach and mood-alleviative consumption approach. The review related to both the approaches has been explained as under:

➢ **Retail therapy as compensatory consumption behavior:**

The clues about existence and importance of compensatory consumption had been highlighted long back by researchers like Gronmo (1988) and Grunert (1993). While, Gronmo (1988) brought forward the concept of compensatory consumption in the form of purchase of cars, appliances and houses by low-income people who suffered lack of respect, status and identity; Grunert (1993) explained it in the form of compensatory eating behavior.

Woodruffe (1997/98) brought out the role of shopping as a compensatory activity and observed that compensatory consumption is a regular and commonly used mood-alleviative activity. The research done by Woodruffe (2001) has been a landmark in the literature on compensatory consumption. The researcher, however, used the terms compensatory consumption and retail therapy to mean one and the same thing. Woodruffe (2001) carried out in-depth interviews with various shoppers to understand their lived experiences of using shopping as a coping mechanism. Based upon the existing literature and the analysis of interview data, a conceptual framework for compensatory consumption was designed by Woodruffe (2001), explaining its precursors, strategies, shopping behavior and outcomes.

Later, Nair (2004) carried out in-depth interviews with 12 female respondents from Delhi (India) to understand their compensatory shopping behavior. In the study, four categories of shoppers were identified, including: 'the information gatherers', 'the no nonsense shoppers', 'the recreationalists' and 'the escapists'. Out of these, the first, third and fourth category belonged to the broad category of compensatory shoppers, especially the escapists who are the true compensatory shoppers because they try to feel control in part of their lives through the shopping activity and use it as a coping strategy for dealing with stress or depression.

Yurchisin et al. (2006) also used the term retail therapy to mean compensatory consumption only and found that liminal state, low self-esteem and negative emotions lead to compensatory consumption. Later, Yurchisin et al. (2008) framed a scale for measuring retail therapy behavior from compensatory consumption viewpoint, which was however later criticized on certain grounds. Some of the researchers also worked on the factors that could predict one's indulgence in compensatory consumption e.g. Chen et al. (2011) found that lack of control motivates one to indulge in shopping to regain control. Similarly, Rose and Segrist (2011) observed that one's distress tolerance level determines usage of retail therapy. It was suggested that people should rely less on compensatory consumption and try out other productive ways of dealing with negative situations.

Kim and Rucker (2012) highlighted that compensatory consumption need not be only reactive; rather it can also be proactive i.e. people may go for consumption even when they are anticipating any threat. The only difference between proactive and reactive compensatory consumption is that in proactive consumption, people usually consume only threat-related products; whereas in reactive condition, the products consumed may or may not be related to the actual threat.

Another study had been carried out by Mandel et al. (2017). It is a review-based study on the psychological effects of self-discrepancy issues. The researchers listed out five different types of compensatory consumption strategies that are used by people to deal with self-discrepancy issues. These strategies include- 'escapism', 'dissociation', 'symbolic self-completion', 'fluid consumption' and 'direct resolution'. Apart from this, a scale for measuring compensatory consumption (in the Indian context), was also framed by Singh (2017). Singh (2017) found four factors i.e. 'conscientiousness', 'powerfulness', 'compulsivity', and 'need attention', to be important components of compensatory consumption.

➢ **Retail therapy as mood-alleviative consumption behavior:**

Role of mood as a motivator for shopping had been brought forward by many earlier researchers like Thayer et al. (1994), Kacen (1994/1998), Luomala (1998/2001/2002) etc. Thayer et al. (1994) and Kacen (1994/98) listed different types of coping strategies that can be used by people to overcome negative mood situations, out of which shopping was also one. On the other hand, Luomala (1998) specifically emphasized on the role of self-gifting in mood-alleviation. Further, Luomala (2001/2002) listed out different types of negative moods and also different types of therapeutic powers of consumption that can help in alleviation of these mood types.

Whereas, some of the earlier researchers (e.g. Woodruffe, 2001; Yurchisin et al., 2006; Yurchisin et al., 2008 etc.) had used the terms retail therapy and compensatory consumption to mean the same thing; it was Kang (2009) and Kang & Johnson (2011) who emphasized that retail therapy was a distinct concept in itself. In fact, compensatory consumption was an umbrella term that included retail therapy. According to Kang (2009), retail therapy is usually motivated by temporary negative mood situations, rather than dealing with major life issues or ongoing problems. Further, the act of retail therapy is mostly successful and it actually helps in mood-alleviation. The first ever scale to measure retail therapy as a mood-alleviative shopping had also been framed by Kang (2009) (/Kang & Johnson, 2011).

Atalay and Meloy (2011) observed retail therapy to be a strategic effort for mood-alleviation. The researchers carried out three studies, including- a field study, a lab study and maintenance of consumption diaries. 220 adult shoppers in a mall participated in the field study and filled up questionnaires comprising of statements related to mood, regulatory focus and loneliness, and also made a list of their intended purchases before entering the mall and their actual purchases afterwards. The results revealed that, people in temporary negative mood indulged more in unplanned self-treats, rather than the lonely people whose main focus was on social interaction through mall shopping. The results of the lab study with 118 undergraduate students revealed that when people exercise restraint knowing the ill consequences of impulse buying, the restraint can also be equally therapeutic. Finally, the researchers asked 69 undergraduate students to note down all the details about the events leading to retail therapy, in two consumption diaries. They were also required to mention the items mostly purchased by them during therapy shopping and whether they had any guilt feeling afterwards. The results showed that more than 40 percent of the participants indulged in self-treat following some bad mood situations. In most of the cases, therapy shopping was not followed by any guilt feeling afterwards.

A study was later conducted by D'Souza (2012) to understand the concept of retail therapy in the Indian context. Twenty one respondents were being interviewed for analyzing their experiences with retail therapy and understanding their pre and post therapy shopping moods and emotions. It was found that shopping led to a change in the pre-shopping and post-shopping mood state of the shoppers and it was the whole shopping process that made their experience good. However, it could not be made clear as to what extent each activity in the shopping process contributed to the same. D'Souza (2012) further identified four types of shopping: 'utilitarian', 'compensatory', 'hedonic' and 'impulse'. It was found that except utilitarian shopping, all other three types of shopping led to mood elevation. Another interview-based study was also carried out in India by Surendran and Vardhan (2014). The researchers tried to understand the psychology of therapy shoppers in India and also determined the role of retail attributes in mood-alleviation. It was found that lighting, ambience, layout etc., encourage shopping for therapeutic reasons.

Rick et al. (2014) brought out the importance of retail therapy in reducing sadness. With the help of three different studies in U.S., it was found that making purchase decisions i.e. actively choosing a product, leads to alleviation of sadness by helping the shopper in restoring personal control. However, such act might not necessarily help in dealing with other types of negative emotions like anger also.

40

A self-gifting perspective of retail therapy was brought forward by Mortimer et al. (2015) through different therapeutic aspects including- therapeutic personal disappointment, therapeutic negative mood reduction, therapeutic positive mood reinforcement and therapeutic motivation. Melindra and Aprianingsih (2016) also observed that different types of therapeutic shopping values and motivation affect one/s purchase intention. Further, retail attributes also play a significant role in this regard. Apart from this, Urkmez and Wagner (2016) carried out 15 in-depth interviews in Turkey and Poland and examined the luxury buying from therapeutic perspective. The results showed that people in Poland go more for compensatory luxury shopping as compared to those in Turkey.

Son and Chang (2016) carried out an online survey with 200 individuals in the United States to determine different personal factors affecting retail therapy. It was found that self-gift motivation and unplanned buying tendency significantly predicted retail therapy, whereas price consciousness did not have a significant relation with it. Apart from this, Lee and Bottger (2017) presented a review-based study highlighting the importance of shopping in mood-alleviation. It was found that people may have different types of therapeutic motivations that they can fulfill with actual purchase and even with window-shopping.

Cifci and Ekinci (2018), on the other hand, brought forward the detrimental effects of retail therapy on consumer emotions. The researchers first framed a scale to measure retail therapy and then determined its impact on emotions. It was found that shoppers feel guilty after therapy shopping and blame themselves as well as the brands they bought. This also leads to negative impact on consumer based brand equity. Apart from this, a study was also carried out by Irwin (2018), highlighting the emotional role of retail therapy as a form of self-care. It was observed that though retail therapy cannot replace actual problem solving; it can at least give temporary relief to the person concerned.

41

In a latest study, Singh and Ahuja (2020) associated the concept of emotional shopping to emotional marketing. It was reflected as to how different therapeutic elements such as self-gifting, shopping emotions etc., can be used to design marketing strategies to positively affect the emotions of shoppers. The Researchers particularly emphasized on studying of the concept of emotional shopping and retail therapy in Indian context so that its relevance in India's diverse cultural setting can be understood.

Based on the review of existing literature, it can be established that compensatory consumption is a wider term as compared to mood-alleviative shopping. It may be motivated by any kind of negative events or problems, starting from any temporary issues to even ongoing and major life problems. On the other hand, when we study retail therapy from mood-alleviative perspective, it includes only temporary negative issues. Further, using compensatory consumption for long-term and ongoing issues can also lead to negative consequences in the long-run in the form of becoming addicted to this behavior. However, this is not so in case of mood-alleviative shopping, which is used only as a temporary solution to problems and thus has less chances of taking form of an addiction. It rather leads to happiness and pleasure in most of the cases. For these reasons, most of the previous researchers (e.g. Luomala, 2002; Kang & Johnson, 2010; Atalay & Meloy, 2011; Rick et al., 2014; Cifci & Ekinci, 2018 etc.) have used the mood-alleviative perspective as a better explanation of retail therapy. Accordingly, for the purpose of this research also, retail therapy has been studied from mood-alleviative perspective only.

Table 2.2 gives a summarized account of previous studies on retail therapy, both as compensatory consumption as well as mood-alleviative consumption.

Table 2.2: Summarized Presentation of Studies on Therapeutic Shopping (Both as Compensatory and Mood-alleviative Shopping)

Researcher/Year/Title	Country	Objectives	Sample/Variables	Findings
Woodruffe (1997) "Compensatory consumption: Why women go shopping when they're fed up and other stories".	U.K.	To understand the role of compensatory consumption in life of women. To advance knowledge in this under-studied topic. To propose agenda for future research.	**Sample-** Case studies with three women from different demographic backgrounds. **Variables-** Compensatory consumption (CCB).	All three women interviewed in this study, mentioned about "lacks" or "deficits" in their lives. They indulged in compensatory shopping for reasons like: treat, prove herself, taking mind off, window shopping, bargaining etc. CCB was found to be a fruitful solution for transient and episodic problems but not for long-term issues. It was also observed that CCB is a commonly used activity.
Luomala (1998) "A mood-alleviative perspective on self-gift behaviors: Stimulating consumer behaviour theory development".	NA	To bring out the role of self-gifting in mood-alleviation and its link to other related shopping behaviors.	**Sample-** Review based study	It was observed that use of self-gifting for mood-alleviation is an under-studied phenomenon. Previous studies had mainly focused on studying mood as an intervening situational variable and only few had studied it as an object of control. This area has important managerial implications because in sad mood, shoppers make more impulse buys, spend more money etc. Even non-buyers may return in future if their experience was good.
Woodruffe (2001) "Retail therapy: An investigation of compensatory consumption and shopping behaviour".	U.K.	To bring out the detailed explanation of the concept of compensatory consumption and its role in life satisfaction.	**Preliminary study-** 3 women. **Final study-** 25 individuals (18 women and 7 men). **Variables-** Compensatory Consumption	Woodruffe (2001) framed a conceptual framework for compensatory consumption through three models covering- the precursors of compensatory consumption, mechanisms used for mood-alleviation, shopping behavior of compensatory shoppers etc. It was found that compensatory consumption represented a continuum, with one extreme having people who do not or rarely indulge in such shopping and the other extreme with those who take on the characteristics of compulsive shoppers.

Researcher/Year/Title	Country	Objectives	Sample/Variables	Findings
Luomala (2001) "Consumption as therapy: A phenomenological inquiry into mood-alleviative consumer behaviors".	Finland	To describe the different types of negative moods. To explore the practice of mood-alleviative consumption. To suggest theoretical and empirical implications for mood-alleviative consumption behavior.	**Sample-** 70 descriptive writings from people approached through advertisements in newspapers and magazines (63 from women). **Variables-** Mood-alleviative consumption.	Luomala (2001) mentioned about three types of therapeutic powers stemming from consumption activity including- distraction, self-indulgence and stimulated elaboration. It was found that consumption can help in alleviating any kind of negative mood including- irritation, stress and dejection. However, in certain circumstances, it can also have negative consequences such as shame, regret, guilt etc.
Luomala (2002) "An empirical analysis of the practices and therapeutic power of mood-alleviative consumption in Finland".	Finland	To build a model for mood-alleviative consumption through empirical investigation about its practices in Finland.	**Sample-** Firstly, questionnaires sent to 1000 residents of Vaasa asking about mood-alleviative activities used by them, for which the response rate was 43%. Out of them, one-third of those whose activities were more related to buying and products consumption participated further. In total, 28 respondents (14 men and 14 women) were interviewed. **Variables-** Mood-alleviative consumption.	Eight types of therapeutic powers of consumption were identified, including- distraction, self-indulgence, stimulated elaboration, outcomes of mood-alleviative activities, recharging, discharging, retreat, and activation. Males and females differed in the usage of mood-alleviative consumption activities. Shopping was found to be more famous amongst women. It was found that different types of mood-alleviative activities can help in alleviating different kinds of negative moods.
Nair (2004) "Compensatory consumption among modern Indian women: A phenomenological exploration".	India	To understand the attitude towards and usage of compensatory consumption among Indian women and to find out the motivations behind it, the products purchased,	**Sample-** In-depth interviews with 12 women, through quota sampling, from Delhi. **Variables-** Compensatory Consumption	Most of the respondents stated that they would prefer to go in the company of somebody for compensatory shopping. They believed in the importance of product purchase in mood-alleviation. Products purchased included clothes, shoes, accessories, jewelry etc. Further, it was found

Researcher/Year/Title	Country	Objectives	Sample/Variables	Findings
		the shopping behavior and shoppers' categories based on compensatory consumption.		that women use shopping as means to escape anxiety, stress and boredom. Different types of shoppers' categories were also identified in the study, including- the information gatherers, the no nonsense shoppers, the recreationalists and the escapists.
Yurchisin, J., Yan, R.N., Watchravesringkan, K. and Chen, C. (2006) "Why retail therapy? a preliminary investigation of the role of self-concept discrepancy, self-esteem, negative emotions, and proximity of clothing to self in the compensatory consumption of apparel products".	U.S.	To study the relationship between liminality and compensatory consumption.	**Sample-** Undergraduates (N = 301; 88% female) from four different state universities. **Variables-** Liminal state, self-esteem, emotional state, proximity of clothing to self, and compensatory consumption behavior.	Researchers found that liminality significantly affects low self-esteem and negative emotional state. Further, low self-esteem and proximity of clothing to self significantly positively affected compensatory consumption. It was also found that gender plays a moderating role in this relationship. According to the researchers, compensatory consumption can be useful to deal with temporary negative emotions, but may become problematic if it takes the form of compulsion.
Rucker and Galansky (2008) "Desire to acquire: powerlessness and compensatory consumption".	U.S.	To study the role of powerlessness on compensatory consumption.	**Sample-** Three experiments: 1. 61 undergraduate students. 2. 127 undergraduates. 3. 65 undergraduates. **Variables-** Powerlessness, mood, product association, willingness to pay, anticipated happiness, sense of power.	It was found that low power state increases the willingness to pay more for status related products. Further, this willingness to pay more is not due to the anticipation of happiness, but with the desire to restore power.
Yurchisin et al. (2008) "Investigating the role of life status changes and negative emotions in compensatory	U.S.	To study the relationship between life-status changes, negative emotional state and	**Sample-** 301 under-graduate students from universities in four states of U.S. (88% females).	Yurchisin et al. (2008) framed a compensatory consumption scale for apparels (46 items) based on the qualitative studies by Woodruffe (1997/98). Apart from this, it was

Researcher/Year/Title	Country	Objectives	Sample/Variables	Findings
consumption among college students".		compensatory consumption.		found that life-status changes (experienced in the past 6 months) and negative emotional state significantly affect compensatory consumption.
Arnold and Reynolds (2009) "Affect and retail shopping behavior: understanding the role of mood regulation and regulatory focus".	U.S.	To examine the role of mood-regulation and regulatory focus in context of retail.	**Sample-** Study 1- lab experiment with 79 under-graduate students from southeastern University. Study 2- field study with 578 respondents selected through online survey (only non-students). **Variables-** Regulatory focus (promotion and prevention focus), affect regulation.	It was found that people who are in negative mood state and also have high promotion focus (i.e. oriented towards achievements and goals), engage more in mood-regulation. Regulatory focus was significantly related to all mood-regulation constructs of mood-monitoring, mood-clarity and mood-repair. Further, all these three constructs were found to be significantly related to hedonic shopping value, which ultimately led to positive word of mouth.
Kang, M. and Johnson, K.K.P. (2010) "Let's shop! Exploring the experiences of therapy shoppers".	U.S.	To enhance the understanding of the concept of retail therapy.	**Sample-** 43 self-identified therapy shoppers taken for in-depth interviews (most of them being women). **Variables-** Retail therapy	The researchers explored consumer experiences at three shopping stages of retail therapy- pre-shopping, shopping and post-shopping stage. All the three types of negative moods were found to be alleviated through shopping. Mood was found to be improved through imagining of consumption, good behavior of the employees, buying of something special, impulse shopping etc. Most of the study participants felt good after shopping. They used the products purchased during therapy shopping and also remembered the shopping experience in the long-run.

Researcher/Year/Title	Country	Objectives	Sample/Variables	Findings
Atalay and Meloy (2011) "Retail therapy: A strategic effort to improve mood".	U.S.	To explain whether indulging in unplanned self-gifting is a strategic effort to improve mood.	**Sample-** Study 1- 220 adults from a mall. Study 2- 11 under-graduates from marketing class. Study 3- 69 under-graduates who completed two consumption diaries. **Variables-** Mood, loneliness, regulatory focus, retail therapy.	It was found that shoppers in sad mood engaged more in unplanned self-gifting. Regulatory orientation and loneliness were not found as predictors. Products purchased as self-treats included- clothing, food, electronics, entertainment, accessories and others. Further, most of the self-treats were found to be motivated by the desire to repair mood, followed by celebratory events and other reasons. It was also found that self-treats bought for mood-alleviation were not much expensive and shoppers did not regret their purchase afterwards. In addition to these findings, the researchers also tested the impact of restraint on therapy shopping. It was found that when consumers are motivated to exercise restraint on their impulse behavior, their therapeutic consumption reduces, while the mood still improves.
Dittmar and Kapur (2011) "Consumerism and well-being in India and the UK: Identity projection and emotion regulation as underlying psychological processes".	India and U.K.	To explain the link between materialism, buying motives and well-being.	**Sample-** 109 respondents from Delhi (India) and 127 from South-east of England in U.K. **Variables-** Materialism, buying motives, and well-being.	The researchers observed that, though, consumption culture is less developed in India, However, the materialistic values are strongly endorsed. Such materialism leads to lower well-being in the long-run. Further, this happens more strongly in case of younger adults as compared to older ones. Materialistic values were also found to predict dysfunctional consumer behavior like compulsive buying. Strong links could also be observed between emotion-regulation and dysfunctional consumer behavior.

Researcher/Year/Title	Country	Objectives	Sample/Variables	Findings
Kang and Johnson (2011) "Retail therapy: Scale development".	U.S.	To establish and validate a scale for measuring retail therapy behavior.	**Sample-** 530 participants chosen on convenience sampling basis and then randomly split into 2 parts- 258 for scale purification and 272 for scale validation. **Variables-** Retail therapy	Based on the interview findings and from previous studies, a 52 items retail therapy scale was framed by the researchers, out of which 31 items were left after EFA. Further, 22 items could be retained after CFA. This 22-items scale was further confirmed and validated on a separate sample. The researchers also found that retail therapy shoppers shop frequently, and spend more time and money on shopping.
Rose and Segrist (2011) "Facets of distress tolerance as predictors of buying in response to self-esteem threats".	U.S.	To study the impact of individual differences in distress tolerance on use of shopping in response to self-esteem threats.	**Sample-** 158 college students (70% females). **Variables-** Distress tolerance including tolerance, regulation, appraisal and absorption.	Distress tolerance has four elements i.e. tolerance, regulation, appraisal, and absorption. Out of these, the researchers observed that 'regulation' was a significant predictor of buying for self-esteem threat. This indicates that people, who have the tendency to engage in avoidance or distraction behavior when stressed out, are also prone to engage in reckless shopping when they experience any kind of threat to their self-esteem.
Kemp and Kopp (2011) "Emotion regulation consumption: When feeling better is the aim".	U.S.	To determine if emotion regulation is attempted by individuals who are experiencing fear or contentment, or for other anxiety, or discrete emotions, as compared to those with neutral affective state.	**Sample-** Study 1- 96 Southern University students in U.S. Study 2- 167 Southern University students in U.S. **Variables-** Emotional states and emotion regulation.	Researchers observed that people indulge in consumption for alleviating negative moods like sadness and fear/anxiety. At the same time, they also use consumption for maintenance of positive mood state i.e. contentment and amusement. In addition, individuals who lack the ability to internally control negative emotions are expected to indulge more in consumption of hedonic products. On the other hand, those who use

Researcher/Year/Title	Country	Objectives	Sample/Variables	Findings
				cognitive reappraisal are better at emotion control and thus make lesser use of compensatory consumption.
D'Souza (2012) "Retail therapy: A study in the Indian context to understand compensatory consumption and its implications on consumers' psyche".	India	To study the motivations of retail therapy in the Indian context and its implications on mood. To study the impact of demographics on retail therapy. To identify products purchased by therapy shoppers.	**Sample-** In-depth interviews with 21 respondents from Delhi and Ahmedabad (15-60 years). Within that projection technique was used. In addition, live interaction with many shoppers at retail spaces was made. **Variables-** Retail therapy	Some of the major findings of this research were- 1) compensatory shopping is used mainly by younger people below 40; 2) women enjoy hedonic and impulse shopping more than men; 3) retail environment plays a vital role in improving ones' mood; 4) sometimes, shoppers also indulge in retail therapy unintentionally. Apart from this, the researchers also identified four types of shoppers i.e. utilitarian, compensatory, hedonic and impulse. Only utilitarian shoppers did not go for therapy shopping.
Kim and Rucker (2012) "Bracing for the psychological storm: proactive versus reactive compensatory consumption".	U.S.	To demonstrate the difference between proactive and reactive compensatory consumption.	**Sample-** Pre-testing- 66 under-graduates for intelligence threat pretest and 53 under-graduates for motivation threat pre-test. Experiment 1- 153 under-graduates from Northwestern University. Experiment 2- 185 under-graduates from Northwestern University. Experiment 3- 105 under-graduates. Experiment 4- 164 under-graduates. Experiment 5- 84 people from online panel.	It was found that people not only indulge in compensatory consumption after a threat or negative situation happens; rather they may also engage in it even when they anticipate a threat. Accordingly, compensatory consumption can be reactive as well as pro-active. The only difference is that when they go for reactive compensation, they mainly look in for distraction and thus may consume any type of products whether they are related or unrelated to the particular threat. On the other hand, people in proactive condition consume only threat-related products.

Researcher/Year/Title	Country	Objectives	Sample/Variables	Findings
			Variables- Self-threat, proactive consumption, compensatory consumption, reactive compensatory consumption.	The researchers observed that it is not only sadness, but a feeling of irrevocable loss and helplessness associated with it that motivates individuals to indulge in compensatory consumption.
Garg and Lerner (2013) "Sadness and consumption".	U.S.	To study the effect of helplessness in relation between sadness and consumption.	**Sample-** Two experimental studies with 104 undergraduate students. **Variable-** Sadness and consumption.	
Lee (2013) "The emotional shopper: Assessing the effectiveness of retail therapy".	NA	To test whether retail therapy really works, through tripartite framework- motivational, behavioral and emotional.	Review-based study	Lee (2013) examined the effectiveness of retail therapy from three perspectives-motivational, behavioral and emotional. It was found that shopping gives values like-sensory stimulation, recreation, bargaining, knowledge about new fashion trends, social interaction etc.
Kim and Gal (2014) "Letting go of compensatory consumption".	U.S.	To study the role of "letting go" as a means of self-acceptance to reduce reliance on compensatory consumption.	**Sample-** Experiment 1- 116 under-graduates. Experiment 2- 93 under-graduates. Experiment 3- 115 under-graduates. **Variables-** Self-acceptance and compensatory consumption.	It was found that letting-go reduces the desire for compensatory consumption, even after a mortality threat. Letting-go was found to be a better and healthier option as compared to compensatory consumption.
Rick, Pereira and Burson (2014) "The benefits of retail therapy- Making purchase decisions reduces residual	U.S.	To explore the role of choice in mood-alleviation, through restoration of personal control.	**Sample-** Study 1: 100 adults (52% females) approached online via M-Turk. Study 2: 141 undergraduate	The act of choosing in shopping, as compared to simply browsing, has more significant role in lowering residual sadness. In a real retail scenario, the positive shopping experience can help in regaining the lost control and

Researcher/Year/Title	Country	Objectives	Sample/Variables	Findings
sadness".			students from a Midwestern University. Study 3: 301 undergraduate students from a Southern University. **Variables-** Personal control and retail therapy.	hence contribute towards mood-alleviation. However, this rule is not as such applicable to the negative mood of anger, which is believed to be caused by some other person, rather than one's environment.
Surendran and Vardhan (2014) "Retail therapy: understanding the phenomenon to improve customer experience".	India	To bring out the motivation and psychology behind retail therapy in India.	**Sample-** 30 In-depth interviews. **Variables-** Retail attributes and retail therapy.	As per the results of the study, most of the shoppers were found making unplanned purchases for mood-alleviation. Further, lighting, layout, ambience, loyalty programs etc. were found to play an important role in encouraging buying while quality and return policies etc., were not found to be much important in retail therapy.
Clarke and Mortimer (2013) "Self-gifting guilt: An examination of self-gifting motivations and post-purchase regret".	Australia	To study the relationship between self-gifting motivations, consumption and post-purchase regret.	**Sample-** 136 under-graduate students in Australia. **Variables-** Hedonic shopping, indulgence, self-gifting and regret.	The researchers identified four types of motivations behind self-gifting, including- reward, hedonic, celebratory and therapeutic. It was found that shopping for hedonic and reward reasons do not lead to any guilt feeling; whereas, when people shop for therapeutic or celebratory reasons, guilt may follow.
Melindra and Aprianingsih (2016) "Retail therapy: The impact of therapeutic motivation, therapeutic value and retail environment on consumers' purchase purchase intention".	Indonesia	To analyze the impact of therapeutic motivations and values and also the retail environment on consumers' purchase intention.	**Sample-** 400 shoppers in Bandung and Jakarta. **Variables-** Retail therapy motivations, shopping values, purchase intention, ambience, spatial layout, signage or symbol.	It was found that the retail environment (including ambience and signage) affects purchase intention. The researchers further observed that therapeutic values play more important role than the therapeutic motivations in affecting one's purchase intention.

Researcher/Year/Title	Country	Objectives	Sample/Variables	Findings
Minghui He, Aimei Li (2016) "The impact of sad-spending on emotional recovery process".	China	To study the relation between sadness and compensatory consumption and sad spending on consumer emotions.	**Sample-** Two lab studies Study 1: 30 respondents for pre-experiment and 128 for final. Study 2: 30 respondents **Variables-** Sad spending, emotional recovery, well-being.	It was found that, though, consumption increases positive emotions but it does not essentially lead to reduction of negative emotions. Further, negative emotions significantly increase the hedonic consumption and consumption sum. This amount spent on consumption further enhances positive emotions and reduces negative emotions.
Son and Chang (2016) "Retail therapy: what makes you feel relieved and happy?".	U.S.	To analyze the impact of self-gift motivation, unplanned buying tendency and price consciousness on retail therapy.	**Sample-** 200 respondents in U.S. selected from Amazon's M-Turk (data collection software). **Variables-** Retail therapy, self-gift motivation, unplanned buying tendency and price consciousness.	Based on the data analysis results in this study, it was found that self-gift motivation and unplanned buying tendency positively affect retail therapy. Price consciousness, on the other hand, did not have as significant effect on retail therapy.
Urkmez and Wagner (2016) "Retail therapy: A European perspective on buying luxury items".	Europe	To study how Europeans experience retail therapy, understanding their motivations and post-purchase behavior.	**Sample-** 15 in-depth interviews in Turkey and Poland. **Variables-** Retail therapy	Most of the participants in this study were found to be non-luxury purchasers. The reasons why people shopped for luxury items for therapy included- socialization, communication, distraction, relaxation etc. Such therapeutic shopping was found to be only a temporary solution to problems. Further, it was observed that about half of the respondents did not carry any guilt feeling following the therapy shopping. Others, who regretted their purchase, mainly felt so either because they spent too much money or bought the same items again and again. While comparing the therapy shopping habits of

52

Researcher/Year/Title	Country	Objectives	Sample/Variables	Findings
				shoppers in Poland and Turkey, it was found that Poland consumers bought more for compensatory reasons than those in Turkey.
Singh (2017) "Indian women and compensatory consumption: A confirmatory factor analysis approach".	India	To develop and validate compensatory consumption scale in the Indian context.	**Sample-** 1482 women from six cities in North India, including- Delhi NCR, Ludhiana, Lucknow, Jaipur, Shimla and Chandigarh. Respondents included- housewives, service women, and professionals. **Variables-** Compensatory consumption.	The researchers framed a thirty six items scale for measuring compensatory consumption. These items were grouped into thirteen constructs through EFA and were named as- 'mood repair', 'gratification', 'consciousness', 'desire to acquire', 'compulsivity', 'loneliness', 'impulsivity', 'exploratory buying', 'depression', 'powerfulness', 'narcissism', 'self-gifting' and 'need attention'. Out of these, four were found to influence compensatory consumption i.e. conscientiousness, powerfulness, compulsivity and need attention.
Lee and Bottger (2017) "The therapeutic utility of shopping: Retail therapy, emotion regulation, and well-being".	NA	To examine the therapeutic utility and value of retail therapy.	Review- based study	It was found that shopping is a very effective tool in mood-alleviation. The researchers mentioned about four types of therapeutic motives i.e. affective preservation, affective growth, cognitive preservation and cognitive growth. It was observed that these entire motives could be achieved both through actual purchase as well as window-shopping.
Mandel, Rucker and Galansky (2017) "The compensatory consumer behavior model: How self-discrepancies drive consumer behaviour".	NA	To bring together the literature on using consumer behavior for self-discrepancy regulation.	Review-based study	The researchers built a model showing psychological consequences of self-discrepancies on consumer behavior and the strategies used to deal with them. These strategies included- direct resolution, symbolic self-completion, dissociation, escapism and fluid consumption.

53

Researcher/Year/Title	Country	Objectives	Sample/Variables	Findings
Cifci and Ekinci (2018) "Undesirable effects of retail therapy on consumer emotions and consumer-based brand equity (CBBE)".	Turkey	To examine and measure retail therapy. To determine the impact of retail therapy on negative emotions. To analyze the impact of retail therapy and negative emotions on consumer-based brand equity.	**Sample-** Focus group interviews with graduate students (4 males and 4 females) from a University in Turkey Final study- 310 graduate students. **Variables-** Retail therapy, negative emotions, consumer-based brand equity.	The researchers framed a scale to measure retail therapy behavior. They initially identified 35 items based on review of literature. Out of these, 9 items were retained after exploratory factor analysis and scale validation, using a sample base of 310 respondents. It was observed that when people experience guilt after therapy shopping, they blame themselves and also the brands, which further negatively affects their purchase decisions.
Gitimu and Waithaka (2018) "Retail therapy: Its relationship to gender, life engagement, and subjective happiness".	U.S.	To study the influence of life engagement and subjective happiness on retail therapy.	**Sample-** 377 students from a Mid-Western university. **Variables-** Life engagement, subjective happiness and retail therapy.	The researchers observed marginal positive differences between the retail therapy scores of those high on life engagement than those scoring low on it. On the other hand, only borderline differences could be observed between individuals scoring high and low on subjective happiness, with regard to their retail therapy behavior.
Irwin (2018) "Emotional outlet malls: Exploring retail therapy".	NA	To explore the therapeutic and emotional role played by shopping as retail therapy.	Review-based study	Irwin (2018) brought forward the positive as well as negative side of using shopping for therapeutic reasons. It was found that retail therapy could be a temporary solution to different problems but it could not replace actual therapy or active problem solving.
Rai et al. (2018) "Shopping is a serious affair: Alleviating negative emotions through retail	India	To assess the use of retail therapy for symbolic self-completion and inadequate self.	**Sample-** Expert interview, focus group discussion and data collection from 844 women.	The researchers emphasized on determining the role of self-discrepancy and different types of negative emotions on retail therapy. From the data analysis results, it was found that dejection and disappointment were the

54

Researcher/Year/Title	Country	Objectives	Sample/Variables	Findings
therapy".			**Variables-** Gender, shopping items, self-discrepancy, retail therapy. Income, age and occupation as extraneous variables and product category as control variable.	antecedents of proactive retail therapy; while symbolic self-completion, self-threat and inadequate self mainly led to reactive retail therapy.
Singh & Ahuja (2020) "Understanding emotional shopping: Some reflections and dynamics"	NA	To explore and give reflections on emotional shopping and use of retail therapy	Review-based study and use of Work Cloud in R-studio 3.6.1.	The researchers observed that self-gifting, compensatory consumption, impulse buying etc. are all forms of emotional shopping, which can be termed as retail therapy. It was also reflected as to how emotional shopping aspects such as gratification, self-esteem, self-love etc. can be used to frame emotional marketing strategies by the marketers, thereby leading to relevance of emotional marketing.

Source: Author's elaboration based on review of literature.

55

2.2.2   Therapeutic Shopping Motivations:

Previous research has shown that people may indulge in therapy shopping under different types of negative mood situations e.g. boredom, loneliness, stress, a feeling of helplessness etc. From compensatory consumption perspective, Woodruffe (1996) observed that when people experience excess work pressure, or poor marital relations or lack of self-confidence etc., they try spending money on themselves as a means of combating the depression and stress caused by such negative situations. Similarly, Woodruffe (2001) listed out different types of factors leading to retail therapy (as compensatory consumption), including- 'Internal Factors' i.e. factors related to self (like self-esteem, self-affirmation, self-anxiety etc.), and 'External Factors' including relationship issues and situational factors. All these factors could be either episodic or ongoing.

Rucker and Galinsky (2009) observed that a state of powerlessness motivates individuals to compensate for the loss of power through consumption of status related products. Also, Kim and Gal (2014) found that it is the perceived self-deficit that leads to compensatory behavior. Some of the other researchers have also mentioned about the self-discrepancy issues as motivators behind retail therapy e.g. doubt about one's own identity, feeling excluded from a reference group etc. (Dommer & Swaminathan, 2013).

As far as the mood alleviative perspective is concerned, Kang (2009) found that shopping is used to overcome all the three basic types of negative moods including-irritation, stress and dejection, caused by any temporary negative situations. Further, according to the findings of a survey of 700 women, carried out by sheconomics.com (2009), retail therapy has been found to be mostly backed by the reasons such as 'cheering oneself up', 'feeling low', 'feeling depressed', 'compensating for something missing in life' etc. Many of the study respondents mentioned that, at times of emotional turmoil, spending money on shopping becomes almost irresistible for them.

Huddleston and Minahan (2011) listed a number of probable reasons behind a retail therapy trip such as- escape from overscheduled life, curing sadness or depression, fighting with anger, overcoming an emotionally distressing situation, compensating for a bad day, getting away with boredom etc. At the same time, Garg and Lerner (2013) opined that it is not only the feeling of low control in negative mood state, rather it is

56

the feeling of irrevocable loss and helplessness associated with sadness that motivates one to indulge in compensatory consumption. Based on the results of two experimental studies with 104 undergraduate students, it was found that helplessness mediates the relationship between negative mood and consumption. Apart from this, Rai et al. (2018) carried out a survey of 844 shoppers and found different types of reasons for different forms of retail therapy i.e. 'pro-active' and 'reactive' retail therapy. It was found that pro-active retail therapy is followed by reasons like dejection, disappointment etc., while reactive retail therapy is due to reasons such as self-threat, symbolic self-completion, inadequate self, etc.

Based on the above discussion, it can be concluded that from the compensatory consumption view-point, retail therapy covers both temporary and ongoing reasons as motivators behind retail therapy; whereas, the mood-alleviative perspective covers only the temporary negative mood situations. Since, the present research focuses only on the mood-alleviative approach of retail therapy, thus, only the temporary negative mood events/situations have been studied as retail therapy motivations.

2.2.3 Shopping Values/Therapeutic Powers of Shopping:

Previous research has shown that shopping may have a number of therapeutic powers that make this activity worthful. Luomala (2001) had listed out the therapeutic powers of any consumption activity as: *Distraction* (shopping helps in attention-diversion of the shoppers from the stressful situation to the sensory environment with soothing sounds, smell and display), *Self-indulgence* (the self-indulgence feature of shopping makes it a pleasurable activity e.g. the activities likes trying on items, browsing etc. act as pain-killers for many shoppers), *Stimulated elaboration* (going into deeper thinking, adopting the 'let-go' policy or changing one's own attitude towards the situation e.g. enjoying in nature's lap, weaving etc.), *Recharging* (having a small break to feel in power again or to accumulate strength to deal with the situation e.g. going for movie, spa etc. It helps to overcome stress or dejection), *Discharging* (basically related to shedding off the negative energy through activities like cleaning, gym, sports etc. It effectively helps in reducing the irritation level, *Retreat* (going to a completely different stimulating environment that helps to reduce the stress level), *Activation* (doing some

57

innovative things where the brain is actively involved to regain the energy e.g. experimental cooking, browsing in stores etc., which can help in coping with dejection), and last but not the least *Outcomes of mood-alleviative activities as a therapeutic power* (sometimes the result or outcome that one gets out of indulging in some therapeutic activity may itself be therapeutic too e.g. appreciation for the products bought during therapy shopping, painting etc.). Out of all these values, three values have been found to be most closely related to the shopping activity i.e. 'distraction', 'self-indulgence' and 'activation' (Kang, 2009).

Kang (2009) and Kang & Johnson (2011) divided the therapeutic values of shopping into two categories including: 'positive reinforcement' and 'negative mood reduction'. The 'positive reinforcement' value indicates the power of shopping activity that helps in maintenance of positive mood state or in boosting it through positive distraction, visual stimulation, knowledge about new trends, pleasant environment etc. On the other hand, the 'negative mood reduction' value includes those aspects of shopping that help one to get rid of negative mood state or stressful environment e.g. offering an escape from loneliness, filling an empty feeling, regaining control etc. Huddleston and Minahan (2011) also mentioned positive distraction, escape, indulgence, elevation of self-esteem, activation of senses, gaining control and social connection as the main therapeutic values derived from shopping.

Lee (2013) examined the effectiveness of retail therapy from three perspectives i.e. motivational, behavioral and emotional. It was observed that one's mood could be enhanced through different acts like- buying hedonic items, through sensory stimulation, getting a desired item, getting deals and offers, learning about the new fashion trends, bargaining, shopping with companions, interacting with fellow shoppers or employees of retail stores etc. The researchers opined that each activity in the shopping process including browsing, interacting with sales people, choosing, paying, acquiring and consuming etc., has its own value in mood-alleviation.

On the basis of the above given literature, it can be concluded that shopping is regarded as a therapeutic activity because of the varied psychological benefits that it offers to the shoppers. These benefits/therapeutic values attract people to engage in it when they experience any kind of negative feelings. The upcoming section further elaborates on whether such therapy shopping trips are successful or not and what outcomes are experienced by these shoppers.

2.2.4 Outcomes of Retail Therapy:

There has been a debate as to whether use of shopping as a therapy has positive or negative outcomes for the consumers. In this regard, most of the research studies have brought forward the positive and constructive role played by retail therapy in one's life. The researchers like Kang (2009), Kang & Johnson (2010), Atalay & Meloy (2011), Deon (2011), D'Souza (2012), Lee (2013), Surendran & Vardhan (2014), Rick et al. (2014) etc. observed that retail therapy successfully alleviates negative mood and this good feeling is also retained for a longer period. Hama (2001) found that spending a considerable amount of money on buying for diversion can help in achieving productive results for the shoppers who seek stress relief.

Kang and Johnson (2010) stated that retail therapy is a normal behavior and shoppers do feel happy and relaxed after shopping. Further, coping with negative mood in this way can as well contribute to the psychological well-being of individuals in the long-run. Apart from this, Deon (2011), Atalay and Meloy (2011) and D'Souza (2012) also observed that most of the people who engage in retail therapy do not experience any guilt or depression afterwards. Emphasizing on the importance of mood-alleviative shopping, Luomala (2001) observed that people engage in it because the positive outcomes of shopping usually outweigh its negative effects.

There have also been studies that have mentioned about the negative consequences of retail therapy, especially in the long-run. In this regard, Woodruffe (2001) observed that though, compensating for short-term problems through shopping might lead to immediate positive emotions, but when shopping is used repeatedly for more intense and ongoing issues, it might start taking the form of addiction. Woodruffe (2001) explained this with the help of a continuum of shopping clearly showing that how beginning from a normal shopping, a person can later become compulsive or addictive shopper. Joji and Raveendran (2007) observed that retail therapy may have positive results in short term, but in the long- run, it may lead to highly negative

59

consequences like falling into the huge debt-traps. Similarly, Kim and Gal (2014) also brought forward the negative side of shopping as a compensatory consumption activity. The researchers suggested that using shopping for coping with negative mood can be detrimental in the long-run and thus, people must try to find out other alternatives e.g. using a 'let go' policy.

In the above discussion, a point worth noting is that most of the studies that have brought forward the negative side of retail therapy have apparently studied it from compensatory view-point. On the other hand, the researchers, who have studied the mood-alleviative perspective of retail therapy, have mostly agreed to its benefits and advantages. It has been found that retail therapy can give relief and happiness to the shoppers at least on a temporary basis and can become problematic only if it takes form of addiction.

In addition to presenting the review related to the concept, motivations, values and outcomes of retail therapy; the role of personal characteristics in this behavior has also been explained in the upcoming section (section 2.3).

2.3   REVIEW   RELATED   TO   THE   IMPACT   OF   PERSONAL CHARACTERISTICS ON RETAIL THERAPY BEHAVIOR

Consumer shopping behavior has been found to be highly influenced by personal characteristics of shoppers. It has been found that the personal characteristics including demographics, personality traits, attitude, perception etc. are a reflection about what type of shopper a person is i.e. for what motives she(/he) uses shopping, what type of shopping decisions that person takes, whether or not the market stimuli influences her(/him) etc. (Verplanken & Herabadi, 2001; Prasad, 2010; Shukla & Babin, 2013). Not only this, importance of personal factors has also been recognized in coping literature in psychology. It has been found that the way a person reacts to stress and the type of strategies that one adopts for emotion regulation, are highly determined by the psychological characteristics of that person (Duhachek & Iacobucci, 2005).

Focusing on studying the role of the personal characteristics in consumption activity, Luomala (2001) mentioned that knowing this relationship can help in getting an understanding as to why people choose consumption for mood-alleviation. Kang

(2009) also emphasized that there is a need to uncover such personal characteristics of individuals that might be leading to retail therapy, because this can further help in profiling of the therapy shoppers. Apart from this, Lee (2013) also stressed on the studying of individual differences in demographics, Big-Five and various other psychological measures like regulatory focus, approach avoidance motivation etc. in retail therapy behavior, for a better understanding of its antecedents.

Till date, only a few studies have actually examined this relationship e.g. Arnold and Reynolds (2009) observed a significant relationship between regulatory focus and retail therapy. The researchers mentioned that although, people are inherently motivated to reduce negative mood and enhance positive mood, they might differ in their approach to do so. Based on the results of two studies- a lab experiment with 79 under-graduate students and a survey with 578 non-student respondents, the researchers found that promotion-focused individuals put in extra effort to repair negative mood. They are also more sensitive towards the hedonic elements of consumption. Arnold and Reynolds (2009) suggested that since, mood regulation is a relatively stable personality trait, retailers can help mood-repairers by providing an up-beat and exploratory kind of shopping environment.

Atalay and Meloy (2011) also observed similar relation between regulatory focus and retail therapy. It was found that people with greater prevention orientation were less expected to engage in retail therapy. Kemp and Kopp (2011) studied the concept of retail therapy under the name of 'emotion regulation consumption', which they defined as consumption activity to repair or manage short-term emotions. The researchers separately studied the impact of different types of emotions including amusement, sadness, fear/anxiety and contentment, on hedonic consumption for emotion-regulation. Side by side, the moderating role of coping strategies had also been determined. Based on the results of two experimental studies with students from a University in the United States, it was found that sad individuals made greater use of hedonic consumption for mood-repair. At the same time, those experiencing mood of amusement also indulged in hedonic consumption for maintenance of positive mood. Further, people who made lesser use of cognitive reappraisal were less able to down-regulate emotions internally and thus indulged more in hedonic consumption.

Chang et al. (2012) carried out a survey with 167 under-graduates and found that hedonic shopping motivation predicts retail therapy, which in turn affects post-shopping emotions. Further, Kang et al. (2013) mentioned about the use of clothing for mood-alteration. It was found that personality variables play an indirect role in this regard e.g. perfectionism and neuroticism lead to social appearance anxiety and proximity of clothing to self. These further lead to use of clothing for mood-regulation while fulfilling different functions like comfort, camouflage, fashion, assurance etc. In another study by Son and Chang (2016), it was found that one's shopping orientation and impulse buying tendency significantly predict retail therapy behavior. The researchers also tried to find if price consciousness also affected retail therapy, but the results were not found to be statistically significant.

Gitimu and Waithaka (2018) carried out a survey with 377 students from a Midwestern University. It was found that retail therapy is affected by one's level of life engagement and also by subjective happiness. As such, people with larger purpose in life, enjoy indulging in retail therapy for the sake of adding more value to their life. At the same time, people who score low on subjective happiness also indulge more in retail therapy for coping with negative mood.

Except for the above mentioned studies, not much of the literature focusing on understanding of the influential role of personal factors in retail therapy could be found. Even the existing research work also suffers from some major weaknesses. First amongst them is that most of the previous researchers have ignored the effect of basic human characteristics (e.g. demographics, personality etc.) that might be predictive of retail therapy. As such, the importance of these factors has been well-known in consumer behavior and marketing field. Their relationship with other emotional shopping types has also been studied by many researchers e.g. the personality traits such as neuroticism, conscientiousness or extraversion etc. have been found to predict impulsive or compulsive buying (e.g. Gustavsson et al., 2003; Joshanloo et al., 2012; Shahjehan et al., 2012; Gohary & Hanzaee, 2014, etc.). Similarly, demographic characteristics of people e.g. their age, income level, gender, etc. have also been found to affect their involvement in shopping for different kinds of motives (e.g. Dhurup,

2008; Tiwari & Abraham 2010; Azizi & Shariffar, 2011 etc.). However, still these factors have been rarely studied in the context of retail therapy.

The purpose of this research has been to fill in the existing gap in the literature and examine the impact of some of the selected individual characteristics in retail therapy. As such, for the purpose of this study, the basic personality traits i.e. the 'Big-Five'; two of the shopping-related personality traits i.e. shopping orientation (chronic) and impulse buying tendency; and also the demographic characteristics of individuals have been studied. The explanation of all these variables, along with their hypothesized relationship with retail therapy, has been presented in the following sections.

2.3.1 Demographic Characteristics and Retail Therapy Behavior:

The proposed relationship of different demographic characteristics including, age, gender, income, occupation etc., with retail therapy has been explained as under:

➤ **Age:** Researchers have highlighted that youngsters are usually more prone to emotional shopping than older people. They visit malls more for reasons like escape and socialization (Tiwari & Abraham, 2010). Kim and Kim (2005) observed that females belonging to Gen Y usually shop more for bargaining and diversion reasons. They have more spending power and are competent shoppers (Javed & Jalbani, 2010). Also, as per the findings of D'Souza (2012), retail therapy is mostly sought by the people belonging to the age group of 21-40 years, whereas people in the age group of less than 20 years and more than 40 years indulge very less in shopping for therapeutic purposes. Based on the evidence available in the past literature, it is hypothesized as under-

H₁: Age negatively relates to Retail Therapy Behavior, such that youngsters are more inclined towards therapy shopping.

➤ **Marital status:** The second element is 'marriage'. Marriage is a major transition is one's life. Married women usually carry far more responsibilities than unmarried women and therefore, experience more anxiety comparatively (APA, 2010). They are more family-oriented and are usually not able to spare time for themselves. Depending upon the requirements of their family, married women usually consider grocery buying as an important part of shopping. On the other hand, for the

63

unmarried women, shopping is more about buying apparels and accessories (Javed & Jalbani, 2010). Li et al. (2015) found that married women above the age of about 40 years usually spend more time and money on their families (especially children) and less on themselves. On the other hand, those who are unmarried have more money to be freely spent on self. Considering particularly the Indian context, married women enjoy less independence in spending their money and are usually accountable to their husband or other elder family members for their purchases (Kishor & Gupta, 2004; Sheth & Vittal, 2007). Based on this available information, it is expected that married women in India might be using shopping for therapeutic reasons comparatively lesser than the unmarried women. It is accordingly hypothesized that-

H₂: Marital Status negatively relates to Retail Therapy Behavior, such that unmarried women are more inclined towards therapy shopping.

➤ **Employment status:** The third important demographic characteristic seems to be employment status of women. Literature states that, due to multiple responsibilities, working women usually experience more stress and anxiety as compared to non-working women (Hashami et al., 2007; Aleem & Danish, 2008; Kermane, 2016). Due to over-burden at work and the constant familial responsibilities, they always strive to find some idle time to relax and regain energy. Since, the present study relates with going out to some retail store for therapy shopping; it is probable that working women might not be having idle time for the same. On the other hand, non-working women are expected to get more free time to be spent on shopping activity. Accordingly, it is hypothesized that-

H₃: Employment Status negatively relates to Retail Therapy Behavior, such that non-working women are more inclined towards therapy shopping.

➤ **Income:** Fourth element in the demographics is the income of a person. Personal income of an individual is made up of disposable income and discretionary income. Whereas, disposable income is the actual income after tax; the income finally left in one's hands after providing for all the necessary expenditures is the discretionary income (Ramya & Ali, 2016). Logically, to buy something for therapeutic reasons can be done only if one has some sort of discretionary income in hand. Although, purchase is not necessary in retail therapy, but most of the therapy shoppers feel good only after they have acquired something (Kang & Johnson, 2010). Further, it has been found that individuals in sad mood like to buy gifts for themselves (Clarke & Mortimer, 2013), spend more impulsively (Atalay & Meloy, 2011), and are usually willing to pay more for given products (Lerner et al., 2004). Thus, based on the expectation that the discretionary income with a person would affect engaging in buying for therapeutic reasons, it is hypothesized that-

H₄: Discretionary Income positively relates to Retail Therapy Behavior, such that women with more discretionary income are more inclined towards therapy shopping.

2.3.2 The Big-Five Personality Traits and Retail Therapy Behavior:

The second type of personal characteristics covered in study is the personality traits. Personality of an individual can be defined as "...the inner psychological characteristics that both determine and reflect how a person responds to his or her environment" (Schiffman & Kanuk, 2010, p. 136). Amongst different psychological factors, personality of an individual has been found to be the one that influences consumer behavior to a great extent (Schiffman & Kanuk, 2010; Solomon, 2011).

There have been a number of theories that help in better understanding of the concept of personality e.g. Psychoanalytic theory, Neo-Freudian theory, Trait theory etc. (Schiffman & Kanuk, 2010). Amongst these, the 'Trait theory' (which explains personality to be made up of different traits that are measurable in quantitative terms), has been most widely accepted (Burger, 2000; Schiffman & Kanuk, 2010). The 'Big-Five' personality traits model identifies these traits as: Extraversion, Agreeableness, Conscientiousness, Neuroticism and Openness to Experience/Intellect (Costa & McCrae, 1985, John & Srivastava, 1999). The expected relationship of these traits to retail therapy has been explained as under:

➢ **Extraversion:** The trait of Extraversion represents one's joy and pleasure in being sociable (Costa, Jr & McCrae, 1992). Extroverts like to interact with others and are livelier. Extraversion has been found to have a positive relation with hedonic

65

shopping behavior (Guido et al., 2007), impulse buying behavior and also compulsive buying (Shahjehan et al., 2011). According to Guido et al. (2007), extroverts seek sensory stimulation and diversion. Since, shopping has been found to have the power of fulfilling the social needs as well as offer diversion from negative situations, it is expected that extroverts might be using it as a coping strategy for dealing with negative mood. Accordingly, it has been hypothesized that-

H₅: Extraversion positively influences Retail Therapy Behavior.

> **Agreeableness:** Agreeableness is related to the need for harmonious relations (Zurawicki, 2010). Agreeable individuals are more sympathetic, helping and forgiving (Costa, Jr & McCrae, 1992; Pervin, 2006). They are better at emotion regulation and do not usually experience negative emotions as strongly as others being low on this trait (Ho et al., 2004). Individuals high on agreeableness are socially adaptable, welcoming and friendly. They experience less inter-personal conflict and less social stress (Asendorpf, 1998). They automatically neutralize negative thoughts and mainly use positive coping strategies such as cognitive reappraisal, for emotion regulation (Sadr, 2016). According to Carver and Smith (2010), agreeable individuals engage lesser in diversion or escape activities for coping with stressors, rather they rely more on social coping. As per the given information, it is expected that individuals who score high on this dimension may be making lesser use of shopping for compensatory reasons. Thus, it is hypothesized as under:

H₆: Agreeableness negatively influences Retail Therapy Behavior.

> **Conscientiousness:** People high on conscientiousness are well-organized, reliable, self-disciplined and dutiful (Costa, Jr & McCrae, 1992; Pervin, 2006; Maltby et al., 2010). They are good at controlling their impulses and delay gratification (Zurawicki, 2010). According to Taylor and Kluemper (2012), conscientious individuals are less likely to respond to negative events. They work towards adaptive emotion regulation, so that they are finally able to reach their goals (Sadr, 2016). They predict and plan for stressors in advance. Accordingly, they are less

exposed to stress (Vollrath 2001). John and Srivastava (1999) specified that conscientious individuals are less likely to engage in any compensatory behaviors and are expected to solve their problems directly or in other responsible ways. Accordingly, based on the findings and opinions of the previous researchers, it is hypothesized that:

H7: Conscientiousness negatively influences Retail Therapy Behavior.

➤ **Neuroticism:** Neuroticism is an individual's tendency of experiencing psychological distress (Costa, Jr. & McCrae, 1992). Neurotic people often complain of worry, nervousness, insecurity and lack of emotional stability (Goldberg, 1990; Pervin, 2006). They usually appraise events as highly threatening (Penley & Tomaka 2002, Suls & Martin 2005) and are also less likely to express their emotions (Sadr, 2016). The previous literature has shown that neuroticism mainly leads to the use of emotion-focused coping strategies (Hooker et al., 1994; Watson & Hubbard, 1996). Since, shopping is also an emotion-focused coping strategy, it is hypothesized that:

H8: Neuroticism positively influences Retail Therapy Behavior.

➤ **Intellect/Openness to Experience:** Individuals high on the trait of Intellect are more open to new experiences and are not conventional in their ideas (Costa, Jr. & McCrae, 1992). They are sensitive to art and beauty (John & Srivastava, 1999). They are intellectually curious and experience the complexity of both positive and negative emotions more keenly than others (Matzler et al., 2006). Because of being more imaginative and excited about new things; they are likely to welcome any kind of emotions (Sadr, 2016). It has also been found that people high on this trait experience more positive affect and make more use of engagement coping strategies such as problem-focused strategies or emotion-focused strategies like social support, acceptance, emotion regulation strategies etc. (Carver & Smith, 2010). Since, shopping is an activity that can fulfill the variety seeking needs of such individuals and offer them an exciting experience; it can be hypothesized that:

H9: Intellect positively influences Retail Therapy Behavior.

67

2.3.3 Shopping Orientation (Chronic) and Retail Therapy Behavior:

Shopping orientation is the general attitude or predisposition of customers towards the act of shopping (Brown et al., 2001). It can basically be of two types- experiential (/hedonic) shopping orientation and task-focused (/utilitarian) shopping orientation. People with experiential orientation usually look for the multi-sensory and emotive aspects of shopping. They are more concerned with emotional quality of products and overall shopping experience (Voss et al., 2003). That is why, many a times, up-lifting mood is a major motivation behind experiential shopping. According to Kang and Johnson (2011), retail therapy seems to belong to the family of hedonic shopping, because it is logical to assume that people, who find shopping as interesting and entertaining, may be choosing it for mood-alleviative reasons as well. On the other hand, those who view shopping as a task shall not be motivated to indulge in it for therapy also (Son & Chang, 2016). Accordingly, it is expected that one's experiential shopping orientation would positively affect retail therapy behavior.

For the purpose of the present research, the experiential shopping orientation has been measured using the 'Chronic Shopping Orientation' scale given by Buttner et al. (2011) and accordingly, the terms shopping orientation and chronic shopping orientation have been used interchangeably. The hypothesis has been as follows:

H_{10}: Chronic Shopping Orientation positively influences Retail Therapy Behavior.

2.3.4 Impulse Buying Tendency and Retail Therapy Behavior:

The impulse buying tendency is the tendency of an individual to engage in impulse or spontaneous purchases, without consideration to the outcomes of such purchase (Rook & Fisher, 1995). Buying on impulse has been closely related to the experiences of boredom and distress. The mood and retail therapy research says that people use impulse buying as an instrument for self-regulating negative feelings or as a self-reward when feeling low (Mick & DeMoss, 1990; Baumeister, 2002; Kang, 2009; Atalay & Meloy, 2011; D'Souza, 2012; Son & Chang, 2016). Given this, impulse buying tendency is expected to have a positive relationship with retail therapy. It is, therefore, hypothesized that:

H_{11}: Impulse Buying Tendency positively influences Retail Therapy Behavior.

2.4 REVIEW RELATED TO THE SHOPPING BEHAVIOR OF THERAPY SHOPPERS AND ROLE OF SHOPPING PROCESS ELEMENTS

This particular section of review covers two sub-sections- First, showing the previous studies' results with regard to the shopping behavior exhibited by the shoppers when they shop for mood-alleviation, and second, covering the review related to the mood-alleviative role of different elements in the shopping process.

2.4.1 Shopping Behavior of Shoppers during Retail Therapy Trip:

Previous research has shown that when people shop for mood-alleviative reasons, they usually behave somewhat differently than how they behave during any usual shopping trips. These behavioral aspects are quite beneficial for the retailers and they can gain more focusing on the therapeutic needs of such shoppers. Some of these shopping behavior elements include-

1. **Therapy shoppers mostly buy on impulse-** It has been found that therapy shoppers are more concerned about getting rid of their negative mood state, following which they are unable to control their impulses and they fall prey for impulse buying (Baumeister, 2002; Atalay & Meloy, 2011; Lee, 2013).

2. **Therapy shoppers prefer to buy self-gifts-** It has been observed that, many a times, therapy shoppers feel good when they buy something for themselves as a gift (Mick & De Moss, 1990; Luomala, 2002; Atalay & Meloy, 2011; Clarke & Mortimer, 2013; Kaur & Kaur, 2016). According to Mick et al. (1992), self-gifts carry a symbolic meaning, especially for women. When they are stressed out due to some major life transitions or due to disturbed inter-personal relations etc., self-gifting makes them feel happy, proud and special. Moreover, due to the specialness feature, use of these self-gifts in future reminds them of the shopping experience too. In rare circumstances, however, self-gifting might lead to a guilt feeling afterwards e.g. in China, Sun (2007) found that many individuals experience a feeling of being selfish if they buy something for themselves. As a solution to this, they also buy something for the other family members to justify their own purchase.

69

3.   **Therapy shoppers are store loyal-** Previous researchers observed that when therapy shoppers find their shopping experience to be enriching; they are expected to visit the same stores whenever they are in a down mood in future also. They are less likely to switch stores (Kang, 2009; Kang & Johnson, 2010).

4.   **Therapy shoppers like to shop alone-** It has been found that therapy shoppers prefer to shop alone when feeling sad or depressed (Woodruffe, 2001). This gives them a chance to think and decide on their own without anyone's interference.

5.   **Therapy shoppers spend more time-** It has been found that therapy shoppers tend to spend more than usual time, when they are out for a therapy shopping trip. In general, such shoppers have also been found to be frequent shoppers (Kang & Johnson, 2010).

6.   **Therapy shoppers spend more money-** Since, the attention of therapy shoppers is more towards mood-alleviation; they usually do not realize about the amount of money they spend (Kang & Johnson, 2010). Previous research also showed that sadness leads to increased willingness to pay for products (Lerner et al., 2004); and this usually happens unconsciously (Cryder et al., 2008).

7.   **Therapy shoppers like to shop at brick-and-mortar stores:** As far as the retail format choice is concerned, Kang (2009) observed that therapy shoppers like to shop at brick and mortar stores, rather than using online shopping or other modes. This is probably due to fact that they get a face to face interaction opportunity as compared to other modes.

8.   **Therapy shoppers are more concerned with experiential aspects of shopping-** Although, the products purchased during therapy shopping are important for shoppers; however, the sensory elements present in the retail environment like ambience and store interiors etc., can also effectively contribute towards mood-alleviation (D'Souza, 2012; Surendran & Vardhan, 2014).

9.   **Therapy shoppers seek social interaction-** It has been found that lonely individuals choose to go for shopping because of the social interaction they can

get at the shopping place (Kim et al., 2005). In general, it has been found that interacting with other fellow shoppers helps individuals in generating good feelings and increases shopping satisfaction (Gray et al., 2011; Borges et al. 2010). Further, the pampering by the sales personnel also makes therapy shoppers feel special. At times, even mere presence of other shoppers can make some people feel good (Lee, 2013).

10.   **Therapy shoppers like to buy more of appearance related products-** The type of products purchased during a retail therapy trip has its own importance in mood-alleviation. In this regard, Kang (2009) found that therapy shoppers mostly like to purchase appearance related products like fashionable clothing, accessories, jewelry etc. and sometimes even certain non-appearance related products such as kitchenware items, household items, electronics, hardware, books, bicycle items etc. Some shoppers even purchase items which they might not ordinarily purchase, such as high-priced items or fashionable and trendy apparel items (Atalay & Meloy, 2011).

Some of the gender differences have also been observed with regard to products purchased during therapy shopping trip e.g. D'souza (2012) found that women across all age groups enjoy shopping. They like to buy apparels, accessories, shoes, jewelry etc. In addition, older women also like to buy something for their home and family. Similarly, Surendran and Vardhan (2014) found that women mostly purchase apparels, food, accessories etc., while men mostly like to purchase food, electronics, movies and games etc. during their therapy shopping trips.

11.   **Therapy shoppers prefer to pay by card-** It has been observed that therapy shoppers mostly like to make credit card payments, instead of paying by cash. This is probably because credit/debit card payments are less transparent because of which shoppers experience lesser pain while using this mode (Loewenstein & O'Donoghue, 2006).

2.4.2   Role of Shopping Process Elements and Retail Environment:

Talking about the role of the shopping process in therapy shopping, different researchers have brought forward different types of factors that help shoppers alleviate

71

their negative mood and feel relaxed. Starting from the simple thought of going for shopping to the post-shopping experience, therapy shoppers may find relief at any stage (Lee, 2013; Kaur & Kaur, 2016). For some, it may be the products purchased, or the bargain price etc. that help in overcoming sadness, while for others, the retail atmosphere, or the personnel behavior etc. may be more important (Lee, 2013).

Luomala (2001) mentioned that sometimes people might also be able to combat negative mood through means of consumption vision i.e. just imagining consumption in their mind, while others might experience that feeling through some external aid e.g. turning over the sales catalogues etc. Hama (2001), further observed that spending more money and buying more expensive products leads to stress release. Similarly, Arnold and Reynolds (2003) observed that many shoppers experience pleasure when they are able to find striking product deals.

A study by Kim et al. (2005), on retail therapy behavior of lonely older shoppers, showed that for experiential oriented shoppers; interacting with other shoppers or sales personnel is more therapeutic than other things. Argo et al. (2005) also found that crowding at retail stores (/presence of other shoppers) can have positive effect on shopping. However, at the same time, when number of non-interacting shoppers increases beyond a limit, the shopping experience starts becoming negative.

The researchers like Woodruffe (2001) and Luomala (2002) emphasized on the importance of the sensory stimulation, created by the retail environment, in mood-alleviation. Surendran and Vardhan (2014) found that product range, ambience and store interiors are the most influencing factors in therapy shopping, while quality of store personnel and exchange/return policies do not carry much relevance.

Rick et al. (2014) found that the act of choosing the products from given variety also helps in gaining a sense of control and thereby helps in alleviating sad mood. Through two studies (one involving only choosing and browsing activity and the other involving real shopping), the researchers proved that when sad shoppers buy a product of their own choice, they are more happy than those who do not get such chance. In addition, deciding on the stores to shop from may also help shoppers experience a sense of control and feel happy (Rick et al., 2014). In another study, Kaur and Kaur (2019) observed that people, who visit malls for mood-alleviative motives, are influenced more by retail factors including, ambience, convenience and entertainment.

From the above discussion, it can be concluded that individuals who shop with mood-alleviative reasons (/therapy reasons) are mostly persuaded by hedonic shopping elements and are less concerned with the utilitarian elements. They pay less attention to the product features, quality elements, price etc. They, rather, prefer entertaining shopping experience and like to buy products that can lead to immediate gratification.

2.5   RESEARCH GAPS AND RATIONALE OF THE STUDY

Based on the review of previous studies on retail therapy, the following research gaps have been observed that lay foundation for the present research.

2.5.1   Problem with Regard to Conceptualization of Retail Therapy:

The concept of retail therapy has been, many a times, confused with other related types of emotional shopping behaviors. Firstly, the terms retail therapy and compensatory consumption have been used interchangeably in a number of studies. At the same time, the concept has also been found to share a close bond with other shopping behaviors like impulse buying, compulsive buying, self-gifting, hedonic shopping etc. This has led to a confusion regarding conceptualization of retail therapy.

The present research has attempted to theoretically clarify these behaviors and present the similarities and dissimilarities that they all share with retail therapy. This has, however, been done only theoretically (in chapter 1) and no empirical data has been analyzed for the same.

2.5.2   Most of the Research Work is Concentrated in Western Countries:

As explained in Chapter 1 also, retail therapy has been found to be a commonly adopted mood-alleviative activity in western countries, especially U.S. and U.K. Accordingly, major portion of the research work in this field is also concentrated in these countries only. Although, the term retail therapy is now being used in India too, however, the research work in this field is just at a nascent stage. Only few of the researchers have worked on exploring the concept and understanding its usage e.g. Nair

73

(2004); D'Souza (2012); Surendran and Vardhan (2014); Rai et al. (2018) etc. Further, most of these studies are either interview-based or review-based and there is a lack of empirical work on this topic in India. Thus, whether and to what extent people in India shop for therapeutic reasons and what kind of shopping behavior they exhibit during such a shopping trip is not much known.

To fill in this gap, the present research has been carried out in the Indian context. The study is particularly focused on women shoppers. It is expected that carrying out research in a country like India where the retail scenario as well as the lifestyle of people (especially women) is much different than that of the western countries, can offer new insights in research on retail therapy.

2.5.3   Lack of Recognition of Shopping as a Coping Strategy:

Although, consumer behavior literature contains a number of studies that have highlighted the usage and importance of retail therapy in mood-alleviation and well-being; shopping activity has still not got a recognizable place amongst the list of coping strategies. It has been found that most of the studies on coping have made use of some standardized coping scales (adopted from psychology literature) that rarely mention shopping activity as any of the items. As a result, these studies have not been able to throw much light on whether or not people recognize shopping as a coping strategy.

The present study has dealt with this issue by particularly asking the women respondents about the different types of strategies and activities that they use to cope with negative mood situations. It has been tried to find out whether shopping is also one of these activities.

2.5.4   Lack of Empirical Work:

Most of the existing studies on retail therapy have either been based on in-depth interviews or experiments or are review-based e.g. Woodruffe (1997/98/2001); Luomala (1998/2001/02); Nair (2004); Kang & Johnson (2010); Kim & Rucker (2012); D'Souza (2012); Garg & Lerner (2013); Lee (2013); Kim & Gal (2013); Rick et al. (2014); Surendran & Vardhan (2014); Mortimer (2015); Urkmez & Wagner (2016); Lee & Bottger (2017), Mandel et al. (2017); Cifci & Ekinci (2018); Irwin (2018) etc. These theoretical and experimental studies have contributed a lot towards the basic understanding of retail therapy behavior and also about its positive role in mood-alleviation and well-being. However, the extent to which people practically make use of shopping for therapeutic reasons; the outcomes they experience; the role of personal or situational factors that lead to retail therapy etc. can be better assessed by taking up of a larger chunk of respondents. As such carrying out a public survey can solve the matter and help in understanding the attitude and behavior of respondents in a better way (The SAGE Encyclopedia of Communication Research Methods). This can also help in authenticating the results of the previous experimental studies while making the research more competent (ukdissertations.in). To fill this gap, data has been collected from Indian women using survey method, to assess their retail therapy behavior.

2.5.5   Role of Personal Factors has been ignored:

Consumer shopping behavior has been found to be highly influenced by the personal characteristics of the shoppers. It has been found that people not only consume products for the mere sake of consumption, rather, the products they consume also reflect their personality and image in the society (Solomon et al., 2010). Many of them prefer to buy those products which they perceive to be similar to their own identity i.e. who they are (Dalton, 2009). Emphasizing on the importance of the personal factors in shopping behavior, Badgaiyan and Verma (2014) suggested that, though, marketers can do nothing about customers' personality, but having knowledge about the same can, at least, help them in devising better policies.

As far as coping with or managing of mood is concerned, research has shown that personal characteristics of individuals affect the way they deal with stress and also the form of stress-relief strategies they use (Andrade, 2005). However, despite their importance, very few studies have attempted to determine the role of such personal factors in retail therapy behavior. Some of the factors covered in the previous literature include- regulatory focus, distress tolerance, shopping orientation etc. The factors that have been mostly ignored by the previous researchers include- basic human characteristics (e.g. personality traits, demographics etc.) that might be predictive of engaging in retail therapy.

75

The present research has attempted to fill this gap by analyzing the influential impact of some of the selected personal factors on retail therapy. These include- the basic/elementary personality traits i.e. The 'Big-five traits'; two shopping-related personality variables i.e. 'Chronic shopping orientation' and 'Impulse buying tendency' and the 'Demographic characteristics' of respondents. The hypothesized relationship of these factors with retail therapy has already been explained in section 2.3 of this chapter.

CONCLUSION

This chapter has covered the review of the existing literature on various topics related to retail therapy. The chapter began with the general understanding of what literature says about coping strategies used by people (especially women) and then explaining as to how shopping is used for coping with negative mood. It further explained the role the personal factors in retail therapy and finally highlighted the different behavioral aspects related to the therapy shopping trip behavior of retail therapy shoppers. While going through the literature, a number of research gaps had been identified, which have also been covered in the chapter. The present research has tried to fill these gaps through statistical analysis shown in different data analysis chapters of this thesis. Further, the methodology adopted for the research has been explained in the upcoming chapter (chapter-3).

REFERENCES

1. Aleem, S. & Danish, L. (2008). Marital satisfaction and anxiety among single and dual career women. *Journal of the Indian Academy of Applied Psychology,* 34,141-144.

2. American Psychological Association (APA) (2010). *Stress on the rise for women.* Retrieved from http://www.apa.org/news/press/releases/stress/2010/ gender-stress.aspx.

3. Andrade, E. B. (2005). Behavioral consequences of affect: Combining evaluative and regulatory mechanisms. *Journal of Consumer Research*, 32(3), 355-362.

4. Argo, J., Dahl, D. & Manchanda, R. (2005). The influence of a mere social presence in a retail context. *Journal of Consumer Research*, 32(2), 207-212.

5. Arnold, M. J. & Reynolds, K. E. (2003). Hedonic shopping motivations. *Journal of Retailing,* 79(2), 77-95.

6. Arnold, M. J. & Reynolds, K. E. (2009). Affect and retail shopping behavior: Understanding the role of mood regulation and regulatory focus. *Journal of Retailing*, 85(3), 308–320.

7. Asendorpf, J. B. (1998). Personality effects on social relationships. *Journal of Personality and Social Psychology*, 74, 1531–44.

8. Atalay, A. S. & Meloy, M. G. (2011). When the going gets tough, the tough go shopping- An examination of self-gifting behaviour. *Advances in Consumer Research,* 33, 259-260.

9. Azizi, S. & Shariffar, A. (2011). Non-functional shopping motives among Iranian consumers. *Management and Marketing*, 9(2), 274-282.

10. Badgaiyan, A. J. & Verma, A. (2014). Intrinsic factors affecting impulsive buying behaviour—Evidence from India. *Journal of Retailing and Consumer Services*, 21(4), 537–549.

11. Baker, J. P. & Berenbaum, H. (2007). Emotional approach and problem-focused coping: A comparison of potentially adaptive strategies. *Cognition and Emotion,* 21(1), 95-118.

12. Barden, N. (2015). *Gender and personality differences in self-gifting behaviour and the impact of locus of control.* 51.

13. Baumeister, R. F. (2002). Yielding to temptation: Self-control failure, impulsive purchasing, and consumer behavior. *Journal of Consumer Research,* 28(4), 670–676.

14. Borges, A., Chebat, J. C. & Babin, B. J. (2010). Does a companion always enhance the shopping experience? *Journal of Retailing and Consumer Services,* 17(4), 294–299.

15. Brown, M., Pope, N. & Voges, K. (2001). Buying or browsing? An exploration of shopping orientations and online purchase intention. *European Journal of Marketing,* 37(11), 1666-1684.

16. Bruchon-Schweitzer, M. (2001). Coping and adjustment strategies for dealing with stress. *Nursing Research,* 68-83.

17. Burger, J. M. (2000). *Personality.* Fifth Ed., Belmont, CA: Wadsworth/ Thompson.

18. Burke, K. (2018). The neuroscience behind retail therapy. *All Regis University Theses.* 864. https://epublications.regis.edu/theses/864.

19. Buttner, O., Florack, A. & Goritz, A. S. (2013). Shopping orientation as a stable consumer disposition and its influence on consumers' evaluations of retailer communication. *European Journal of Marketing,* 48(5/6), 1026-1045.

20. CALM (2016). *Masculinity audit 2016: Understanding modern masculinity and the causes of male suicide.* Available at http://bit.ly/masculinity2016.

21. Carver, C. S. & Smith, J. C. (2010). Personality and coping. *Annual Review of Psychology,* 61, 679–704.

22.   Chang, H. J., Son, J. & Yurchisin, J. (2012). The impact of retail therapy on apparel consumers' post-purchase emotions. *2012, International Textile and Apparel Association, Inc. ITAA Proceedings, #69 – www.itaaonline.org*

23.   Chen, C. Y. & Pham, M. T. (2019). Affect regulation and consumer behavior. *Consumer Psychology Review*, 2, 114-144.

24.   Chen, C. Y., Lee, L. & Yap, A. J. (2017). Control deprivation motivates acquisition of utilitarian products. *Journal of Consumer Research*, 43(6), 1031-1047.

25.   Chen, Y., Peng, Y., Xu, H. & O'Brien, William H. (2017). Age differences in stress and coping: Problem-focused strategies mediate the relationship between age and positive affect. *Psychology Faculty Publications*. 39, available at https://scholarworks.bgsu.edu/psych_pub/39.

26.   Cifci, S. & Ekinci, Y. (2018). Undesirable effects of retail therapy on consumer emotions and consumer-based brand equity (CBBE). Paper presented at the *Management International Conference, Bled, Slovenia*, 30 May- 2 June, 2018, 169-176.

27.   Clarke, P. & Mortimer, G. (2013) Self-gifting guilt: An examination of self-gifting motivations and post-purchase regret. *Journal of Consumer Marketing*, 30(6), 472-483.

28.   Costa, P. T. & McCrae, R. R. (1985). The NEO personality inventory. *Psychology Assessment Resources*, Odessa, Florida, USA.

29.   Costa, P. T. & McCrae, R. R. (1992). NEO personality inventory professional manual. Odessa, FL: Psychological Assessment Resources.

30.   Cryder, C. E., Lerner, J. S., Gross, J. J. & Dahl, R. E. (2008). Misery is not miserly: Sad and self-focused individuals spend more. *Psychological Science*, 19(6), 525-530.

31.   D'Souza, D. (2012). *Retail therapy: A study in the Indian context to understand compensatory consumption and its implications on consumer's psyche*, Dissertation in partial fulfillment of the requirements for the Post Graduate Programme for Communications Management Diploma.

32.   Dalton, A. (2009). Look on the bright side: Self-expressive consumption and consumer self-worth. *ACR North American Advances*, 36, 131-134.

33.   Deon, T. (2011). The prevalence of impulsive, compulsive and innovative shopping behaviour in the economic retail hub of South Africa: A marketing segmentation approach. *African Journal of Business Management*, 5(14), 5424-5434.

34.   Dhurup, M. (2008). A generic taxonomy of shopping motives among hypermarkets (hyper-stores) customers and the relationship with demographic variables. *Acta Commercii*, 64-79.

35.   Dittmar, H. & Kapur, P. (2011). Consumerism and well-being in India and the UK: Identity projection and emotion regulation as underlying psychological processes. *Psychological Studies*, 56(1), 71-85.

36.   Dommer, S. L. & Swaminathan, V. (2013). Explaining the endowment effect through ownership: The role of identity, gender, and self-threat. *Journal of Consumer Research,* 39(5), 1034–1050.

37.   Duhachek, A. & Iacobucci, D. (2005). Consumer personality and coping: Testing rival theories of process. *Journal of Consumer Psychology*, 15(1), 52–63.

38.   Faber R. J. & Vohs, K. D. (2004). To buy or not to buy? Self-control and self-regulatory failure in purchase behavior. In: *Handbook of Self-regulation: Research, Theory, and Application* (ed. R. F. Baumeister), 509–524. New York: Guilford Press.

39.   Folkman, S., Lazarus, R. S., Gruen, R. J. & DeLongis, A. (1986). Appraisal, coping, health status, and psychological symptoms. *Journal of personality and social psychology*, 50(3), 571.

40.   Garg, N. & Lerner, J. S. (2013). Sadness and consumption. *Journal of Consumer Psychology*, 23(1), 106-113.

41.   Garnefski, N., Kraaij, V. & Spinhoven, P. (2001). Negative life events, cognitive emotion regulation and emotional problems. *Personality and Individual Differences*, 30, 1311-1327.

42. Gitimu, P. N. & Waithaka, A. G. (2018). Retail therapy: Influence of life engagement and subjective happiness. *Journal of Behavioural Studies in Business*, 10.

43. Gohary, A. & Hanzaee, K. H. (2014). Personality traits as predictors of shopping motivations and behaviors: A canonical correlation analysis. *Arab Economics and Business Journal*, 9(2014), 166-174.

44. Goldberg, L. R. (1990). An alternative 'description of personality': The Big-five factor structure. *Journal of Personality and Social Psychology*, 59(6), 1216-1229.

45. Golpelwar, M. (2014). Action and cognition in task oriented coping: Factor structure and internal consistency of the CISS-21 with an Indian sample. DOI: 10.7287/peerj.preprints.519v2.

46. Gray, H. M., Ishii, K. & Ambady, N. (2011). Misery loves company: When sadness increases the desire for social connectedness. *Personality and Social Psychology Bulletin*, 37(11), 1438–1448.

47. Gronmo, S. (1988). *Compensatory consumer behaviour: Elements of a critical sociology of consumption.* In Otnes, P. (ed), The Sociology of Consumption, Solum Forag Norway: Humanities Press, New York.

48. Grunert, S. C. (1993). On gender differences in eating behaviour as compensatory consumption. In Costa, (ed), *Proceedings of the Second Conference on Gender and Consumer Behaviour, Salt Lake City,* 74-86.

49. Guido, G., Capestro, M. & Peluso, A. M. (2007). Experimental analysis of consumer stimulation and motivational states in shopping experiences. *International Journal of Market Research,* 49(3), 365-386.

50. Gustavsson, J. P., Jonsson, E. G., Linderb, J. & Weinryb, R. M. (2003). The HP5 inventory: Definition and assessment of five health relevant personality traits from a five-factor model perspective. *Personality and Individual Differences*, 35(1), 69–89.

51. Hama, Y. (2001). Shopping as a coping behavior for stress. *Japanese Psychological Research, Special Issue- Consumer Behavior,* 43(4), 218-224.

52. Hashami, H. A., Khurshid, M. & Hassan, I. (2007). Marital adjustment, stress and depression among working and non-working married women. *Journal of Medical Science,* 2, 19-26.

53. Ho, V. T., Weingart, L. R. & Rousseau, D. M. (2004). Responses to broken promises: Does personality matter? *Journal of Vocational Behavior,* 65(2), 276–293.

54. Hooker, K., Frazier, L. D. & Monahan, D. J. (1994). Personality and coping among caregivers of spouses with dementia. *The Gerontologist,* 34, 386-392.

55. Huddleston, P. & Minahan (2011). *Consumer behavior: Women and shopping.* Business Expert Press.

56. Hussain, S. A. (2018). A study on stress and coping strategies for its management in hospital organizations in Patna District. *IJRAR- International Journal of Research and Analytical Reviews,* 2, 1084-1091.

57. Irwin, C. (2018). Emotional outlet malls: Exploring retail therapy. *BU Well,* 3(1), 8.

58. Javed, W. F. & Jalbani, A. A. (2010). A qualitative study on Gen Y women and shopping competence. *Journal of Independent Studies and Research,* MSSE, 8(1), 41-52.

59. John, O. P. & Srivastava, S. (1999). *The Big-five trait taxonomy: History, measurement, and theoretical perspectives.* In L. A. Pervin & O. P. John (Eds.), Handbook of Personality: Theory.

60. Joji, Alex N. & Raveendran, P.T. (2007). Compulsive buying behavior in Indian consumers and its impact on credit default- An emerging paradigm. *International Marketing Conference on Marketing & Society.*

61. Joshanloo, M., Rastegar, P. & Bakhshi, A. (2012). The Big Five personality domains as predictors of social wellbeing in Iranian university students. *Journal of Social and Personal Relationships,* 29(5), 639–660.

62.   Kacen, J. J. (1994). *Moods and motivations: An investigation of negative moods, consumer behaviors, and the process of mood management.* Unpublished doctoral dissertation in business administration. The University of Illinois at Urbana-Champaign, Illinois, USA.

63.   Kacen, J. J. (1994). Phenomenological insights in mood and mood-related consumer behaviors. In NA - *Advances in Consumer Research*, 21, eds. Chris T. Allen and Deborah Roedder John, Provo, UT: Association for Consumer Research, 519-525.

64.   Kacen, J. J. (1998). Retail therapy: Consumers' shopping cures for negative moods. *Advances in Consumer Research,* 25(1), 75-87.

65.   Kang, J.-Y. M., Johnson, K. K. P. & Kim, J. (2013). Clothing functions and use of clothing to alter mood. *International Journal of Fashion Design, Technology and Education*, 6(1), 43–52.

66.   Kang, M. & Johnson, K. K. P. (2010). Let's shop! Exploring the experiences of therapy shoppers. *Journal of Global Fashion Marketing*, 1(2), 71-79.

67.   Kang, M. & Johnson, K. K. P. (2011). Retail therapy: Scale development. *Clothing and Textiles Research Journal,* 29(1), 3-19.

68.   Kang, M. (2009). *Retail therapy: A qualitative investigation and scale development.* Doctoral dissertation, University of Minnesota.

69.   Kaur, J. & Kaur, C. (2016). *How they buy? –Analyzing the shopping behaviour of retail therapy shoppers.* Paper presented at International conference on Marketing, Technology and Society, at Indian Institute of Management, Kozhikode (Kelara), on September 29- October 1, 2016.

70.   Kaur, J. & Kaur, C. (2019). *Impact of mall attributes on mood related hedonic motives.* Paper presented in the International conference on the theme "Strategic Marketing Initiatives in Emerging Markets" in collaboration with North American Society for Marketing Education in India (NASMEI) on March 15-16, 2019.

71.   Keita, G. P. (2007). Psychosocial and cultural contributions to depression in women: Considerations for women midlife and beyond. *Journal of Managed Care Pharmacy*, 13(9 Supp A), 12-15.

72.   Kelly, M. M., Tyrka, A. R., Price, L. H. & Carpenter, L. L. (2008). Sex differences in the use of coping strategies: Predictors of anxiety and depressive symptoms. *Depression and Anxiety*, 25(10), 839-846.

73.   Kemp, E. & Kopp, S. W. (2011). Emotion regulation consumption: When feeling better is the aim. *Journal of Consumer Behaviour*, 10(1), 1–7.

74.   Kermane, M. M. (2016). A psychological study on stress among employed women and housewives and its management through progressive muscular relaxation technique (PMRT) and mindfulness breathing. *Journal of Psychology and Psychotherapy,* 6, 244.

75.   Kim, S. & Gal, D. (2014). From compensatory consumption to adaptive consumption: The role of self-acceptance in resolving self-deficits. *Journal of Consumer Research*, 41, 526–542.

76.   Kim, S. & Rucker, D. (2012). Bracing for the psychological storm: Proactive versus reactive compensatory consumption. *Journal of Consumer Research*, 39, 815-830.

77.   Kim, Y. K., Kang, J. & Kim, M. (2005). The relationship among family and social interaction, loneliness, mall shopping motivation and mall spending of older consumers. *Psychology and Marketing,* 22(12), 995-1015.

78.   Kishor, S. & Gupta, K. (2004). Women's empowerment in India and its states: Evidence from the NFHS. *Economic and Political Weekly*, 39, 694-712.

79.   Lazarus (1993). Coping theory and research: Past, present and future. *Psychosomatic Medicine*, 55, 234-247.

80.   Lazarus, R. S. & Folkman, S. (1984). *Stress, appraisal, and coping.* Springer. New York. 40-48.

81.   Lee, L. & Bottger, T. M. (2017). The therapeutic utility of shopping: Retail therapy, emotion regulation, and well-being. *The Routledge Companion to Consumer Behavior.*

82.   Lee, L. (2013). The emotional shopper: Assessing the effectiveness of retail therapy. *Foundations and Trends in Marketing,* 8(2), 69-145.

83.   Lerner, J. S., Small, D. A., & Loewenstein, G. (2004). Heart strings and purse strings: Carryover effects of emotions on economic decisions. *Psychological Science,* 15(5), 337-341.

84.   Li, Y., Li, Z., Liu, Y. & Teng, Y. (2015). The impact of women consumers' psychology and behavior on marketing strategies. *International Symposium on Social Science,* published by Atlantis Press, 405-408.

85.   Liddon, L., Kingerlee, R. & Barry, J.A. (2017). Sex differences in preferences for therapy, coping strategies, and help-seeking behavior. *British Journal of Clinical Psychology.*

86.   Loewenstein, G. & O'Donoghue, T. (2006). We can do this the easy way or the hard way: Negative emotions, self-regulation, and the law. *The University of Chicago Law Review,* 73(1), 183-206.

87.   Luomala, H. (1998). Self-regulation of negative moods in a consumption context. Irritation-, stress-, and dejection-alleviative self-gift behaviours in focus. *Vaasa: Universitas Wasaensis, 1998.* ISBN 951-683-743-3.

88.   Luomala, H. T. (2001). Consumption as therapy: A phenomenological inquiry into mood-alleviative consumer behaviors. *ACR Asia-Pacific Advances.*

89.   Luomala, H. T. (2002). An empirical analysis of the practices and therapeutic power of mood-alleviative consumption in Finland. *Psychology & Marketing,* 19(10), 813-836.

90.   Maltby, J., Day, L. & Macaskill, A. (2010). *Personality, individual differences and intelligence.* Essex: Pearson.

91.   Mandel, N., Rucker, D. D., Levav, J. & Galinsky, A. D. (2017). The compensatory consumer behaviour model: How self-discrepancies drive consumer behaviour. *Journal of Consumer Psychology,* 27(1), 133-146.

85

92. Matud, M. P. (2004). Gender differences in stress and coping styles. *Personality and Individual Differences*, 37, 1401-1415.

93. Matzler, K., Bidmon, S. & Grabner-Kräuter, S. (2006). Individual determinants of brand affect: The role of the personality traits of extraversion and openness to experience. *Journal of Product & Brand Management,* 15(7), 427-434.

94. Melindra, E. & Aprianingsih, A. (2016). Retail therapy: The impact of therapeutic motivation, therapeutic value and retail environment on consumer's purchase intention. Paper Presented at the 7th *Smart Collaborations for Businesses in Technology and Information Industries (SCBTII) Conference*, 2016.

95. Mezulis, A. H., Abramson, L. Y. & Hyde, J. S. (2002). Domain specificity of gender differences in rumination. *Journal of Cognitive Psychotherapy*, 16, 421–434.

96. Mick, D. G. & DeMoss, M. (1990). Self-gifts: Phenomenological insights from four contexts. *Journal of Consumer Research*, 17(3), 322-32.

97. Mick, D. G., M. DeMoss & Faure, Corinne (1992). A projective study of motivations and meanings of self-gifts: Implications for retail management. *Journal of Retailing,* 68(2), 122-144.

98. Miedziun, P. & Czabała, J. C. (2015). Stress management techniques. *Archives of Psychiatry and Psychotherapy*, 4, 23–30.

99. Mortimer, G., Bougoure, U. S. & Fazal-E-Hasan, S. (2015). Development and validation of the self-gifting consumer behaviour scale: The self-gifting consumer behaviour scale. *Journal of Consumer Behaviour*, 14(3), 165–179.

100. Nair, K. (2004). *Compensatory consumption among modern Indian women: A phenomenological exploration*, Submitted in partial fulfillment of post-graduate diploma in communications, Mudra Institute of Communications, Ahmedabad.

101. Penley, J., Tomaka, J. & Wiebe, J. (2002). The association of coping to physical and psychological health outcomes: A meta-analytic review. *Journal of Behavioral Medicine,* 25(6), 551-603.

102. Pervin, L. A. (2006). *The science of personality.* (3rd ed.), New York: Oxford University Press.

103. Prasad, C. J. (2010). Effect of consumer demographic attributes on store choice behavior in food and grocery retailing- An empirical analysis. *Management and Labour Studies*, 35(1), 35-58.

104. Rai, K. A., Joseph, A. S. & Mayya, S. (2018). Shopping is a serious affair: Alleviating negative emotions through retail therapy. *IOSR Journal of Business and Management (IOSR-JBM)*, 1-7.

105. Ramya, N. & Ali, S. A. M. (2016). Factors affecting consumer buying behavior. *International Journal of Applied Research*, 2(10), 76-80.

106. Rick, S. I., Pereira, B. & Burson, K. A. (2014). The benefits of retail therapy: Making purchase decisions reduces residual sadness. *Journal of Consumer Psychology*, 24(3), 373-380.

107. Rook, D.W. & Fisher, R.J. (1995). Trait and normative aspects of impulsive buying behavior. *Journal of Consumer Research*, 22 (3), 305-13.

108. Rose, P. & Segrist, D. (2011). Facets of distress tolerance as predictors of buying in response to self-esteem threats. *ACR North American Advances,* 39, 709-710.

109. Rucker, D. D. & Galinsky, A. D. (2008). Desire to acquire: Powerless and compensatory consumption. *Journal of Consumer Research*, 35(October), 257–267.

110. Ryan, K. (2013). *How problem focused and emotion focused coping affects college students' perceived stress and life satisfaction.* Submitted in Partial fulfilment of the requirements of the Bachelor of Arts degree (Psychology Specialization) at DBS School of Arts, Dublin.

111. Sadr, M. M. (2016). The role of personality traits predicting emotion regulation strategies. *International Academic Journal of Humanities*, 3(4), 13-24.

112. Schiffman, L. & Kanuk, L.L. (2010). *Consumer behavior.* Global Tenth Ed., United States of America: Pearson Education, Inc.

113. Schnider, K. R., Elhai, J. D. & Gray, M. J. (2007). Coping style use predicts posttraumatic stress and complicated grief symptom severity among college students reporting a traumatic loss. *Journal of Counseling Psychology*, 54(3), 344-350.

114. Shahjehan, A., Qureshi, J. A., Zeb, F. & Saifullah, K. (2012). The effect of personality on impulsive and compulsive buying behaviors. *African Journal of Business Management*, 6(6), 2187-2194.

115. Sheth, K. K. & Vital, l. (2007). *India: Shopping with the family*. The McKinsey Quarterly, 74-5.

116. Shukla, P. & Babin, B. J. (2013). Effects of consumer psychographics and store characteristics in influencing shopping value and store switching. *Journal of Consumer Behaviour*, 12, 194–203.

117. Silvera, D. H., Lavack, A. M. & Kropp, F. (2008). Impulse buying: The role of affect, social influence, and subjective well-being. *Journal of Consumer Marketing,* 25(1), 23-33.

118. Singh, S. (2017). Indian women and compensatory consumption: A confirmatory factor analysis approach. *International Journal of Engineering Technology Science and Research (IJETSR)*, 4(9), 19-31.

119. Singh, S. & Ahuja, D. (2020). *Understanding emotional shopping: Some reflections and dynamics*. In Collectanea: A Glimpse of Contemporary Business and Management Research, Ed. Narwal, K. P., Saini, V. P. & Bhaker, S. K., 360-371. Available at https://www.researchgate.net/publication/339446098.

120. Solanki, H. K., Kaur, A., Das, M., Awasthi, S. & Jain, S. (2019). Coping mechanism used by homemakers in Kumaon region (Uttarakhand, India) to deal with stress in their day-to-day life. *Journal of Family Medicine and Primary Care*, 1138-1144.

121. Solomon, M. R. (2011). *Consumer behavior: Buying, having, and being*. Global Edition. Pearson, 14(2), 116-124.

122. Son, J. & Chang, H. J. J. (2016). Retail therapy: What makes you feel relieved and happy? In the *Blending Cultures, International Textile and Apparel Association (ITAA) Annual Conference Proceedings*, 2016.

123. Suls, J. & Martin, R. (2005). The daily life of the garden-variety neurotic: Reactivity, stressor exposure, mood spillover, and maladaptive coping. *Journal of Personality,* 73, 1485–509.

124. Sun, L. (2007). *Understanding self-gift consumer behaviour (SGCB) in China: How culture influences SGCB.* Dissertation for MA in Marketing. Available at http://citeseerx.ist.psu.edu/viewdoc/download?doi=10.1.1.458.6058&rep=rep1& type=pdf.

125. Surendran, J. & Vardhan, R. (2014). Retail therapy: Understanding the phenomenon to improve customer experience. Available at http://tejas.iimb. ac.in/articles/Tejas_ December%20Edition_Article%204.pdf.

126. Taylor, S. G. & Kluemper, D. H. (2012). Linking perceptions of role stress and incivility to workplace aggression: The moderating role of personality. *Journal of Occupational Health Psychology*, 17(3), 316-329.

127. Thayer, R. E., Newman, R. & McClain, T. M. (1994). Self-regulation of mood: Strategies for changing a bad mood, raising energy, and reducing tension. *Journal of Personality and Social Psychology*, 67(5), 910–925.

128. Tiwari, R. K. & Abraham, A. (2010). Understanding the consumer behavior towards shopping malls in Raipur city. *International Journal of Management and Strategy.* 1(1).

129. Tobin, D. L. Holroyd, K. A., Reynolds, R. V. & Wigal, J. K. (1989). The hierarchical factor structure of the Coping Strategies Inventory. *Cognitive Therapy and Research*, 14, 343–361.

130. Urkmez, T. & Wagner, R. (2016). *Retail therapy: A European perspective on buying luxury items.* Paper presented in the Marketing Trends Conference, Venice, January 2012-13.

89

131. Verplanken, B. & Herabadi, A. (2001). Individual differences in impulse buying tendency: Feeling and no thinking. *European Journal of Personality*, 15(1), 71–83.

132. Vollrath, M. (2001). Personality and stress. *Scandavian Journal of Psychology*, 42, 335–47

133. Voss, K. E. & Spangenberg, E. R. & Grohmann, B. (2003). Measuring the hedonic and utilitarian dimensions of consumer attitude. *Journal of Marketing Research*, 40 (3), 310-320.

134. Watson, D. & Hubbard, B. (1996). Adaptational style and dispositional structure: Coping in the context of the five-factor model. *Journal of Personality*, 64, 737-774.

135. Woodruffe, H. (1997). Compensatory consumption: Why women go shopping when they're fed up and other stories. *Marketing Intelligence & Planning*, 15(7), 325-334.

136. Woodruffe, H. (1998). Private desires, public display: Consumption, postmodernism and fashion's "New Man". *International Journal of Retail & Distribution Management*, 26(8), 301-310.

137. Woodruffe, H. (2001). *Retail therapy: An investigation of compensatory consumption and shopping behavior*, Thesis submitted to Lancaster University for the Degree of Doctor of Philosophy (Phd).

138. Workman, L. & Paper, D. (2010). Compulsive buying: A theoretical framework. *Journal of Business Inquiry*, 9, 89–126.

139. Yurchisin, J., Yan, R. N., Watchravesringkan, K. & Chen, C. (2006). Why retail therapy? A preliminary investigation of the role of liminality, self-esteem, negative emotions, and proximity of clothing to self in the compensatory consumption of apparel products. *Psychology*, 60(6), 895-910.

140. Yurchisin, J., Yan, R., Watchravesringkan, K. & Chen, C. (2008). Investigating the role of life status changes and negative emotions in compensatory consumption among college students. *College Student Journal*, 42(3), 860-868.

141. Zurawicki, L. (2010). Neural bases for segmentation and positioning. *Neuromarketing*, 163-178, New York: Springer.

CHAPTER 3

OBJECTIVES AND
RESEARCH METHODOLOGY

CHAPTER-3

OBJECTIVES AND RESEARCH METHODOLOGY

Carrying out a research is a step-by-step process. It begins with carving out the aims and objectives based on existing literature and logic. This is followed by selection of the appropriate study design; defining the target population and selecting the method for data collection; deciding on the sample size; designing the survey instrument; and deciding on the statistical analysis techniques to be used (Binu et al., 2014). As the review of literature, the research gaps and rationale of the study have already been explained in the previous chapter (chapter-2); this chapter gives a detailed account of the methodology followed for fulfilling the objectives of the research.

The chapter has been organized into ten different sections. Section 3.1 covers the objectives of the present research. Section 3.2 highlights the scope of the study. Section 3.3 covers the research design. Section 3.4 shows the details of the preliminary study, followed by pilot study details in Section 3.5 and sampling details of the final study in Section 3.6. Section 3.7 shows section-wise details of the survey instrument used for the present study. Section 3.8 gives details about reliability of the instruments, while the details for validity tests have been shown in Section 3.9. Finally Section 3.10 lists out all the statistical techniques used for this study.

3.1 OBJECTIVES OF THE PRESENT RESEARCH

Based on the gaps identified in the existing literature and the rationale of the study, the following objectives have been framed for the present research.

1. To explore different types of coping strategies/activities adopted by Indian women to overcome negative mood (with special focus on determining the usage of shopping for coping).

2. To analyze the retail therapy behavior of women in India. Within that, to analyze the-

    ➤ Therapeutic shopping motivations

    ➤ Therapeutic shopping values, and

    ➤ Therapeutic shopping outcomes.

91

3.   To assess the influential impact of personal characteristics on retail therapy behavior of women in India. Within that, to assess the impact of-

➢   Demographic characteristics

➢   Big-five personality traits

➢   Chronic shopping orientation, and

➢   Impulse buying tendency.

4.   To analyze the retail therapy trip behavior of women therapy shoppers in India. Within that, to analyze-

➢   The shopping decisions undertaken by Indian women during a retail therapy trip (e.g. decisions relating to retail format, products, payment mode, person accompanying, time and money etc.), and

➢   The role of shopping process elements in mood-alleviation (including the role of retail attributes).

3.2   SCOPE OF THE STUDY

Deciding on the scope of a research study is essential for explaining its focus and direction. It helps in explaining as to what the study includes and what not. The scope of the present research has been explained in different sections, as given below:

3.2.1   Concept-wise Scope:

As explained in the introduction (Chapter-1) and review of literature (Chapter-2), the concept of retail therapy has been explained in two ways- as compensatory consumption and as mood-alleviative shopping. The scope of this study has been limited to the mood-alleviative perspective of retail therapy only, which is also more commonly accepted by the previous researchers like Atalay and Meloy (2011); Kang and Johnson (2010), Rick et al. (2014), Luomala (2002) etc. Accordingly, for this research, the term retail therapy has been used to mean use of shopping to overcome negative mood caused by temporary negative situations like an argument with someone, a bad day at work, feeling bored or lonely etc.

Apart from this, following Kang (2009), the term 'retail therapy' includes both buying as well as shopping without buying (i.e. window shopping) and is also limited to shopping for non-perishable products only e.g. clothing, accessories etc. Thus, it shall not include grocery shopping, eating or consumption of services.

3.2.2   Gender-wise Scope:

Based on the review of existing literature, it has been observed that many of the research studies on retail therapy have either taken up the sample of women only (e.g. Woodruffe, 1997; Nair, 2004; Singh, 2017; Rai et al., 2018 etc.); or majority of the research participants therein have been women as compared to men (e.g. Woodruffe, 2001; Luomala, 2002; Yurchisin et al., 2006; Rose & Segrist, 2011; D'Souza, 2012 etc.). Researchers have found that women experience the emotional value of shopping more intensely and significantly than men and thus retail therapy is also more commonly prevalent among them (Luomala, 2002, Arnold & Reynolds, 2003; Noble et al., 2006).

Accordingly, for the purpose of the present research, the focus has been exclusively on the women shoppers only.

3.2.3   Variables-wise Scope:

The purpose of this study has been to understand the usage and adoption of retail therapy by the Indian women and to study the role of personal characteristics in it. Within the personal characteristics, the basic personality traits (Big-five traits) and demographic variables (age, employment status, marital status and discretionary income) have been covered. In addition, two shopping-related personality variables i.e. shopping orientation (Chronic) and impulse buying tendency; have also been studied. In addition to this, the shopping behavior exhibited by women, during a retail therapy trip, has also been analyzed.

In nutshell, the variables used in the study include- 'Retail Therapy Behavior', 'Big-Five Personality Traits' (extraversion, agreeableness, conscientiousness, neuroticism and intellect), 'Chronic Shopping Orientation', 'Impulse Buying Tendency', 'Demographics' and 'Shopping Trip Behavior Elements'.

3.2.4   Geographical Area-wise Scope:

Area-wise, the scope of the study has been limited to some of the major cities of Punjab (Northern India). The state of Punjab has been one of the most prosperous states in India (Tata Strategic Management Group, 2013) and has witnessed tremendous transformations in the retailing sector over the past one and a half decade. Opening up of a large number of malls, hypermarkets, departmental stores etc. in different cities has been a sign of increased affinity of Punjabi's towards organized retailing. According to a report by the Retailers Association of India, compiled by Valsan and Bhola (2014), three cities including the capital city Chandigarh, Ludhiana and Amritsar, have seen maximum retail developments and they also show huge retail investment potential for future as well. In addition, SAS Nagar (Mohali) and Jalandhar have also been the choice of organized retailers (Jhamb & Kiran, 2011; Sharma et al., 2011). All these cities of Punjab had also been listed amongst the top thirty developed retail markets in India (India Retail Report, 2013). Due to the retail modernization, it is expected that people in these cities might be using shopping for reasons over and above the utilitarian reasons. Accordingly, women from these cities have been chosen to form the target population of the study.

3.3   RESEARCH DESIGN

A research design is the framework showing the procedures used for data collection and its analysis (Churchill & Iacobucci, 2002). A scientific and appropriate research design and sample selection requires it to be suitable for the research problem and research objectives in hand. The present research study uses descriptive research design, and within that the cross-sectional data has been collected and analyzed. The decision has been based on different aspects including the following-

3.3.1   Type of Information Required:

It is important to list out the information to be gathered from the respondents, because this helps in deciding about the research design to be used. As far as the needs of this research study have been concerned, the information to be collected has been about the usage of shopping for mood-alleviation, the personal characteristics and the therapy shopping behavior of women.

3.3.2   The Kind of Respondents:

Another decision by the researcher is regarding the type of respondents to be approached i.e. whether they should belong to a particular group or should be from the general population. As explained earlier also, the scope of this study has been limited to women only. However, within this segment, no particular class or category has been further chosen; rather, women with diverse demographic characteristics have been selected to make the sample representative.

3.3.3 Requirement of any Detailed Data Description:

The next decision is regarding the depth of the information required for the study. Usually, in cases, where the researcher wants to explore something new or to know it in depth, exploratory research methods like- literature search, depth-interviews, focus group or case analysis etc., are undertaken. On the other hand, when the purpose is to describe the characteristics of the population or the phenomenon in hand, the descriptive design tools such as longitudinal or cross-section methods are used. For the requirements of this study, the information could be collected in a better way by collecting cross-sectional data through field survey. Thus, conducting any in-depth interviews etc. was not found to be necessary.

3.3.4 Prior Information to the Respondents about the Purpose of the Study:

The fourth question relates to whether any prior information is required to be given to the participants regarding the purpose of the research and about the effects of the study on them. For this study, the purpose of the research had been clearly explained both for the pilot-testing as well as final survey. Further, the respondents had also been informed that they could leave the survey at any point of time and that it would not adversely affect them in any way. They were also assured that their identity would never be disclosed and information from them would be used for academic purposes only.

3.4 PRELIMINARY STUDY

To get an initial insight about what Indian women do to cope with stress and whether shopping activity is used by them as a coping strategy; a preliminary study had been carried out with twenty five women respondents selected on convenience basis from a University in Amritsar (Punjab). In total three questions had been asked:

1.   Frequency of experiencing negative mood (e.g. irritation/ stress/ depression) in a month, on an average.

2.   Activities indulged in to cope with negative mood.

3.   Frequency of using shopping for dealing with negative mood.

The detailed explanation of the findings of this study has been given in chapter 4.

3.5   PILOT STUDY

Following the preliminary study, a survey instrument had been designed and got evaluated from academicians (researcher's own supervisor and two others) and industry experts (retail managers of two different multi-brand retail stores in Jalandhar city). Based on their suggestions, some explanations and examples had been added up to certain statements to make them more understandable to the respondents e.g. meaning of certain terms like 'seldom feel blue', 'vivid imagination', 'abstract ideas' etc. had been explained in brackets along with the statements. Similarly, examples explaining different types of retail formats had also been added.

Using the designed survey questionnaire, a pilot study with 169 respondents from five cities of Punjab i.e. Chandigarh, Mohali, Ludhiana, Amritsar and Jalandhar, had been carried out. The results had been found to be satisfactory, with all the research scales being reliable. The respondents, at this stage, found layout of the questionnaire to be appealing and most of them filled in the information with enthusiasm. On an average, they took around 15-20 minutes to complete the questionnaire.

3.6   FINAL STUDY

3.6.1   Universe of the Study:

All the women within the Punjab state (Northern India), whether working or non-working and who are above the age of 21 years, form the universe of this study.

3.6.2   Sample Size:

The appropriate sample size for a research depends upon the objectives of the study, the number of variables to be studied and also on the statistical techniques to be used. For deciding on the sample size for this study, the criteria used have been explained as under:

1. Hair et al. (2010) observed that the sample size needs to be preferably ten times the number of variables to be analyzed. In this study, the total number of scale items had been 58 (retail therapy- 22; impulse buying tendency- 9; chronic shopping orientation- 7; and personality traits- 20). In addition, 12 more questions relating to shopping behavior had been asked. Thus, the total being 70, thereby requiring minimum data for 700 respondents.

2. As far as sample requirements for particular statistical techniques are concerned, Hair et al. (2010) mentioned that for use of SEM (confirmatory factor analysis and path analysis), a sample size of 500 or more is required, if the number of constructs is greater than seven (which is there in case of the present study).

3. There are also different standard formulae available to help in deciding about the correct sample size. Out of these, one of the widely used formula is that given by Krejcie & Morgan (1970), according to which, the required sample size can be determined as under-

$$\text{Sample size} = \frac{X^2 \, N \, P \, (1\text{-}P)}{d^2(N\text{-}1) + X^2 P(1\text{-}P)}$$

Where, X^2 is the chi-square value at particular degrees of freedom and at desired confidence level

N is the Population size

P is the Population proportion

d is the degree of accuracy expressed as a proportion

As suggested by Krejcie & Morgan (1970), X^2 has been calculated at d. f. = 1, for a confidence level of 0.05, which comes out to be 3.84. 'N' i.e. the population size, for this study, is the total size of female population in the selected cities i.e. **2,186,260;** the population proportion has been assumed to be 0.5 and degree of accuracy as 0.05. This results in the required minimum sample size of 384 respondents.

4. Last, but not the least, while finalizing the decision regarding sample size, the researcher must also provide for any missing data, normality issues etc. (Hair et al., 2010).

Keeping all the above mentioned points in mind and giving due consideration to the probable data loss due to missing data, it had finally been decided to distribute questionnaires to about 800 respondents in total.

3.6.3 Sampling Design and Sample:

For the purpose of data collection, different types of sampling techniques have been used, including- purposive/judgmental sampling, quota sampling technique, convenience sampling, snowball sampling etc. Firstly, using purposive sampling, it was decided to select only those cities within Punjab that have witnessed retail developments over past few years so that women therein at least have opportunity to go for therapeutic kind of shopping. Further, since the size and population of these cities is quite different, it was decided to select sample from each city in proportion to the women population of that city, just like it is done in stratified sampling. Following this, quota sampling had been used to evenly distribute the questionnaires in the selected cities to fairly represent both working and non-working women segments. Again, using judgment, it had been decided to take up working women from some common occupations where women could be easily found. These occupations included- teaching, banking and insurance and other occupations (including some other government and private office employees). At individual level, data from these working women had been collected at their convenience during their free time or break time, after getting a verbal permission from their branch/staff head.

The non-working class, on the other hand, included college/university students and housewives. It was purposely decided to collect data only from post-graduate students with the expectation that they could better understand the questionnaire than junior students. Data had been collected from them during their free lectures, so that they could comfortably answer to the survey questions. Housewives, on the other hand, had been approached through snowball sampling. For this, references had first been taken from working women and then from other housewives. Data had been collected from them either at their home by employing door to door survey or meeting them at some get-togethers like kitty parties.

Out of the total 800 questionnaires distributed, 703 (87.9% response rate) had been found to be complete and consistent in all respects. The details of the city-wise women population, minimum required sample and usable sample, have been shown in Table 3.1.

Table 3.1: City-Wise Women Population Data, the Desired Sample and the Usable Sample

City	Women Population (Census India, 2011)	Desired Sample	Usable Sample
Chandigarh	435,958	160	131
SAS Nagar (Mohali)	69,706	26	45
Ludhiana	743,971	272	219
Amritsar	531,375	194	172
Jalandhar	405,250	148	136
Total	**2,186,260**	**800**	**703**

Source: Authors elaboration based on Census 2011 (https://www.census2011.co.in/)

3.6.4 Sampling Period:

The pilot study had been carried out in year 2017 during the months of January-February, while the final data collection had been done during the period July, 2017-April, 2018.

3.6.5 Demographic Profile of the Respondents:

The final usable sample of 703 women comprises of 372 (53%) working women, out of whom 50 percent are teachers, 23 percent are from banking/insurance line and remaining 27 percent from other occupations. Amongst the non-working category, 70 percent are the students, while 30 percent are housewives. The mean age of the respondents has been found to be 30 years and more than half of the study respondents have been found to be post-graduates. As far as the marital status is concerned, about 60 percent of the respondents have been found to be unmarried.

Further, since, the study included both working and non-working women, thus, to maintain parity for comparison of income available with both the groups, their monthly discretionary income (i.e. what is left in their hands after deducting for the necessary expenses like grocery, bills etc.) out of the monthly family income, was asked for. As per the given data, discretionary income with most of the respondents (i.e. 61%) was found to be less than Rs. 10,000 (Refer Table 3.2).

Table 3.2: The Demographic Profile of the Respondents

DEMOGRAPHICS		FREQUENCY	PERCENT
Employment status	Working	372	52.9
	Non-working	331	47.1
Occupation	Teacher	188	26.7
	Student	232	33.0
	Housewife	99	14.1
	Bank/insurance	86	12.2
	Others	98	13.9
Marital Status	Married	286	40.7
	Un-married	417	59.3
Education	Under-graduate	80	11.4
	Graduate	243	34.6
	Post-graduate and above	380	54.1
Monthly Discretionary Income (Rs.)	Less than 10000	429	61.0
	10001-20000	172	24.5
	20001-30000	44	6.3
	More than 30000	58	8.3
Age → Range (22-65 years); Mean (30 years)			

Source: Authors elaboration based on own survey data

3.7   SURVEY INSTRUMENT

The survey instrument used for the data collection has been organized into five different sections explained as under:

100

Section A:

This part of the questionnaire covers questions related to frequency of experiencing negative mood, the coping strategies used to deal with negative mood and frequency of using shopping for mood-alleviation. Respondents had to mention any three activities that they indulged in to up-lift their mood.

Section B:

The second section (Section B) includes different scales related to the shopping behavior of the respondents including- 'Retail Therapy' scale (by Kang & Johnson, 2011/ Kang, 2009); the 'Impulse Buying Tendency' scale (by Rook & Fisher, 1995) and the 'Chronic Shopping Orientation' scale (by Buttner et al., 2013). All the statements in these scales have been measured on seven-point Likert scale ranging from '1= strongly disagree' and '7= strongly agree'.

For the purpose of getting information related to 'Retail Therapy Behavior', the twenty two- item scale developed by Kang & Johnson (2011) (/Kang, 2009) has been used. This is the only known scale that comprehensively measures the retail therapy behavior. It contains different items covering the motivations for retail therapy, the values derived from shopping and the outcomes of retail therapy. Different dimensions of the scale represent different stages in the shopping process including- pre-shopping stage, shopping stage and the post-shopping stage. The scale had been originally developed in context of the U.S. population and all the items had been checked for their reliability and validity on two separate samples (developmental sample and validation sample). In Kang's study, all the factor loadings had been found to be greater than 0.6, the reliability scores being greater than 0.8 and all the fit indices being within the threshold limits.

For determining the second variable i.e. 'Impulse Buying Tendency', a widely used scale, developed by Rook & Fisher (1995) has been used. It is a nine-item single factor scale which originally had a Cronbach alpha value of 0.88 and with all the factor loadings being above 0.6. The fitness indices for the scale had also been found by Rook & Fisher (1995), to be within the prescribed limits.

101

The third variable had been 'Chronic Shopping Orientation', for which the chronic shopping orientation scale, developed by Buttner et al. (2013), has been used. The originally designed scale comprised of seven items that reflected both task-focused as well as experiential shopping orientation. Buttner et al. (2013) had framed the scale, based on the data collected through an online survey of 387 respondents. The scale had been checked for its consistency over time and across different retail domains.

Section C:

The third section (i.e. Section C) relates to the 'Big-Five Personality Variables'. For this, the twenty items Mini-IPIP Scale developed by Donnellan et al. (2006) has been used. This scale is a short-form of the 50-item 'International Personality Item Pool' developed by Goldberg (1999). It comprises of five sub-scales measuring different personality traits i.e. 'Extraversion', 'Agreeableness', 'Conscientiousness', 'Neuroticism' and 'Intellect'. All the scale items have been measured on a seven-point Likert scale ranging from '1= strongly disagree' and '7= strongly agree'.

All the research scales used in the present study, along with their sources have been given in Table 3.3.

Table 3.3: Research Scales Used for the Present Study

SCALE	SOURCE
Retail Therapy Behavior	Kang & Johnson (2011)/ Kang (2009)
Chronic Shopping Orientation	Buttner et al. (2013)
Impulse Buying Tendency	Rook & Fisher (1995)
Big-Five Personality Traits	Donnellan et al. (2006)

Source: Authors elaboration

Section D:

Section D contains various questions related to the therapy shopping trip behavior of the retail therapy shoppers, including- the retail formats they like to visit for therapy shopping, the person they like to accompany them, the products that help them in getting rid of sad mood, extent of unplanned buying, time and money spend, mode of payment, etc. Since, these questions were related to a therapy shopping trip; they could be answered only by retail therapy shoppers. Accordingly, a note had been given in the beginning of this section, asking the respondents to answer it only if they actually went for retail therapy shopping. In other words, the section had been filled in only by self-identified therapy shoppers.

Section E:

The last section (Section E) in the survey instrument consists of the general questions related to the demographics of the respondents including their age, marital status, education level, occupation, monthly family income and monthly discretionary income (after deducting all necessary expenses like grocery, bills etc.).

3.8   RELIABILITY OF THE MEASUREMENT INSTRUMENT

The term reliability refers to the stability and dependability of a scale over time and across situations (Hair et al., 2010). Although, not sufficient, reliability is regarded as a necessary condition for testing the usability of an instrument. This is because apart from being reliable, the instrument also needs to be backed by validity (Thompson, 2013). There are different types of reliability tests out of which the internal consistency reliability is widely used because of the ease of using it (Tang et al., 2014). It is based on the assumption that the items measuring the same construct should correlate.

For the purpose of this research, one of the most commonly used types of internal consistency reliability measure i.e. Cronbach Alpha, has been calculated (Kimberlin & Wintersten, 2008). It reflects the degree of homogeneity among the scale items. The value of Cronbach Alpha ranges from 0 to 1 (Sekaran, 2003). Ideally, its value should be greater than 0.7 (Hair et al., 2010). The Cronbach Alpha values for the variables used in this research have been: 0.90 (Therapeutic shopping motivation); 0.90 (Therapeutic shopping value- positive reinforcement); 0.88 (Therapeutic shopping value- negative mood reduction); 0.89 (Therapeutic shopping outcomes); 0.81 (Extraversion); 0.79 (Agreeableness); 0.80 (Conscientiousness); 0.82 (Neuroticism); 0.74 (Intellect); 0.86 (Chronic shopping orientation); and 0.89 (Impulse buying tendency). Thus, all the values have been found to be above minimum threshold of 0.7.

3.9   VALIDITY OF THE INSTRUMENT

Validity of a measurement instrument is an essential condition. It indicates the extent to which an instrument measures what it is supposed to measure (Thatcher,

103

2010). Validity, in fact, is not the test of the instrument itself; rather it is the extent to which the results of that instrument are warranted based on its intended use (Kimberlin & Wintersten, 2008). Different types of validity measures include:

3.9.1 Content Validity:

Content validity is the extent to which an instrument adequately represents a construct under study. As such, there is no statistical test to check this. It rather depends upon judgment and opinion of experts (Kimberlin & Wintersten, 2008). In order to meet the condition of content validity, the measurement scales used in this study have been chosen cautiously. Care has been taken to confirm the adequacy of the items they cover and their reliability and validity in the previous studies has also been accounted for. In addition, modifications (adding explanations or examples to certain questions) have also been done on the basis of experts' opinions.

3.9.2 Construct Validity:

The construct validity is the extent to which the measured items actually reflect the theoretical latent constructs that they are designed to measure (Hair et al., 2010). For checking the construct validity, tests related to convergent validity and discriminant validity have been undertaken. Details have been explained in the following sub-sections.

➤ **Convergent validity:**

A high proportion of common variance among the indicators of a construct reflects convergent validity (Hair et al., 2010). It can be examined through several measures including- Factor Loadings, Average Variance Extracted (AVE) and Composite Reliability (CR). High factor loadings on a construct, indicates that all its items are converging on a common point. According to Hair et al. (2010), the factor loading values should ideally be greater than 0.7, but a value greater than at least 0.5 is also acceptable. The average variance extracted (AVE), on the other hand, is the mean variance for the items of a construct. Its value should also be greater than 0.5 (Hair et al., 2010). The third measure i.e. composite reliability indicates the internal consistency among the items of a construct. The value of composite reliability (CR) should ideally be greater than 0.7 (Hair et al., 2010). To summarize, in order to meet the condition of convergent validity, following rules apply:

1. Factor loadings > 0.7

2. CR> 0.7

3. CR>AVE

4. AVE> 0.5

In the present study, all the above mentioned conditions have been met, thereby proving convergent validity. Results have been shown in data analysis chapters (Chapter 5 and 6).

➤ **Discriminant validity:**

Discriminant validity is the extent to which a construct is different from another construct. It is a proof that items in a particular construct measure some unique information that other constructs do not measure (Hair et al., 2010). It also means that the items or variables of a particular construct represent only that construct. Discriminant validity can be established if the values of Average Variance Extracted (AVE) for the constructs exceed the values of Maximum Shared Variance (MSV) and Average Shared Variance (ASV) for that construct (Fornell & Larcker, 1981). In the present study, both the conditions have been met and discriminant validity has been proved. The results have been shown in data analysis chapters (chapter 5 and 6).

3.10 STATISTICAL TECHNIQUES USED

Depending upon the objectives of this research, different types of statistical techniques have been applied using the SPSS 19 and AMOS 19 software. A brief description of these techniques has been given as under:

3.10.1 Descriptive Data Analysis:

The descriptive statistics including frequency and percentage have been used for understanding the usage of different mood-alleviative techniques; frequency of experiencing negative mood and frequency of using shopping for mood-alleviation. Further, frequencies, percentage and ranks have been calculated for understanding the shopping behavior of the retail therapy shoppers. In addition to this, mean, standard deviation, frequencies have also been calculated for assessing responses to the retail therapy scale items. Demographic-wise mean values have also been calculated.

3.10.2 Exploratory Factor Analysis (EFA):

Exploratory factor analysis has been used to check the dimensionality of the scale items for all the scales used in this research. Within that, principal component analysis with varimax rotation has been used for scales including- chronic shopping orientation scale, impulse buying tendency scale and Big-five personality traits scale. On the other hand, as suggested by Kang & Johnson (2011)/ Kang (2009), the Oblique rotation method has been used for the retail therapy scale, because the factors were expected to be correlated. Different items like Eigen value, factor loadings, communalities and cross loadings have been considered while deciding on the retention or deletion of any scale item, in order to make the scale fit and usable for further analysis.

3.10.3 Confirmatory Factor Analysis (CFA):

CFA has been applied to test the extent to which the theoretical pattern of variables, demonstrating different constructs, represents the actual data. It helps in confirming the factor structure that has been established through exploratory factor analysis (Hair et al, 2010). This confirmation is based on a number of criteria including-model fitness based on chi-square, normed chi-square and fit indices; factor loadings, modification indices, squared multiple correlations etc. (Hair et al, 2010). Apart from this, CFA also accommodates the testing of various kinds of validities related to the measurement instrument. In this study, CFA has been applied on all the scales including retail therapy scale, impulse buying tendency, chronic shopping orientation and personality traits scale.

3.10.4 Correlation Analysis:

Correlation refers to the linear relationship between two variables (Hair et al, 2010). Correlation analysis has been used to check the relationship between the frequency of experiencing negative mood and the frequency of using shopping for

106

mood-alleviation. Also, correlation values among different constructs used in this study have been calculated as a part of exploratory and confirmatory factor analysis. Correlation analysis has also been used to check the relationship between age and retail therapy behavior.

3.10.5 One-way Anova:

One-way Anova is a technique used to compare two or more groups based on the mean scores of a dependent variable under study. This technique is used when the dependent variable is metric and the independent variables are categorical (Chawla & Sondhi, 2011). The null hypothesis in Anova is that mean values of dependent variable for all the population groups are equal. If this is not accepted, it would mean that the groups differ with each other on the particular criterion under study (McDonald, 2009). While using One-way Anova, the multiple comparison analysis called as post-hoc analysis can also be carried out in cases where the number of groups is more than two (McDonald, 2009). In the present study, One-way Anova has been used to compare groups of women having different levels of discretionary income, based on their retail therapy behavior.

3.10.6 Independent Sample T-test:

Independent Sample T-test is a technique used to compare two groups of individuals based on a particular criterion. In the present study, Independent sample T-test has been used to check if married and unmarried women; and working and non-working women differ with respect to their retail therapy behavior.

3.10.7 Path Analysis (SEM):

Path Analysis, in Structural Equation Modeling, is a technique used to test the impact of one or more independent variables on one or more dependent variables (Hair et al., 2010). It is similar to regression analysis technique, but with a difference that it may work simultaneously on multiple independent and dependent variables and can even show the impact of any moderators and mediators in one go. In the present study, Path analysis has been used to test the influential impact of personal characteristics (i.e.

shopping orientation, impulse buying tendency and Big-five personality traits) on retail therapy behavior.

CONCLUSION

This chapter has given a detailed account of the methodology followed for the present research. It began with listing out the different objectives of the research, followed by the scope of the study, the research design, the information regarding pilot survey, final survey, sample of the study, the survey instrument details, the reliability and validity measures used and also the different statistical techniques used for the study. It has, thus, helped in explaining the scope and design on which the present research is based. The data analysis for fulfilling the objectives of the research has been presented further in the upcoming chapters (Chapter- 4 to Chapter-7).

REFERENCES:

1. Arnold, M. J. & Reynolds, K. E. (2003). Hedonic shopping motivations. *Journal of Retailing*, 79(2), 77-95.

2. Atalay, A. S. & Meloy, M. G. (2011). When the going gets tough, the tough go shopping- An examination of self-gifting behaviour. *Advances in Consumer Research,* 33, 259-260.

3. Binu, V.S., Mayya, S. S. & Dhar, M. (2014). Some basic aspects of statistical methods and sample size determination in health science research. *AYU- An International Quarterly Journal of Research in Ayurveda*, 35(2), 119-123.

4. Buttner, O., Florack, A. & Goritz, A. S. (2013). Shopping orientation as a stable consumer disposition and its influence on consumers' evaluations of retailer communication. *European Journal of Marketing,* 48(5/6), 1026-1045.

5. Chawla, D. & Sondhi, N. (2011). *Research methodology: Concepts and cases.* Vikas Publishing House, New Delhi.

6. Churchill, G & Iacobucci, D. (2002). *Marketing research: Methodological foundations*, 12th edition. Dawn Iacobucci and Gilbert Churchill Nashville, TN: Earlie Lite Books, Inc.

7. D'Souza, D. (2012). *Retail therapy: A study in the Indian context to understand compensatory consumption and its implications on consumer's psyche*, Dissertation in partial fulfillment of the requirements for the Post Graduate Programme for Communications Management Diploma.

8. Donnellan, M. B., Oswald, F. L., Baird, B. M. & Lucas, R. E. (2006). The mini-IPIP scales: Tiny-yet-effective measures of the Big Five factors of personality. *Psychological Assessment*, 18(2), 192.

9. Fornell, C. & Larcker, D. F. (1981). *Structural equation models with unobservable variables and measurement error: Algebra and statistics.*

10. Goldberg, L. R. (1999). A broad-bandwidth, public-domain, personality inventory measuring the lower-level facets of several five-factor models. In I. Mervielde, I. J. Deary, F. De Fruyt, and F. Ostendorf (Eds.), *Personality Psychology in Europe*, 7, 7–28.

11.   Hair, Jr. J. F., Black, W. C., Babin, B. J. & Anderson, R. E. (2010). *Multivariate data analysis.* Pearson Education Inc., New Delhi, India.

12.   https://www.census2011.co.in/

13.   *India's next 100 retail markets.* India Retail Report (2013), http://www.asipac. com/uploaded/pdfFiles/1366786671full_IRR_Indias_Next_100_Retail__Market s_2013.pdf, retrieved on 12.08.2017.

14.   Jhamb, D. & Kiran, R. (2011). Organized retail in India- Drivers facilitator and SWOT analysis. *Asian Journal of Management Research*, 2(1), 264-273.

15.   Kang, M. (2009). *Retail therapy: A qualitative investigation and scale development.* Doctoral dissertation, University of Minnesota.

16.   Kang, M. & Johnson, K. K. P. (2010). Let's shop! Exploring the experiences of therapy shoppers. *Journal of Global Fashion Marketing*, 1(2), 71-79.

17.   Kang, M. & Johnson, K. K. P. (2011). Retail therapy: Scale development. *Clothing and Textiles Research Journal,* 29(1), 3-19.

18.   Kimberlin, C. L. & Wintersten, A. (2008). Validity and reliability of measurement instruments used in research. *American Journal of Health-Syst Pharm*, 65, 2276-2284.

19.   Krejcie, R. V. & Morgan, D. W. (1970). Determining sample size for research activities. *Educational and Psychological Measurement*, 30, 607-610.

20.   Luomala, H. T. (2002). An empirical analysis of the practices and therapeutic power of mood-alleviative consumption in Finland. *Psychology & Marketing,* 19(10), 813-836.

21.   McDonald, J. H. (2009). *Handbook of biological statistics*, 2, 6-59. Baltimore, MD: Sparky House Publishing.

22.   Nair, K. (2004). *Compensatory consumption among modern Indian women: A phenomenological exploration*, Submitted in partial fulfillment of post-graduate diploma in communications, Mudra Institute of Communications, Ahmedabad.

23.   Noble, S. M., Griffith, D. A. & Adjei, M.T. (2006). Drivers of local merchant loyalty: Understanding the influence of gender and shopping motives. *Journal of Retailing*, 82(3), 177–188.

24.   Rai, K. A., Joseph, A. S. & Mayya, S. (2018). Shopping is a serious affair: Alleviating negative emotions through retail therapy. *IOSR Journal of Business and Management (IOSR-JBM)*, 1-7.

25.   Rick, S. I., Pereira, B. & Burson, K. A. (2014). The benefits of retail therapy: Making purchase decisions reduces residual sadness. *Journal of Consumer Psychology*, 24(3), 373-380.

26.   Rook, D. W. & Fisher, R. J. (1995). Trait and normative aspects of impulsive buying behavior. *Journal of Consumer Research*, 22 (3), 305-13.

27.   Rose, P. & Segrist, D. (2011). Facets of distress tolerance as predictors of buying in response to self-esteem threats. *ACR North American Advances,* 39, 709-710.

28.   Sekaran, U. (2003). *Research methods for business: A skill building approach* (2nd Edition). New York: John Wiley & Sons, Inc.

29.   Sharma, G., Mahendru, M. & Singh, S. (2011). Impact of organized retail on the economy of Punjab, *Global Journal of Management and Business Research*, 11(2), 94-102.

30.   Singh, S. (2017). Indian women and compensatory consumption: A confirmatory factor analysis approach. *International Journal of Engineering Technology Science and Research (IJETSR)*, 4(9), 19-31.

31.   Tang, W., Cui, Y. & Babenko, O. (2014). Internal consistency: Do we really know what it is and how to assess it? *Journal of Psychology and Behavioral Science*, 2(2), 205-220.

32.   Tata Strategic Management group (2013). *Well-being and female security indices.*

33.   Thatcher, R. (2010). Validity and reliability of quantitative electroencephalography. *Journal of Neurotherapy*, 14, 122-152.

34.   Thompson, N. A. (2013). *Reliability and validity.* White Paper, Assessment Systems Worldwide.

35.   Valsan, S. & Bhola, S. (2014). *Retail reality in India: Evolution and potential. A comparison and contrast with the emerging cities of Asia.* Retailers association of India. Published by Jones Lang LaSalle.

36.   Woodruffe, H. (2001). *Retail therapy: An investigation of compensatory consumption and shopping behavior,* Thesis submitted to Lancaster University for the Degree of Doctor of Philosophy (Phd).

37.   Woodruffe, H. (1997). Compensatory consumption: Why women go shopping when they're fed up and other stories. *Marketing Intelligence & Planning,* 15(7), 325-334.

38.   Yurchisin, J., Yan, R. N., Watchravesringkan, K. & Chen, C. (2006). Why retail therapy? A preliminary investigation of the role of liminality, self-esteem, negative emotions, and proximity of clothing to self in the compensatory consumption of apparel products. *Psychology,* 60(6), 895-910.

COPING STRATEGIES AND USE OF SHOPPING FOR MOOD REGULATION

CHAPTER- 4

COPING STRATEGIES AND USE OF SHOPPING FOR MOOD REGULATION

Based on the review of existing literature, it has been found that when people experience any kind of negative mood, they start feeling helpless and try to get rid of the negative feeling as soon as possible (Andrade, 2005). For this, they either fight with the problem directly (problem-focused coping), or use some indirect means to compensate for the felt negative mood (emotion-focused coping) (Lazarus & Folkman, 1984; Chen et al., 2017). Many a times, they also make use of consumption for mood-management e.g. intake of hedonic food items, consuming alcohol, shopping etc. (Gronmo, 1988; Grunert, 1993; Woodruffe, 2001; Zheng & Peng, 2014).

The present chapter brings forward the different types of coping strategies adopted by Indian women when they are in a down mood. At the same time, it has also been explored whether they make use of shopping activity also for coping with negative mood. Further, it has been analyzed if any significant correlation exists between their frequency of experiencing negative mood and the frequency of using shopping for mood-alleviation.

METHODOLOGY

For the purpose of fulfilling the first objective of this research, covered in this chapter, a preliminary study had first been carried out, followed by an extensive survey. The motive behind preliminary study had been to have an idea about usage of shopping as a coping strategy. For this, 25 women (including seven graduate students, six housewives, three teachers and nine PhD research fellows) had been chosen on convenience basis from Amritsar. Using descriptive statistics (frequency and percentage), there responses had been scrutinized. The final sample, on the other hand, comprised of 703 women respondents (refer chapter-3 for details). Final sample data has been analyzed using descriptive statistics (frequency and percentage) and correlation analysis.

The data analysis in the present chapter has been organized into four sections. Section 4.1 shows the results of preliminary study; Section 4.2 covers the final study results, while showing the frequency of negative mood experienced by Indian women, the detail of mood management/coping strategies used by them, and the frequency of using shopping for mood alleviation; Section 4.3 shows the data analysis results for relationship between the frequency of experiencing negative mood and the frequency of using shopping for mood-alleviation. This is followed by Section 4.4 that briefly discusses and concludes the analysis findings.

4.1   PRELIMINARY STUDY

As mentioned earlier, the preliminary study has been done with twenty five women who had been asked to think of certain times when they are upset or they feel stressed out or sad. They, then, had to pen down any three activities, which they most often use to get rid of the negative mood. After compiling the list of these activities based on their responses, it has been found that **'social media usage'** is the most popular activity used for mood-alleviation, with 11 out of 25 women mentioning it in their response.

This has been followed by **'talking to some family member or friend'** (n=8) at the second position; **'listening to music'** and **'watching television'** both at the third place (with n=7), **'eating hedonic items'** like ice-cream, chocolates etc. (n=6) at fourth place, **'meditation'** and **'internet surfing'** at fifth place (n=5) and **'shopping'** at sixth place (n=4). This has been further followed by other activities like- **reading, cooking, playing games, sleeping, writing, cleaning and walking.**

Though, as per the results, only 4 out of 25 women (i.e. 16%) have mentioned that they use shopping for mood-alleviation; however, the results have given an idea that, at least, they recognize it as a mood management/coping strategy. Based on these results, the final survey had been planned and the questionnaire had been designed with the first section asking the participants about the different coping strategies that they use to overcome negative mood. The data analysis results for the final study have been shown in Section 4.2.

114

4.2 FINAL STUDY

In the final survey, the respondents had been asked about- 1) the frequency of experiencing negative mood in a month on an average; 2) any three activities used for mood-alleviation (same as asked in preliminary study); and 3) the frequency of using shopping for mood-alleviation. The results have been explained in the following sub-sections.

4.2.1 Frequency of Experiencing Negative Mood:

The first question has been regarding frequency of experiencing negative mood, in a month, on an average. For this question, respondents had been given five options, out of which they had to select one. These were- 'never', 'rarely', 'sometimes', 'frequently' and 'always'. The results have been shown in Table 4.1.

Table 4.1: Frequency and Percentage of Respondents Experiencing Negative Mood

Negative Mood Experience in a Typical Month	Number of Respondents	Percentage
Never	12	1.7%
Rarely	163	23.2%
Sometimes	397	56.5%
Frequently	115	16.4%
Always	16	2.3%
Total	**703**	**100%**

Source: Authors elaboration based on own survey data

Table 4.1 shows that approximately 57 percent of the respondents have mentioned that they experience negative mood only sometimes. This has been followed by 23 percent who rarely experience negative mood and approximately 16 percent who have said that they frequently experience negative mood. There have also been sixteen such women (2.3%) who have said that they always experience negative mood.

4.2.2 Mood-Alleviative Activities:

The next question has been regarding the activities used by women for mood-alleviation. For this, the respondents had not been given any pre-defined options. They

115

had only been required to mention any first three things they do when they are stressed out or upset. In order to understand the popularity of each coping strategy; the frequency and percentage of respondents choosing it has been determined. The results have been shown in Table 4.2.

Table 4.2: Number and Percentage of Women using Different Mood-Alleviative/ Coping Strategies

S. no.	Activity	Frequency	Percentage	Rank
1	Active problem solving/ Dealing with the source of stress	83	11.8%	X
2	Not talking to anyone/ person concerned	98	13.9%	VIII
3	Reading/ Studying	71	10.1%	XII
4	Listening to music	193	27.5%	IV
5	Cooking	62	8.8%	XIII
6	Religious practice/ Meditation	74	10.5%	XI
7	Surfing on internet/Social media	213	30.3%	II
8	Meeting friends	197	28%	III
9	Talking on phone with family/friends	272	38.7%	I
10	*Shopping (including online shopping or other shopping modes)*	*171*	**24.3%**	**V**
11	Comfort eating	101	14.4%	VII
12	Crying	62	8.8%	XIII
13	Watching television	123	17.5%	VI
14	Going out for a movie/ Dining out	46	6.5%	XV
15	Cleaning or other household work	83	11.8%	X
16	Indulging in hobbies	74	10.5%	XI
17	Exercise/Dance	34	4.8%	XVI
18	Sleeping	84	11.95%	IX
19	Acceptance/ Doing nothing	53	7.54%	XIV
20	Others	15	2.1%	XVII

Source: Authors elaboration based on own survey data

The results in Table 4.2 show that for women, **'talking on phone to someone in the family or friends'** is an ultimate stress-buster (approximately 39% women chose it). Seeking social support is in fact an approach-oriented coping strategy that has many benefits (Stanton et al., 2000). At times, it may also give meaningful solutions to an underlying problem.

Following this, 30 percent of the respondents have mentioned that they use **'social media platform'** to divert their attention when they are stressed out. This seems logical because today, surfing on the internet or using social media tools has, in fact, become the most common time-pass. It is a commonly used way of escaping from bad mood (Liddon et al., 2017).

The activity that has got the third rank in the list is **'meeting friends'**. Friends are usually the like-minded people whose company can create a positive environment. Thus, it seems quite obvious for the women to meet their friends, spend good time and burn out their stress (Anbumalar et al., 2017). Further, **'listening to music'** has been the next most resorted activity. Music has been found to easily divert one's attention. It has been found that listening to music can reduce stress in daily life, especially if it is intentionally listened to for relaxation (Linnemann et al., 2015).

'Shopping' has been placed at the fifth rank, with 24 percent of the women mentioning it in their list. It includes in-store shopping as well as online shopping or other shopping modes e.g. Tele-shopping. Since, many of the respondents had not clearly mentioned the type of shopping, thus, all the modes have been taken together. Being at the fifth position amongst more than twenty listed activities, it gives a clear understanding that people do find shopping to be therapeutic. This might be because, while shopping, the energy of individuals gets diverted to different activities like browsing, choosing, making price comparisons, looking at other shoppers etc. and they are able to forget about the negative situation, at least for some time (Kang, 2009; Atalay & Meloy, 2011; Surendran & Vardhan, 2014).

The next in the list is **'watching television'**. Television is an easy source of distraction. Watching one's favorite dramas or movies or other programs can divert one's attention (Solanki et al., 2019). Here, some respondents specifically mentioned that they watch comedy shows to forget about the stressful situations.

117

This has further been followed by **'comfort eating'**, which includes consuming of items like chocolates, fast-food etc. 14 percent of the women have said that they treat themselves with some nice food item to cheer up their mood. A number of previous studies have also highlighted the consumption of hedonic food items by women under stressful situations (Liddon et al., 2017; Miedziun & Czabała 2015).

Nearly 14 percent of the women have said that they **'remain quiet and stop talking to anyone or at least to the person concerned'** whom they feel had been responsible for the negative mood. This type of coping strategy might be successful in situations where expressing emotions might be more problematic. However, in the long run, such suppression may lead to worst results and adversely affect the well-being of the person concerned (John & Gross, 2004).

About 12 percent of the participants mentioned that they actually go to **'sleep'** when they feel stressed out. It might be because sleeping gives them a break from the stressful situation, where after they might be able to handle it in a better way. Similarly, nearly 12 percent of the women have said that they **'actively and directly handle the stressful situation'** and try to resolve the problem. This percentage is quite low, but at the same time, in line with the findings of the previous studies that say that women make lesser use of problem-focused coping (Matud, 2004). Also, this might be because, women (especially in India) are usually taught to suppress emotions and adjust with given situations. Lack of this feeling of authority might create hindrance in actively dealing with the problem, especially when some other person is the source of stress.

The same percentage (i.e. 12 percent) of the respondents, have also mentioned **'cleaning or doing household work'** as a diversion activity to cope with negative mood. Apart from this, some other activities mentioned by the respondents include- **'religious practice/meditation'** (10.5%) and **'indulging in hobbies** (10.5%), followed by **'reading/studying'** (10%), **'cooking'** (8.8%), **'crying'** (8.8%), **'doing nothing and accepting the situation as such'** (7.5%), **'going out for a movie/ dining out'** (6.5%), **'exercise/dance'** (4.8%), and **'others'** (2.1%). Here, 'others' includes certain other items like **spending time with kids, walking, singing, writing** etc., that had very low frequencies and hence they have been clubbed together under this head.

4.2.3 Usage of Shopping for Mood-Alleviation:

After asking the respondents about the usage of different activities for mood-alleviation, they had been particularly asked about their frequency of using shopping for up-lifting negative mood. For this, they had been given five options- 'never', 'rarely', 'sometimes', 'frequently' and 'always'. Table 4.3 shows the frequency and percentage of the respondents agreeing to either of the five options.

Table 4.3: Frequency of using Shopping for Mood-Alleviation

Frequency of using Shopping for Mood Alleviation	Frequency	Percentage
Never	132	18.8%
Rarely	198	28.2%
Sometimes	258	36.7%
Frequently	91	12.9%
Always	24	3.4%
Total	**703**	**100%**

Source: Authors elaboration based on own survey data

The data in Table 4.3 shows that there are approximately 37 percent of females who have said that they sometimes go for shopping when they are stressed out or experiencing any other kind of negative mood. At the same time, 28 percent of them have said that they rarely go for shopping for mood-alleviation, followed by approximately 19 percent who never go for mood-alleviative shopping. Further, there are 91 (12.9%) females who have said that they frequently make use of shopping when they are upset or stressed out. This is followed by 3.4 percent of the women who have said that they always go for shopping for mood-alleviation.

4.3 RELATION BETWEEN FREQUENCY OF EXPERIENCING NEGATIVE MOOD AND FREQUENCY OF USING SHOPPING

The next step in the analysis has been, to understand whether any relationship exists between the frequency of experiencing negative mood and the frequency of using shopping for mood-alleviation. As per the existing research, it is the negative mood arising from negative events or situations that creates discomfort among individuals and motivates them to go for therapeutic shopping (Lee, 2013). But, according to Kang

(2009), it is not necessary that, those who experience negative mood more frequently than others; also make more use of shopping to alleviate it and vice-versa. The present study has attempted to test this relationship statistically. For that, correlation analysis has been run using SPSS 19.0 software. The null hypothesis has been:

H_0: There is no significant relation between frequency of experiencing negative mood and frequency of using shopping for mood-alleviation.

The results of the correlation analysis have been shown in Table 4.4. As per the results, the correlation between frequency of experiencing negative mood and frequency of going for therapeutic shopping has not been found to be significant, thereby supporting the null hypothesis. The results are thus, in line with the observations of Kang (2009). This indicates the probability that some people might rarely experience negative mood, but may always choose to go for shopping in such situations, or on the contrary, some of them might experience negative mood quite frequently, but use shopping for coping with it only rarely.

Table 4.4: Correlation between Frequency of Experiencing Negative Mood and Frequency of using Shopping for Mood- Alleviation

		Frequency of experiencing negative mood	Frequency of shopping for mood-alleviation
Frequency of experiencing negative mood	Pearson correlation	1	.051
	Sig (two-tailed)		.179
	N	703	703

Source: Authors elaboration based on own survey data

4.4   DISCUSSION AND CONCLUSION

The objective covered in this chapter has been about exploring the type of coping styles used by Indian women to deal with negative mood. According to the previous literature, there can be two basic types of coping strategies i.e. problem-focused and emotion-focused strategies. As far as the results of this study are concerned, it has been found that Indian women mostly make use of emotion-focused

120

strategies, rather than going for problem-focused coping. Amongst these, the most resorted coping strategies include: talking to friends or family, surfing internet, meeting friends, listening to music, shopping, watching television, comfort eating, remaining quiet, sleeping, doing household work, meditation, reading, walking etc. Most of these acts fall under the category of emotion-focused style. On the other hand, very few respondents i.e. (just 12%) mentioned that they directly work towards dealing with the problematic situation. Apart from these, there have also been certain activities like- not talking to the person concerned, talking to friends/family etc. that may be considered as either problem-focused or emotion-focused, depending upon the particular situation.

In addition to knowing about the coping strategies used by Indian women, another purpose of this research has been to find out whether shopping is also used as a coping strategy. As per the results, nearly one-fourth (i.e. 24.3%) of the study participants have been found to be using shopping activity for coping with negative mood. Not only this, when specifically being asked about the frequency of going for shopping for mood-alleviation; nearly 37 percent of the study participants agreed that they do so sometimes, about 13 percent said that they frequently go for shopping and about 3 percent of them admitted that they always go for shopping whenever they are stressed out or experiencing negative mood, thus making a total of 53 percent. Usage of retail therapy has already been found to be quite common among people in western countries and the findings of this study indicate that Indian women are no exception to that. They too use shopping for therapeutic reasons.

Another finding of the present study has been that the frequency of experiencing negative mood and the frequency of using shopping for mood-alleviation are not significantly correlated to each other. This means that it is not necessary that people who are more frequently upset always go for shopping for mood-alleviation. Nor does it mean that people, who experience negative mood less frequently, do not go for mood-alleviative shopping. It might be that one may be sad only occasionally, but she/he always goes for shopping for getting rid of negative mood. Similarly, one may get sad or stressed out very frequently, but may rarely go for shopping or may not at all use shopping for mood-alleviation. This finding is an indirect indication that it is not necessarily the experiencing of negative mood only that leads to indulgence in retail therapy; rather, there might be some other factors also that play a crucial role in this regard e.g. one's personal characteristics, one's way of dealing with stress, the situational factors etc.

To summarize, the findings from this analysis give an understanding, that along with a number of other activities being used by Indian women to cope with stress, shopping is also being actively used. The further questions such as negative situations leading to retail therapy, the therapeutic benefits of shopping, outcomes of therapy shopping etc. have been covered in the upcoming chapter (i.e. chapter- 5) of the thesis.

REFERENCES

1. Anbumalar, C., Dorathy, A. P., Jaswanti, V. P., Priya, D. & Reniangelin, D. (2017). Gender differences in perceived stress levels and coping strategies among college students. *International Journal of Indian Psychology*, 4(4).

2. Andrade, & Eduardo, B. (2005). Behavioral consequences of affect: Combining evaluative and regulatory mechanisms. *Journal of Consumer Research*, 32, 355–362.

3. Atalay, A. S. & Meloy, M. G. (2011). When the going gets tough, the tough go shopping- An examination of self-gifting behaviour. *Advances in Consumer Research,* 33, 259-260.

4. Chen, Y., Peng, Y., Xu, H. & O'Brien, William H. (2017). Age differences in stress and coping: Problem-focused strategies mediate the relationship between age and positive affect. *Psychology Faculty Publications*. 39, available at https://scholarworks.bgsu.edu/psych_pub/39.

5. Gronmo, S. (1988). *Compensatory consumer behaviour: Elements of a critical sociology of consumption.* In Otnes, P. (ed), The Sociology of Consumption, Solum Forag Norway: Humanitites Press, New York.

6. Grunert, S. C. (1993). *On gender differences in eating behaviour as compensatory consumption.* In Costa, (ed), Proceedings of the second conference on gender and consumer behaviour, Salt Lake City, 74-86.

7. John, O. P. & Gross, J. J. (2004). Healthy and unhealthy emotion regulation: Personality processes, individual differences, and life span development. *Journal of Personality*, 72 (6), 1301-1333.

8. Kang, M. (2009). *Retail therapy: A qualitative investigation and scale development.* Doctoral dissertation, University of Minnesota.

9. Lazarus, R. S. & Folkman, S. (1984). *Stress, appraisal, and coping.* Springer. New York. 40-48.

10. Lee, L. (2013). The emotional shopper: Assessing the effectiveness of retail therapy. *Foundations and Trends in Marketing,* 8(2), 69-145.

11. Liddon, L., Kingerlee, R. & Barry, J. A. (2017). Gender differences in preferences for psychological treatment, coping strategies, and triggers to help-seeking. *British Journal of Clinical Psychology.*

12. Linnemann, A., Ditzen, B., Strahler, J., Doerr, J. & Nater, U. (2015). Music listening as a means of stress reduction in daily life. *Psychoneuroendocrinology.* 60.

13. Matud., M. P. (2004). Gender differences in stress and coping styles. *Personality and Individual Differences,* 37(7), 1401-1415.

14. Miedziun, P. & Czabała, C. (2015). Stress management techniques. *Archives of Psychiatry and Psychotherapy*, 4, 23–30.

15. Solanki, H. K., Kaur, A., Das, M., Awasthi, S. & Jain, S. (2019). Coping mechanism used by homemakers in Kumaon region (Uttarakhand, India) to deal with stress in their day-to-day life. *Journal of Family Medicine and Primary Care*, 1138-1144.

16. Stanton, A. L., Kirk, S. B., Cameron, C. L. & Danoff-Burg, S. (2000). Coping through emotional approach: Scale construction and validation. *Journal of Personality and Social Psychology*, 78(6), 1150.

17. Surendran, J. & Vardhan, R. (2014). Retail therapy: Understanding the phenomenon to improve customer experience. Available at http://tejas.iimb. ac.in/articles/Tejas_December%20Edition_Article%204.pdf

18. Woodruffe, H. (2001). *Retail therapy: An investigation of compensatory consumption and shopping behavior*, Thesis submitted to Lancaster University for the Degree of Doctor of Philosophy (Ph.D).

19. Zheng, X. Y. & Peng, S. Q. (2014). Consumption as psychological compensation: A review of compensatory consumption. *Advances in Psychological Science*, 22, 1-8.

RETAIL THERAPY MOTIVATIONS, THERAPEUTIC SHOPPING VALUES AND OUTCOMES

CHAPTER- 5

RETAIL THERAPY MOTIVATIONS, THERAPEUTIC SHOPPING VALUES AND OUTCOMES

The previous chapter (chapter 4) has highlighted that there are a considerable number of Indian women who choose to go for shopping to cope with negative mood. But what situations lead them to do so, what they get from shopping and whether or not their mood is eventually uplifted is still a question. The present chapter gives an answer to this by bringing forward the underlying motivations, therapeutic values and outcomes of retail therapy as experienced by the Indian women.

5.1   BACKGROUND

Although, the detailed review has been given in chapter-2 of the thesis, the following sections give only a brief up of the motivations behind retail therapy, the therapeutic shopping values and the outcomes of such behavior.

5.1.1   Retail Therapy Motivations:

The previous researchers have brought forward different factors that motivate individuals to choose shopping for therapeutic reasons. Depending upon the approach used in these studies to define retail therapy, these motivations can be categorized into two groups i.e. motivations behind retail therapy as compensatory consumption and motivations behind retail therapy as mood-alleviative consumption, as explained in Table 5.1.

Table 5.1: Motivations for Retail Therapy

Retail Therapy as Compensatory Consumption	Retail Therapy as Mood-Alleviative Consumption
Internal factors related to self (issues related to self-esteem, self-affirmation, self-deficit, self-anxiety etc.) (Woodruffe, 2001; Yurchisin et al., 2006; Kim & Gal, 2014; Mandel et al., 2017).	**Relieve stress** (Kang, 2009)
Relationship issues (including personal or official relations) (Woodruffe, 2001)	**Feel good about oneself** (Kang & Johnson, 2010; Kang, 2009)

125

Retail Therapy as Compensatory Consumption	Retail Therapy as Mood-Alleviative Consumption
Situational factors (including death of someone close, a rejection letter, exam pressure, day-to-day irritations etc.) (Woodruffe, 2001)	**Escape from over-scheduled life** (Huddleston & Minahan, 2011)
Liminality (Yurchisin et al., 2006)	**Cope with boredom** (Kang & Johnson, 2010; Kang, 2009)
Deprivations in life (D'Souza, 2012)	**A bad day at work** (Kang & Johnson, 2010; Kang, 2009)
Proving oneself (Woodruffe, 1997)	**Feeling of emptiness** (Kang, 2009)
Powerlessness (Rucker & Galansky, 2008)	**Socialization** (Urkmez & Wagner, 2016)
Foreseeing of a negative situation (pro-active compensatory consumption) (Kim & Rucker, 2012)	**Lack of control** (Kang, 2009) (Luomala, 2002) (Lee, 2013)
Lack of control (Chen et al., 2010)	**Loneliness** (Kim et al., 2005; Kang, 2009; Huddleston & Minahan, 2011)
	Argument with someone (Huddleston & Minahan, 2011)

Source: Authors elaboration based on review of literature.

The list of motivational factors shown in Table 5.1 leads to an understanding that the underlying reasons for retail therapy, as a compensatory consumption behavior, may be anything from minor to major 'lacks' in one's life. Sometimes, even deeper life issues may be involved behind a shopping trip that cannot be cured easily (Woodruffe, 2001). On the other hand, from mood-alleviative perspective, retail therapy is motivated by short-term and temporary mood-regulatory reasons only, that are comparatively easy to deal with (Kang, 2009). The examples include- getting rid of boredom or loneliness, a bad day at work, argument with someone etc. (Kang & Johnson, 2010).

5.1.2 Therapeutic Shopping Values:

The different types of therapeutic values stemming from shopping forms the basic reason for why at all people choose it for mood-alleviation. Some of these values include- positive distraction, escape, indulgence, sense of control, social connection etc. (Luomala, 2002; Huddleston & Minahan, 2011). It has been found that the courteous behavior of employees, attractive displays and product offers etc., make the shoppers feel happy and relaxed (Kang, 2009). Surendran and Vardhan (2014) found that product range, ambience and store interiors are the most influencing factors in therapy shopping. According to Lee (2013), the therapeutic values derived include- relaxation, distraction, feeling of power, happiness from imagining product ownership etc. Kang & Johnson (2011)/ Kang (2009) divided the therapeutic shopping values into two parts- positive mood reinforcement values and negative mood alleviation values. It was found that some of the shopping values like stimulation, getting knowledge of new fashion trends, courteous behavior of employees etc., help in maintaining the positive mood state of a person, while the features like social interaction, gaining control, distraction etc., help in mood-alleviation.

5.1.3 Retail Therapy Outcomes:

As explained in the literature review chapter also, retail therapy has been found to be mostly followed by positive outcomes at least on temporary basis. At the same time, it might lead to certain detrimental outcomes in the long-run due to over-reliance or due to becoming addict to its usage. Some of the researchers who have agreed to the positive psychological benefits from retail therapy include- Hama (2001); Kang (2009), Kang & Johnson (2011), Deon (2011), Atalay and Meloy (2011), Lee (2013), Rick et al. (2014) etc. On the other hand, some of the researchers who have brought forward that retail therapy can also have negative consequences in the long-run include- Woodruffe (2001), Joji and Raveendran (2007), D'Souza (2012); Kim and Gal (2014) etc. (These researchers have mainly worked on the compensatory perspective of retail therapy).

5.1.4 Measuring Retail Therapy Behavior:

Although, indulging in retail therapy has been found to be quite common phenomenon, still there are very few scales that have been developed to measure the behavior. The first ever scale for measuring retail therapy as compensatory consumption had been framed by Yurchisin et al. (2008). The scale was, however, criticized for being based only on Woodruffe's (1997/98) work, where only six individuals in total had been interviewed and also because of certain validity issues. Later Kang (2009)/ Kang & Johnson (2011) came up with a scale on retail therapy as mood-alleviative shopping. The scale represented different stages of shopping. The pre-shopping stage detailed out

127

different motivations behind retail therapy, shopping stage indicated different therapeutic values derived from shopping, and post-shopping stage highlighted different outcomes of retail therapy.

Certain dimensions of the scale framed by Kang & Johnson (2011)/ Kang (2009) were, later, used by Tunjungsari (2011) to measure retail therapy perception of Indonesian consumers and to extend its relation to brand preferences. Similarly, Gitimu and Waithaka (2018) used all the dimensions of scale for analyzing the relationship of retail therapy with life engagement and subjective well-being in U.S. In a later study, Cifci and Ekinci (2018) framed a nine items retail therapy scale covering its motivations and outcomes. Apart from these, no other scales on retail therapy could be found in the existing literature.

As the scope of this study is limited to the mood-alleviative perspective of retail therapy and since the scale developed by Kang & Johnson (2011)/Kang (2009) is the only known scale that comprehensively measures it; thus the same has been used for analyzing the motivations, values and outcomes of retail therapy among Indian women.

5.2 METHODOLOGY

All the respondents i.e. 703 females (refer chapter 3 for details) form the base for analysis in this chapter. During data collection, all the respondents had been asked to mark their level of agreement or disagreement to the items contained in the Kang's retail therapy scale. The responses had been measured on a seven point likert scale ranging from "7= strongly agree" to "1= strongly disagree". The data analysis techniques include- exploratory factor analysis, confirmatory factor analysis, descriptive statistics including the mean values, frequencies and standard deviations.

The data analysis results in this chapter have been shown in different sections. Section 5.3 shows the results of exploratory factor analysis and scale reliability. This is followed by Section 5.4 showing the results of scale validation and model fitness through confirmatory factor analysis. Section 5.5 covers the mean responses for different dimensions of retail therapy scale, along with the number of respondents agreeing or disagreeing to each particular scale item. Discussion for each section of the data analysis has been given at the end of that particular section only.

5.3   EXPLORATORY FACTOR ANALYSIS (EFA)

The purpose of exploratory factor analysis (EFA) is to reduce the data into a meaningful factor structure (Yong & Pearce, 2013). EFA is used when the underlying factor structure is not known to the researcher (Kim & Mueller, 1978). In other cases where it is already known, using confirmatory factor analysis (CFA) is recommended. However, sometimes, if the scale is used for some other population, cultural factors might lead to a change in the original factor structure and this shall not be reflected in the CFA model. In such cases, Orcan (2018) suggested that, firstly EFA should be run before going with CFA.

In case of the present study also, the retail therapy scale being used, had been designed about 10 years back and had been based on the responses of shoppers from U.S. Thus, exploratory factor analysis has first been used to test whether each of the scale items loads onto their respective factors as originally designed. A slight difference in using of this scale in the present study has been regarding measuring of the responses on a seven-point Likert scale instead of original five-point scale. This has been done so that more variability in the responses could be extracted (Malhotra, 2006).

For checking the dimensionality through exploratory factor analysis, the Oblique rotation method has been used, as suggested by Kang & Johnson (2011)/ Kang (2009), because the factors were expected to be correlated to each other. All the items with Eigen values of over 1.00, communalities greater than 0.5 and factor loadings above 0.5 have been retained (Hair et al., 2010). This has resulted into the formation of the same four factors as in the original scale, explaining the total variance of 70.32%. The KMO measure of sampling adequacy has been found to be 0.95. The communalities for all the items range between 0.633 and 0.778 i.e. greater than the minimum standardized value of 0.5 (Hair et al., 2010). The factor loadings range between 0.533 and 0.925, again above the minimum threshold of 0.5 (Hair et al., 2010). The factor naming has remained the same as in the original scale i.e. 'Therapeutic Shopping Motivation', 'Therapeutic Shopping Value: Positive Reinforcement', 'Therapeutic Shopping Value: Negative

Mood Reduction', and 'Therapeutic Shopping Outcomes'. The factor loadings, communalities, total variance explained, KMO value and Cronbach Alpha values for all the items have been shown in Table 5.2.

5.3.1 Factors Extracted:

➢ **Therapeutic shopping motivation:**

The first set of statements is related to the negative mood experiences that lead to use of shopping for therapy. It includes different reasons such as 'to relieve stress' (M1), 'to cheer oneself up' (M2), 'to feel better' (M3) and 'relaxed' (M5), 'to feel good about oneself' (M6), and 'to compensate for a bad day' (M4). Amongst these, M2 has the highest factor loading value (0.925), followed by M1 (.0910), M3 (0.858), M4 (0.674), M5 (0.663) and M6 (0.533). The reliability score of this construct is 0.903.

➢ **Therapeutic shopping value: positive reinforcement:**

The second and third construct answer the why part of retail therapy i.e. why people engage in retail therapy. These items show the respondents' general perception about the therapeutic values derived from shopping. The positive reinforcement construct includes the items like 'shopping as a positive distraction' (V1), finding the shopping environment to be 'stimulating' (V3) and 'pleasant' (V5), 'getting knowledge of new fashion trends' (V4), 'getting positive feelings about oneself' (V6) and 'a sense of achievement' (V2). Amongst these, V4 has the highest factor loading (0.906), followed by V3 (0.889), V6 (0.851), V5 (0.815), V2 (0.705) and V1 (0.666). The reliability score for this factor is 0.901.

➢ **Therapeutic shopping value: negative mood reduction:**

The items in this construct are related to the perception of people with regard to those therapeutic values derived from shopping that help in alleviating negative mood. It includes items such as 'diverting one's attention from stressful' (V8) or 'bothersome environment' (V9), 'relieving from a feeling of loneliness' (V7), 'gaining control' (V11) and 'filling an empty feeling' (V10). Within this construct, the highest factor loading value has been for V7 (0.921), followed by V9 (0.777), V8 (0.761), V11 (0.668) and V10 (0.667). The reliability score of this construct is 0.882.

Table 5.2: The Factor Structure of Retail Therapy Dimensions

ITEM	STATEMENTS (22 SCALE ITEMS)	Factor Loadings	Commu nalities
	THERAPEUTIC SHOPPING MOTIVATION (TSM)		
M2	I shop to cheer myself up	.925	.739
M1	I shop to relieve my stress	.910	.760
M3	I shop to make myself feel better	.858	.720
M4	I shop to compensate for a bad day	.674	.645
M5	I shop to feel relaxed	.663	.681
M6	I shop to feel good about myself	.533	.633
	THERAPEUTIC SHOPPING VALUE: POSITIVE REINFORCEMENT (TSV-P)		
V4	Shopping provides me with knowledge of new styles	.906	.731
V3	I like the visual stimulation shopping provides	.889	.678
V6	Finding a great deal reinforces positive feelings about myself	.851	.673
V5	I enjoy being in a pleasant environment that shopping provides	.815	.710
V2	Shopping gives me a sense of achievement	.705	.634
V1	Shopping is a positive distraction	.666	.652
	THERAPEUTIC SHOPPING VALUE: NEGATIVE MOOD REDUCTION (TSV-N)		
V7	Shopping is an escape from loneliness	.921	.778
V9	Shopping is a way to take my mind off things that are bothering me	.777	.721
V8	Shopping is a way to remove myself from stressful environment	.761	.768
V11	Shopping is a way to control things when other things seem out of control	.668	.675
V10	Shopping for something new fills an empty feeling	.667	.690
	THERAPEUTIC SHOPPING OUTCOMES (TSO)		
O4	I use items I bought during my shopping to relieve a bad mood	.863	.733
O2	After a shopping trip to make myself feel better, the good feelings generated last at least for the rest of the day	.851	.719
O3	I feel good immediately after my shopping trip to relieve a bad mood	.839	.717
O5	When I use items I bought during my shopping to relieve my bad mood, I remember the shopping experience	.811	.715
O1	My shopping trip to relieve my bad mood is successful	.745	.700
	Overall Reliability (Cronbach Alpha)		**0.93**
	KMO		**0.95**
	Total Variance Explained		**70.32%**

Source: Authors elaboration based on own survey data
: Scale used- Kang & Johnson (2011)/ Kang (2009).

➤ **Therapeutic shopping outcomes:**

Responses to the statements in this construct indicate the ultimate outcomes derived from therapeutic shopping. The items include, 'shopping trip being successful' (O1), 'getting an immediate relief from stress' (O3), 'retention of the positive feelings' (O2), 'using the items purchased during therapy shopping' (O4) and 'remembering of the shopping experience while using the items' (O5). Amongst these, O4 has the highest factor loading value of 0.863, followed by O2 (0.851), O3 (0.839), O5 (0.811) and O1 (0.745). The reliability score for this factor is 0.897.

5.3.2 Discussion:

Based, on the results of factor analysis, the formation of the same four-factor structure of the retail therapy scale in India is an indication of the reliability and generalizability of the scale over time and across different populations. All the items have successfully loaded on to their respective factors and all the values including KMO, Cronbach's alpha, factor loadings, communalities etc. have been found to be within the prescribed limits given by Hair et al. (2010).

5.4 CONFIRMATORY FACTOR ANALYSIS (CFA)

After checking the dimensionality through exploratory factor analysis, the four factor confirmatory model has been estimated based on the maximum likelihood procedure using AMOS 19 software. While running the CFA model, a number of factors have been considered including: model fit, factor loadings, modification indices and squared multiple correlations. Further, the reliability and validity of the scale have also been tested. For testing the model's fitness, the chi square, the associated degrees of freedom and various other fit indices have been checked for (Hair et al., 2010). The results have been shown in Table 5.3. As per the results, all the standardized factor loadings have been found to range between 0.74 and 0.85 i.e. above the minimum threshold value of 0.5 and also the ideal value of 0.7, suggested by Hair et al. (2010). The squared multiple correlation values have been found to range between 0.54 and 0.72 i.e. above the minimum threshold value of 0.5 (Hair et al., 2010). Further, a graphic representation of the measurement model has also been shown in Figure 5.1.

132

Table 5.3: Parameter Estimates, Standard Errors, Critical Ratios, and Squared Multiple Correlations (SMC) for the Measurement Model Items

FACTORS	STATEMENTS	Standardized Factor Loadings	Unstandardized Factor Loadings	Standard Error	Critical Ratios (T-values)	SMC
	THERAPEUTIC SHOPPING MOTIVATION (TSM)					
M1	I shop to relieve my stress	.81	1.03	.046	22.36	.66
M2	I shop to cheer myself up	.78	.961	.045	21.39	.61
M3	I shop to make myself feel better	.79	.996	.046	21.79	.63
M4	I shop to compensate for a bad day	.76	1.00	a	a	.57
M5	I shop to feel relaxed	.80	1.00	.046	22.05	.64
M6	I shop to feel good about myself	.74	.910	.045	20.05	.55
	THERAPEUTIC SHOPPING VALUE: POSITIVE REINFORCEMENT (TSV-P)					
V1	Shopping is a positive distraction	.78	.993	.043	23.11	.61
V2	Shopping gives me a sense of achievement	.76	1.02	.045	22.37	.57
V3	I like the visual stimulation shopping provides	.76	.930	.042	22.40	.58
V4	Shopping provides me with knowledge of new styles	.80	.906	.038	23.95	.64
V5	I enjoy being in a pleasant environment that shopping provides	.82	1.00	a	a	.67
V6	Finding a great deal reinforces positive feelings about myself	.75	.920	.042	22.15	.57
	THERAPEUTIC SHOPPING VALUE: NEGATIVE MOOD REDUCTION (TSV-N)					
V7	Shopping is an escape from loneliness	.75	.997	.047	21.31	.57
V8	Shopping is a way to remove myself from stressful environment	.85	1.10	.045	24.64	.72
V9	Shopping is a way to take my mind off things that are bothering me	.82	1.04	.044	23.79	.68
V10	Shopping for something new fills an empty feeling	.80	1.00	.044	23.04	.64
V11	Shopping is a way to control things when other things seem out of control	.79	1.00	a	a	.61
	THERAPEUTIC SHOPPING OUTCOMES (TSO)					
O1	My shopping trip to relieve my bad mood is successful	.79	1.01	.041	24.36	.66
O2	After a shopping trip to make myself feel better, the good feelings generated last at least for the rest of the day	.80	1.00	a	a	.67
O3	I feel good immediately after my shopping trip to relieve a bad mood	.81	1.05	.043	24.48	.67
O4	I use items I bought during my shopping to relieve a bad mood	.79	1.00	.047	21.17	.54
O5	When I use items I bought during my shopping to relieve my bad mood, I remember the shopping experience	.80	1.04	.048	21.66	.56

Source: Authors elaboration based on own survey data
: Scale used- Kang & Johnson (2011)/ Kang (2009).

Note: 'a' indicates a parameter fixed at 1.0 in the original solution

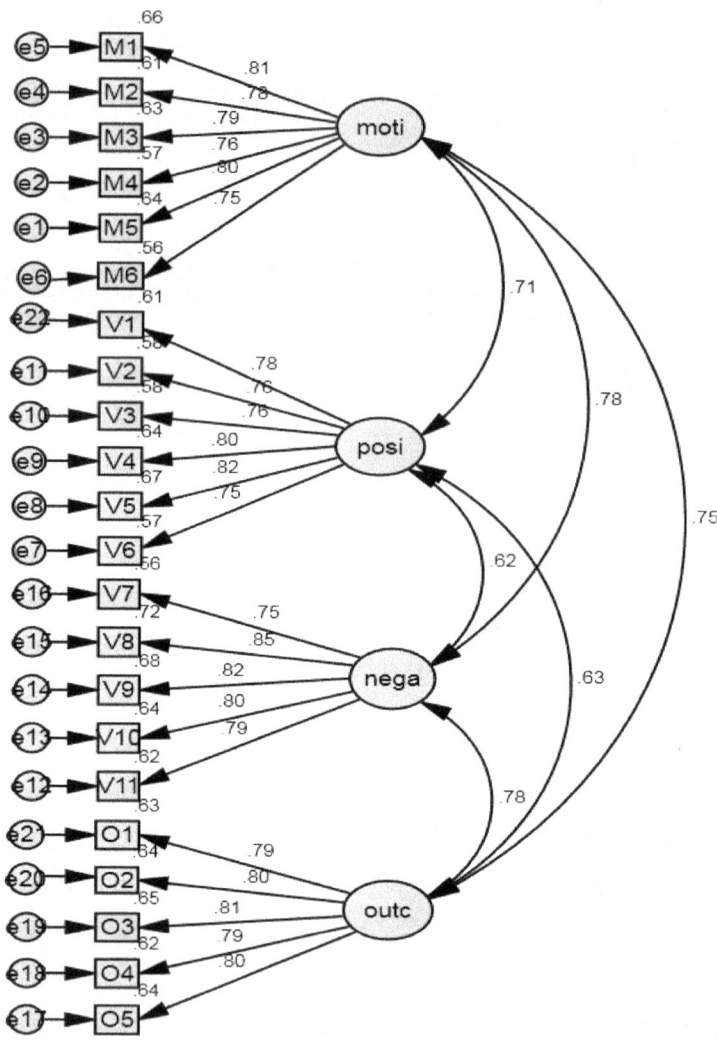

Figure 5.1: Standardized Factor Loadings for Measurement Model (Therapeutic Shopping Motivation, Positive Reinforcement, Negative Mood Reduction, Therapeutic Shopping Outcomes)

Source: Authors elaboration based on own survey data

5.4.1 Model Fit:

For testing the model fitness, Chi-square value and various fit indices have been calculated. The summarized results for the model fitness have been shown in Table 5.4. As per the results, the Chi square value ($\chi2$) has been found to be 1016.23 with 203 degrees of freedom. The Normed chi square ($\chi2/df$) is 5.00, which is not indicative of a best fit, but at least it shows an acceptable fit (Hair et al., 2010). The Tucker-Lewis Index (TLI) is 0.914, which is slightly above the minimum required value of 0.90, while the comparative fit index (CFI) is 0.924, which is again above the threshold value of 0.90 (Hair et al., 2010). The root mean square error of approximation (RMSEA) has been found to be 0.07, which is below the maximum threshold value of 0.08 (Hair et al., 2010). Further, the value of standardized root mean residual (SRMR) has been found to be 0.048, which is again within the maximum limit of 0.08 (Hair et al., 2010). Since, the results have indicated an acceptable fit, thus no changes have been made to the model.

Table 5.4: The Measurement Model Evaluation (Retail Therapy)

Indices	Criteria (Hair et al., 2010)	Final Model Fit
$\chi2$	Significant p-values expected for large samples	1016.23**
Normed $\chi2$ or $\chi2/df$	<2= very good; Up to 5= acceptable	5.00
TLI	> 0.90	0.914
CFI	> 0.90	0.924
RMSEA	< 0.08	0.070
SRMR	< 0.08	0.048

Source: Authors elaboration based on own survey data

** p-value significant at 0.01 level of significance

Note: $\chi2/df$– Chi-square divided by degrees of freedom; TLI- Tucker Lewis Index; CFI- Comparative Fit Index; RMSEA- Root Mean Squared Error of Approximation; SRMR- Standardized Root Mean Residual.

5.4.2 Construct Validity of the Measurement Model:

The construct validity is the extent to which the measured items actually reflect the theoretical latent constructs that they are designed to measure (Hair et al., 2010). For checking the construct validity, two tests i.e. relating to the convergent validity and discriminant validity have been conducted. The details have been shown in the following sub-sections:

135

➢ **Convergent validity:**

A high proportion of common variance among the indicators of a construct reflects convergent validity. It can be examined through several measures including-factor loadings, average variance extracted (AVE) and composite reliability (CR) (Hair et al., 2010). In order to meet the condition of convergent validity, following rules apply:

1. Factor loadings > 0.7

2. CR> 0.7

3. CR>AVE

4. AVE> 0.5

In the CFA model, factor loadings for all the items have been found to be exceeding the threshold value of 0.5 (Hair et al., 2010). Average variance extracted (AVE) has been calculated for each construct using the Stats Tool Package and all the values have been found to be greater than the threshold value of 0.5 (refer Table 5.5). Similarly, the composite reliability scores have also been found to be greater than the threshold value of 0.7 (Hair et al., 2010). Results have been shown in Table 5.5.

Table 5.5: The Psychometric Properties of Retail Therapy Scale (Convergent and Discriminant Validity)

CONSTRUCTS	CR	AVE	MSV	ASV
TSM	0.904	0.612	0.601	0.554
TSV-P	0.902	0.606	0.510	0.424
TSV-N	0.901	0.644	0.618	0.533
TSO	0.897	0.636	0.608	0.516

Source: Authors elaboration based on own survey data

Note: TSM- Therapeutic Shopping Motivation; TSV-P- Therapeutic Shopping Values- Positive Mood Reinforcement; TSV-N- Therapeutic Shopping Values- Negative Mood Reduction; TSO- Therapeutic Shopping Outcomes; CR- Composite Reliability, AVE- Average Variance Extracted, MSV- Maximum Shared Variance, ASV- Average Shared Variance.

➢ **Discriminant validity:**

The discriminant validity for the constructs has also been established by comparing the values of Average Variance Extracted with that of the Maximum Shared Variance and Average Shared Variance. According to Fornell and Larcker (1981), in order to prove discriminant validity, the values of AVE must exceed the values of MSV and ASV. The results shown in Table 5.5 are accordingly a proof of the discriminant validity.

5.4.3 Discussion:

The results of confirmatory factor analysis (CFA) indicate that the retail therapy scale developed by Kang & Johnson (2011)/ Kang (2009) is valid and reliable for use in India. No validity issues have been found with the scale. The CFA model shows at least an acceptable fit, if not the best one. At the same time, the factor loadings, variance extracted, correlations etc. have all been found to be within the threshold limits.

5.5 DESCRIPTIVE ANALYSIS OF RETAIL THERAPY SCALE ITEMS

After checking the psychometric properties of the retail therapy scale, the mean responses have been analyzed. The purpose has been to understand the overall attitude and perception of women towards retail therapy. For this, the mean responses for every item as well as for the underlying constructs have been calculated. In addition, the number of respondents agreeing or disagreeing to a particular item has also been analyzed. Details have been shown in the following sections.

5.5.1 Therapeutic Shopping Motivation:

As far as the first construct of the retail therapy scale i.e. 'Therapeutic Shopping Motivation' is concerned, an agreement with the items means that respondents actually shop for those therapeutic reasons (Kang, 2009). It lists out different type of situations that motivate one to go for retail therapy. As shown in Table 5.6, for Indian women, the highest agreement lies with the motivation of 'feeling good about myself' (M6), with mean of 4.43 and with 397 women i.e. 56.5 percent agreeing to it. This is followed by 'cheering oneself up' (M2) (mean=4.36) with 374 women (53%) on agreement side, 'feeling better' (M3) (mean=4.28), again with same number of women agreeing to it. There are 332 women who have agreed that they use shopping 'to feel relaxed' (M5) (mean= 4.09).

The other two reasons (that otherwise appear to be more intensely related to negative mood experience) i.e. 'relieving stress' (M1) and 'compensating for a bad day' (M4), have comparatively lower mean values i.e. 3.91 and 3.59 respectively. Whereas, 250 (i.e. 35.6%) women agreed that they shop to compensate for a bad day, there have been 328 women (i.e. 46.6%) who disagreed to this. Thus, importance-wise, therapeutic motivations can be listed as- 'feeling good', 'cheering up', 'feeling better', 'feeling relaxed', 'relieving stress', and 'compensating for a bad day'.

5.5.2 Therapeutic Shopping Value- Positive Reinforcement:

The second and third sets of statements are related to the perception about therapeutic values derived from shopping. These include- 'Positive Reinforcement' and 'Negative Mood Reduction'. According to Kang (2009), items in these constructs can be expected to be very useful in predicting one's likelihood of engaging in retail therapy. As per the results (refer Table 5.6), almost all the statements in the positive reinforcement values have comparatively higher mean values. This indicates that Indian women believe that they get positive values from shopping. Amongst these, 'getting knowledge about new styles' (V4) has been found to have the highest mean value (mean= 5.58) with 600 women (i.e. 85%) agreeing to it.

This is followed by 'enjoying in the pleasant environment' (V5) with mean value of 5.08 and 71.4 percent women showing an agreement towards it. For the remaining items i.e. 'finding a great deal' (V6), 'positive distraction' (V1), 'visual stimulation' (V2), and 'sense of achievement' (V3), the mean values have been found to be 4.91, 4.80, 4.79 and 4.48 respectively. Further, the percentage of women agreeing to these items has been 67%, 63%, 62% and 53% respectively (percentage calculated based on frequencies in Table 5.6).

Table 5.6: Descriptive Data Analysis of Retail Therapy Constructs (Frequencies, Mean Values and Standard Deviations)

CONSTRUCTS	FREQUENCY							MEAN	St. Dev.
	SD	D	SWD	N	SWA	A	SA		
THERAPEUTIC SHOPPING MOTIVATION								**4.11**	**1.52**
I shop to relieve my stress.	92	114	75	106	157	121	38	3.91	1.82
I shop to cheer myself up.	68	62	73	126	152	161	61	4.36	1.76
I shop to make myself feel better.	75	76	65	113	165	152	57	4.28	1.80
I shop to compensate for a bad day.	138	112	78	125	116	91	43	3.59	1.89
I shop to feel relaxed.	76	101	67	127	153	129	50	4.09	1.79
I shop to feel good about myself	58	80	54	114	168	162	67	4.43	1.76
THERAPEUTIC SHOPPING VALUE: POSITIVE REINFORCEMENT								**4.94**	**1.29**
Shopping is a positive distraction.	24	71	46	120	157	187	98	4.80	1.63
Shopping gives me a sense of achievement.	32	88	85	124	138	154	82	4.48	1.72
I like the visual stimulation shopping provides.	27	52	51	134	169	187	83	4.79	1.56
Shopping provides me with knowledge of new styles.	21	28	16	38	148	261	191	5.58	1.45
I enjoy being in a pleasant environment that shopping provides.	23	46	41	91	159	225	118	5.08	1.56
Finding a great deal reinforces positive feelings about myself.	24	49	51	108	184	187	100	4.91	1.56
THERAPEUTIC SHOPPING VALUE: NEGATIVE MOOD REDUCTION								**4.16**	**1.46**

Retail Therapy Motivations, Therapeutic Shopping Values and Outcomes

CONSTRUCTS	FREQUENCY							MEAN	St. Dev.
	SD	D	SWD	N	SWA	A	SA		
Shopping is an escape from loneliness.	66	85	96	127	137	128	64	4.17	1.78
Shopping is a way to remove myself from stressful environment.	50	104	77	120	146	145	61	4.26	1.75
Shopping is a way to take my mind off things that are bothering me.	53	79	93	119	166	141	52	4.28	1.70
Shopping for something new fills an empty feeling.	52	90	82	138	150	147	44	4.22	1.69
Shopping is a way to control things when other things seem out of control.	70	109	107	144	130	103	40	3.89	1.71
THERAPEUTIC SHOPPING OUTCOMES								**4.41**	**1.38**
My shopping trip to relieve my bad mood is successful.	37	68	93	142	183	140	40	4.35	1.56
After a shopping trip to make myself feel better, the good feelings generated last at least for the rest of the day.	28	51	85	134	178	164	63	4.60	1.55
I feel good immediately after my shopping trip to relieve a bad mood.	35	69	79	141	162	157	60	4.48	1.62
I use items I bought during my shopping to relieve a bad mood.	46	98	86	116	138	166	53	4.30	1.73
When I use items I bought during my shopping to relieve my bad mood, I remember the shopping experience.	49	102	80	114	134	162	62	4.30	1.72

Source: Authors elaboration based on own survey data

: Scale used- Kang & Johnson (2011)/ Kang (2009).

140

5.5.3   Therapeutic Shopping Value- Negative Mood Reduction:

As far as negative mood reduction values are concerned, the item with highest mean value has been 'taking mind off the things that are bothering' (V9) (mean= 4.28) to which 51 percent of the women have agreed, 17 percent have been neutral and 32 percent have disagreed (refer Table 5.6). This is followed by V8 i.e. 'removing from stressful environment' with mean of 4.26 and about half of the women agreeing to it.

For other items including 'filling an empty feeling' (V10), 'escaping from loneliness' (V7), and 'way of controlling things when other things seem out of control' (V11), mean scores have been 4.22, 4.17 and 3.89 respectively, along with 49%, 47% and 39% respondents respectively agreeing to their belief in these therapeutic values. Out of the total 703 women, nearly 41 percent have disagreed that shopping helps them in gaining control, while 35 percent have disagreed to the fact that shopping helps them to escape from loneliness (percentage calculated based on frequencies in Table 5.6).

5.5.4   Therapeutic Shopping Outcomes:

The last set of statements is related to the outcomes of retail therapy. Research shows that retail therapy is not a problematic shopping experience and shoppers rarely feel guilty afterwards (Atalay & Meloy, 2011). Thus, a positive response to these items would indicate that people actually feel relieved after shopping and these positive feeling are also retained with them. Amongst these statements, the maximum mean value has been secured by 'good feelings last at least for the rest of the day' (O2) (mean= 4.60), followed by 'immediate good feelings' (O3) (mean= 4.48), 'therapy trip being successful' (O1) (mean= 4.35).

The remaining two items i.e. 'using the products purchased during therapy shopping' (O4) and 'remembering the shopping experience while using them' (O5) have the same mean scores i.e. 4.30. It has been found that at least more than 50 percent of the respondents have shown an agreement to all the items in this construct (percentage calculated based on frequencies in Table 5.6).

5.5.5   Discussion:

The findings from the descriptive analysis show that, overall, Indian women shoppers have a positive attitude towards retail therapy. Most of the responses have

141

been towards the agreement side. The detailed descriptive analyses of the items shows that the most resorted mood situations for which retail therapy is used by Indian women includes- feeling good about oneself, followed by cheering up, feeling better and relaxed. The remaining two items (i.e. relieving stress and compensating for a bad day) have been agreed to by comparatively lesser number of women. Further, it has been found that majority of the women believe in the positive mood reinforcement values of shopping and mention that shopping helps them in getting knowledge about new fashion trends, offers a pleasant environment, gives them sensory stimulation and sense of achievement.

For negative mood alleviation values also, nearly 50 percent of the women have agreed that shopping distracts them from stress in one or the other way; helps in filling an empty feeling; helps in gaining control and even in dealing with loneliness. Further, as far as the outcomes are concerned; at least more than half of the women have agreed to the fact that their retail therapy trips are successful. Further, these good feelings are also retained for at least that day. They also use the products purchased during retail therapy trip, which reminds them of the pleasurable shopping experience. This is also an indication that they do not carry a guilt feeling after therapy shopping.

CONCLUSION

The primary purpose of this chapter has been to bring forward the different types of motivations, values and outcomes of retail therapy as experienced by Indian women. Simultaneously, it has also covered validation of the existing retail therapy scale (by Kang & Johnson, 2011/ Kang, 2009). The scale had originally been designed in the U.S. context and has also been found to be valid and reliable in Indian context too. Based on the responses to the scale items, retail therapy has been found to be commonly adopted shopping behavior among Indian women. The average number of respondents agreeing to the usage of retail therapy and its success in mood-alleviation has been more than half. Further, a considerable number of respondents have also agreed towards the therapeutic shopping values derived from retail therapy. The upcoming chapter further covers different types of personal characteristics that might be predictive of one's indulgence in therapy shopping.

REFERENCES

1. Atalay, A. S. & Meloy, M. G. (2011). Retail therapy: A strategic effort to improve mood. *Psychology and Marketing*, 28(6), 638-659.

2. Chen, C. Y., Lee, L. & Yap, A. J. (2010). Control deprivation and compensatory shopping. *Advances in Consumer Research*, 38, 185–186.

3. Cifci, S. & Ekinci, Y. (2018). *Undesirable effects of retail therapy on consumer emotions and consumer-based brand equity (CBBE)*. Paper Presented at the Management International Conference, Bled, Slovenia, 30 May- 2 June, 2018, 169-176.

4. D'Souza, D. (2012). *Retail therapy: A study in the Indian context to understand compensatory consumption and its implications on consumer's psyche*, Dissertation in partial fulfillment of the requirements for the post graduate programme for communications management diploma.

5. Deon, T. (2011). The prevalence of impulsive, compulsive and innovative shopping behaviour in the economic retail hub of South Africa: A marketing segmentation approach. *African Journal of Business Management*, 5(14), 5424-5434.

6. Fornell, C. & Larcker, D. F. (1981). *Structural equation models with unobservable variables and measurement error: Algebra and statistics*.

7. Gitimu, P. N. & Waithaka, A. G. (2018). Retail therapy: Influence of life engagement and subjective happiness. *Journal of Behavioural Studies in Business*, 10.

8. Hair, Jr. J. F., Black, W. C., Babin, B. J. & Anderson, R. E. (2010). *Multivariate data analysis*. Pearson Education Inc., New Delhi, India.

9. Hama, Y. (2001). Shopping as a coping behavior for stress. *Japanese Psychological Research, Special Issue- Consumer Behavior*, 43(4), 218-224.

10. Huddleston & Minahan (2011). *Consumer behaviour: Women and shopping*. Business Expert Press.

11.   Joji, Alex N. & Raveendran, P. T. (2007). Compulsive buying behaviour in Indian consumers and its impact on credit default- An emerging paradigm. Paper Presented in the *International Marketing Conference on Marketing and Society*.

12.   Kang, M. & Johnson, K. K. P. (2011). Retail therapy: Scale development. *Clothing and Textiles Research Journal,* 29(1), 3-19.

13.   Kang, M. (2009). *Retail therapy: A qualitative investigation and scale development*. Doctoral dissertation, University of Minnesota.

14.   Kim, J. & Mueller, C.W. (1978). *Introduction to factor analysis: What it is and how to do it*. Beverly Hills, CA: Sage Publications.

15.   Kim, S. & Rucker, D. (2012). Bracing for the psychological storm: Proactive versus reactive compensatory consumption. *Journal of Consumer Research*, 39, 815-830.

16.   Kim, S. & Gal, D. (2014). From compensatory consumption to adaptive consumption: The role of self-acceptance In resolving self-deficits. *Journal of Consumer Research*, 41, 526–542.

17.   Kim, Y. K., Kang, J. & Kim, M. (2005). The Relationship among family and social interaction, loneliness, mall shopping motivation and mall spending of older consumers. *Psychology and Marketing,* 22(12), 995-1015.

18.   Lee, L. (2013). The emotional shopper: Assessing the effectiveness of retail therapy. *Foundations and Trends in Marketing,* 8(2), 69-145.

19.   Luomala, H. T. (2002). An empirical analysis of the practices and therapeutic power of mood-alleviative consumption in Finland. *Psychology and Marketing,* 19(10), 813-836.

20.   Malhotra, N. (2006). Chapter 5- Questionnaire design and scale development. *In the Handbook of Marketing Research: Uses, Misuses, and Future Advances*, 176-202, retrieved from https://www.researchgate.net/publication/ 266864633 _Questionnaire_design_and_scale_development.

21. Mandel, N., Rucker, D. D., Levav, J. & Galinsky, A. D. (2017). The compensatory consumer behaviour model: How self-discrepancies drive consumer behaviour. *Journal of Consumer Psychology*, 27(1), 133-146.

22. Orcan, F. (2013). Exploratory and confirmatory factor analysis: Which one to use first? *Journal of Measurement and Evaluation in Education and Psychology*, 9(4), 414-421.

23. Rick, S. I., Pereira, B. & Burson, K. A. (2014). The benefits of retail therapy: Making purchase decisions reduces residual sadness. *Journal of Consumer Psychology*, 24(3), 373-380.

24. Rucker, D. D. & Galinsky, A. D. (2008). Desire to acquire: Powerless and compensatory consumption. *Journal of Consumer Research*, 35(October), 257–267.

25. Surendran, J. & Vardhan, R. (2014). Retail therapy: Understanding the phenomenon to improve customer experience. Retrieved from http://tejas.iimb. ac.in/articles/Tejas_December%20Edition_Article%204.pdf.

26. Tunjungsari, H. K. (2011). *Retail therapy: Do foreign brands give more satisfaction than local brands?* Proceedings of 15th Society for Global Business and Economic Development Conference, 1461-1469.

27. Urkmez, T. & Wagner, R. (2016). Retail therapy: A European perspective on buying luxury items. Paper Presented in the *Marketing Trends Conference, Venice*, January 2012-13.

28. Woodruffe, H. (1997). Compensatory consumption: Why women go shopping when they're fed up and other stories. *Marketing Intelligence and Planning*, 15(7), 325-334.

29. Woodruffe, H. (1998). Private desires, public display: Consumption, postmodernism and fashion's "New Man". *International Journal of Retail and Distribution Management*, 26(8), 301-310.

30. Woodruffe, H. (2001). *Retail therapy: An investigation of compensatory consumption and shopping behaviour*. Thesis submitted to Lancaster University for the Degree of Doctor of Philosophy (Phd).

31. Yong, A. G. & Pearce, S. (2013). A beginner's guide to factor analysis: Focusing on exploratory factor analysis. *Tutorials in Quantitative Methods for Psychology*, 9(2), 79-94.

32. Yurchisin, J., Yan, R. N., Watchravesringkan, K. & Chen, C. (2006). Why retail therapy? A preliminary investigation of the role of liminality, self-esteem, negative emotions, and proximity of clothing to self in the compensatory consumption of apparel products. *Psychology*, 60(6), 895-910.

33. Yurchisin, J., Yan, R., Watchravesringkan, K. & Chen, C. (2008). Investigating the role of life status changes and negative emotions in compensatory consumption among college students. *College Student Journal,* 42(3), 860-868.

CHAPTER 6

IMPACT OF PERSONAL
CHARACTERISTICS ON RETAIL
THERAPY BEHAVIOR

CHAPTER-6

IMPACT OF PERSONAL CHARACTERISTICS ON RETAIL THERAPY BEHAVIOR

The previous chapter (Chapter-5) dealt with validating Kang & Johnson (2011)/ Kang (2009) retail therapy scale in the Indian context. The chapter explained different types of negative mood situations that lead to retail therapy, along with the perception of Indian women with regard to the therapeutic values derived from shopping. Finally, outcomes of therapy shopping had also been presented. The present chapter deals with the third objective of this research i.e. 'To examine the influential impact of personal characteristics on retail therapy behavior of women in India'. For the purpose of this research, four types of personal characteristics have been studied i.e. (i) Demographic characteristics, (ii) 'Big-Five' personality traits, and two shopping related personality traits i.e. (iii) Chronic shopping orientation, and (iv) Impulse buying tendency. The detailed explanation of all these variables, and their hypothesized relationship with retail therapy, has been given in the literature review chapter (chapter-2).

METHODOLOGY

The data for this objective has been analyzed using different statistical techniques including- correlation analysis, independent sample T-test, one-way Anova, exploratory factor analysis (EFA), confirmatory factor analysis (CFA) and path analysis. The analysis begins with testing the relationship between different demographic variables and retail therapy (Section 6.1). This is followed by testing the dimensionality, reliability and validity of the measurement scales using EFA and CFA in Section 6.2. Finally, the hypotheses testing results for the impact of Big-Five personality traits, shopping orientation and impulse buying tendency on retail therapy behavior, have been shown in Section 6.3. This is further followed by conclusion for the chapter.

6.1   RELATION BETWEEN DEMOGRAPHICS AND RETAIL THERAPY

The analysis related to the role of demographics in retail therapy behavior has been explained in the following sub-sections:

6.1.1   Age and Retail Therapy Behavior:

Based on the review of previous literature (refer chapter-2), the following had been hypothesized:

H₁: Age negatively relates to Retail Therapy Behavior, such that youngsters are more inclined towards therapy shopping.

In order to statistically test the hypothesized relationship, correlation analysis has been used. The relationship of age has been determined with overall retail therapy measure as well as with each of its constructs separately. Results have been shown in Table 6.1.

Table 6.1: Correlation between Age and Retail Therapy

Age	TSM	TSV-P	TSV-N	TSO	Retail Therapy Behavior
Pearson Correlation	-.107**	-.089*	-.065	-.073*	-.099**

Source: Authors elaboration based on own survey data
**Correlation significant at 0.01 level (2-tailed)
*Correlation significant at 0.05 level (2-tailed)
Note: TSM- Therapeutic Shopping Motivation; TSV-P- Therapeutic Shopping Values- Positive Mood Reinforcement; TSV-N- Therapeutic Shopping Values- Negative Mood Reduction; TSO- Therapeutic Shopping Outcomes.

As shown in Table 6.1, age has been found to have a negative relation with all the retail therapy constructs separately as well as with the overall measure of retail therapy. A negative relation of age with therapeutic shopping motivation (at 1% level of significance) means that as age increases, people make lesser use of shopping for therapeutic reasons. Similarly, the inverse relation of age with both the types of therapeutic values i.e. positive mood reinforcement (at 5% level of significance) and negative mood reduction (at 10% level of significance), indicates that with increase in age, people's belief about the therapeutic benefits from shopping gets reduced. At the same time, a negative relation of age with therapeutic shopping outcomes (at 5% level of significance) means that as the age increases, the effectiveness of shopping as a therapeutic activity also falls down. To summarize, it can be concluded that as women get older, their inclination towards retail therapy gets reduced. The results are also in line with the existing literature e.g. Tiwari & Abraham (2010); Huddleston & Minahan (2011).

6.1.2   Marital Status and Retail Therapy Behavior:

With regard to the marital status, the following hypothesis had been framed based on previous literature (for details refer chapter-2):

H₂: Marital Status negatively relates to Retail Therapy Behavior, such that unmarried women are more inclined towards therapy shopping.

The relationship of marital status of the women respondents (i.e. whether they are 'married' or 'un-married/divorced/separated') with retail therapy has been examined using Independent Sample T-test. The results have been shown in Table 6.2 below:

Table 6.2: Relationship between Marital Status and Retail Therapy Behavior

	Levene's Test for Equality of Variances		T-test for Equality of Means					95% Confidence Interval of the Difference	
	F	Sig.	T	Df	Sig. (2-tailed)	Mean Difference	Std. Error Difference	Lower	Upper
TSM	1.40	.237	-.714	701	.475	-.075	.105	-.283	.132
TSV-P	1.88	.171	-.490	701	.624	.046	.094	-.138	.230
TSV-N	.009	.926	-.098	701	.922	-.009	.099	-.205	.185
TSO	.024	.876	-.088	701	.930	.008	.093	-.174	.190
RTB	1.09	.296	-.325	701	.745	-.023	.071	-.162	.116

Source: Authors elaboration based on own survey data

Note: TSM- Therapeutic Shopping Motivation; TSV-P- Therapeutic Shopping Values- Positive Mood Reinforcement; TSV-N- Therapeutic Shopping Values- Negative Mood Reduction; TSO- Therapeutic Shopping Outcomes; RTB- Retail Therapy Behavior

The results in Table 6.2 show that marital status does not have any statistically significant relation with retail therapy or any of its constructs. This implies that whether a female is married or unmarried, it does not affect her perception and attitude towards retail therapy. This is also clear from the average (mean) responses of married as well as unmarried women as shown in Table 6.3. Further, the mean responses for both the groups are positive (greater than the neutral response of 4 on 7-point Likert scale). This indicates that both married as well as unmarried women go for therapy shopping, although their reasons may or may not be the same.

Table 6.3 Mean Values for Retail Therapy Constructs (Demographic Variables-Wise)

Demographics/ Retail Therapy Constructs	Motivation	Positive	Negative	Outcome
Married	4.12	4.99	4.47	4.32
Unmarried	4.20	4.95	4.47	4.31
Working	4.06	4.88	4.40	4.23
Non-working	4.30	5.06	4.56	4.42
Cash- less than 10000	4.16	4.97	4.50	4.33
10001-20000	4.18	4.99	4.40	4.30
20001-30000	4.37	5.13	4.66	4.38
Above 30000	4.04	4.67	4.46	4.21

Source: Authors elaboration based on own survey data

6.1.3 Employment Status and Retail Therapy Behavior:

Based on the existing literature (refer chapter-2), it had been hypothesized that:

H₃: Employment Status negatively relates to Retail Therapy Behavior, such that non-working women are more inclined towards therapy shopping.

At the time of data collection, women had been asked to state whether they were working or not (non-working includes retired). In order to test the relationship of work status with the retail therapy dimensions, Independent Sample T-test has been used. The results have been shown in Table 6.4 below:

Table 6.4: Relationship between Employment Status and Retail Therapy Behavior

	Levene's Test for Equality of Variances		T-test for Equality of Means						95% Confidence Interval of the Difference	
	F	Sig.	T	Df	Sig. (2-tailed)	Mean Diff	Std. Error Diff		Lower	Upper
TSM	2.12	.146	-2.13	701	.033*	-.221	.104		-.425	-.017
TSV-P	9.17	.319	-1.89	701	.050*	-.174	.092		-.355	.007
TSV-N	1.447	.229	-1.50	701	.060	-.146	.097		-.337	.045
TSO	.486	.486	-2.07	701	.039*	-.188	.091		-.366	-.009
RTB	3.75	.063	-2.15	701	.032*	-.150	.069		-.287	-.013

Source: Authors elaboration based on own survey data

*Significant at 0.05 level (2-tailed)

Note: TSM- Therapeutic Shopping Motivation; TSV-P- Therapeutic Shopping Values- Positive Mood Reinforcement; TSV-N- Therapeutic Shopping Values- Negative Mood Reduction; TSO- Therapeutic Shopping Outcomes; RTB- Retail Therapy Behavior.

The results in Table 6.4 show that employment status has a significant negative relation with retail therapy and all its constructs, meaning thereby that non-working women indulge more in retail therapy as compared to the working women. This is also clear from the mean responses of both the groups as shown in Table 6.3. As per the results, the average response of non-working women towards all the constructs of retail therapy has been more positive and higher in comparison to the working women, although the responses are positive in both the groups. This might probably be because of the reason that due to over-scheduled lives, working women might be able to spare comparatively lesser time for shopping as compared to the non-working women.

6.1.4 Discretionary Income and Retail Therapy Behavior:

As far as the relation between income and retail therapy is concerned, the following hypothesis had been framed (for details refer chapter 2):

H₄: Discretionary Income positively relates to Retail Therapy Behavior, such that women with more discretionary income are more inclined towards therapy shopping.

As per the mean values in Table 6.3, women with monthly discretionary income between Rs. 20000 and Rs. 30000, have been found to have more positive response towards the retail therapy constructs than other categories. However, in order to statistically test the relationship between discretionary income and retail therapy, One-way Anova has been used. The results have been presented in Table 6.5 and 6.6. Table 6.5 shows the results for the homogeneity of variances in the groups, the results of which indicate that variances are homogenous and thus Anova is appropriate to use.

Table 6.5: Levene's Test for Homogeneity of Variances

	Levene's Statistic	df1	df2	Sig.
TSM	.246	3	699	.864
TSV-P	1.371	3	699	.250
TSV-N	1.696	3	699	.166
TSO	.508	3	699	.677
RTB	.892	3	699	.445

Source: Authors elaboration based on own survey data
Note: TSM- Therapeutic Shopping Motivation; TSV-P- Therapeutic Shopping Values- Positive Mood Reinforcement; TSV-N- Therapeutic Shopping Values- Negative Mood Reduction; TSO- Therapeutic Shopping Outcomes; RTB- Retail Therapy Behavior.

This is followed by Table 6.6 that shows the results for significance of differences in the mean responses of women belonging to different income categories.

Table 6.6: Relationship between Discretionary Income and Retail Therapy Behavior

		Sum of Squares	Df	Mean Square	F	Sig.
TSM	Between Groups	6.435	3	2.145	1.131	.336
	Within Groups	1325.859	699	1.897		
	Total	1332.294	702			
TSV-P	Between Groups	1.702	3	.567	.377	.769
	Within Groups	1051.343	699	1.504		
	Total	1053.046	702			
TSV-N	Between Groups	5.287	3	1.762	1.056	.367
	Within Groups	1167.030	699	1.670		
	Total	1172.317	702			
TSO	Between Groups	1.065	3	.355	.244	.866
	Within Groups	1019.264	699	1.458		
	Total	1020.330	702			
RTB	Between Groups	1.944	3	.648	.758	.518
	Within Groups	597.424	699	.855		
	Total	599.368	702			

Source: Authors elaboration based on own survey data

Note: TSM- Therapeutic Shopping Motivation; TSV-P- Therapeutic Shopping Values- Positive Mood Reinforcement; TSV-N- Therapeutic Shopping Values- Negative Mood Reduction; TSO- Therapeutic Shopping Outcomes; RTB- Retail Therapy Behavior.

As per the results in Table 6.6, F-values are not significant; thereby indicating that discretionary income does not have a significant effect on retail therapy behavior. In other words, the amount of discretionary income available with the women does not affect their perception and usage of retail therapy. The summarized hypotheses testing results for all the demographics and retail therapy behavior have also been presented in Table 6.7.

Table 6.7: Summary of Hypotheses Testing Results

Hypothesis	Hypothesized Relationship	Result
H₁	Retail Therapy Behavior <-- Age	*Supported*
H₂	Retail Therapy Behavior <-- Marital Status	*Not Supported*
H₃	Retail Therapy Behavior <-- Employment Status	*Supported*
H₄	Retail Therapy Behavior <-- Discretionary Income	*Not Supported*

Source: Authors elaboration

Based on the above results, it can be concluded that age and employment status of Indian women, significantly affect their retail therapy behavior, whereas marital status and discretionary income do not play a significant role in this regard.

6.2 DIMENSIONALITY, RELIABILITY AND VALIDITY OF THE PROPOSED MEASUREMENT MODEL

6.2.1 RESULTS OF EXPLORATORY FACTOR ANALYSIS (EFA)

6.2.1.1 Retail Therapy Scale:

The factor structure, reliability and validity details for the retail therapy scale being used for this study, have already been explained in the previous chapter (chapter-5).

6.2.1.2 The MINI-IPIP Scale:

For measuring the Big-five personality traits of the respondents, the twenty items Mini-IPIP Scale developed by Donnellan et al. (2006) has been used. The scale has been checked for its dimensionality using exploratory factor analysis (EFA). Before doing that, eleven negatively worded items have been reverse coded in SPSS software.

Based on the EFA results, two of the scale items i.e. 'I have frequent mood swings- P13 (Neuroticism)' and 'I have a vivid imagination- P17 (Intellect)', have been removed because of cross loading issues and low communality values (0.29, which is far below the minimum threshold value of 0.5 as suggested by Hair et al., 2010) respectively. Following this, the factor analysis has been re-run. The final results have been shown in Table 6.8.

153

Table 6.8: Factor Loadings, Communalities, Cronbach Alpha, and Variance Explained for Big-Five Personality Traits, Chronic Shopping Orientation and Impulse Buying Tendency

FACTORS	STATEMENTS	Factor Loadings	Communalities	Cronbach Alpha Value	Variance Explained (%age)
EXTRAVERSION					
P2	I don't talk a lot.	.84	.73		
P3	I talk to a lot of different people at parties.	.81	.66		
P4	I keep in the background.	.79	.66		
P1	I am the life of the party.	.66	.58	**.81**	**14%**
AGREEABLENESS					
P5	I sympathize with others' feelings	.84	.72		
P8	I am not really interested in others.	.78	.62		
P7	I feel others' emotions.	.77	.60		
P6	I am not interested in other people's problems.	.75	.59	**.79**	**13.7%**
CONSCIENTIOUSNESS					
P12	I make a mess of things.	.84	.70		
P10	I often forget to put things back in their proper place	.79	.65		
P11	I like order.	.77	.60		
P9	I get chores done right away.	.74	.64	**.80**	**13.2%**
NEUROTICISM					
P14	I am relaxed most of the time.	.86	.76		
P15	I get upset easily.	.83	.70		
P16	I seldom feel blue.	.77	.63	**.82**	**11.3%**
INTELLECT					
P18	I am not interested in abstract ideas.	.84	.71		

FACTORS	STATEMENTS	Factor Loadings	Communalities	Cronbach Alpha Value	Variance Explained (%age)
P20	I do not have a good imagination.	.80	.65		
P19	I have difficulty understanding abstract ideas.	.77	.62	.74	10.2%
Overall Cronbach Alpha value and Variance Explained				**.65**	**62.4%**
CHRONIC SHOPPING ORIENTATION					
SO4	When shopping, I am usually looking for entertainment.	.78	.72		
SO1	When shopping, I often have fun.	.77	.66		
SO7	When shopping, I like to browse around.	.76	.66		
SO6	I like to kill time by shopping.	.74	.58		
SO3	When shopping, I act as deliberately and goal-focused as possible.	.63	.78		
SO2	When shopping, I try to get it over with as soon as possible.	.61	.69	.86	52.8%
IMPULSE BUYING TENDENCY					
IB1	I often buy things spontaneously.	.80	.64		
IB2	"Just do it" describes the way I buy things.	.79	.63		
IB6	Sometimes I feel like buying things on the spur of the moment.	.78	.66		
IB5	"Buy now, think about it later" describes me.	.77	.58		
IB3	I often buy things without thinking.	.76	.58		
IB4	"I see it, I buy it" describes me.	.76	.57		
IB9	Sometimes, I am bit reckless/careless about what I buy.	.73	.54		
IB7	I buy things according to how I feel at the moment.	.71	.51	.89	58.8%

Source: Authors elaboration based on own survey data.

: Scales used- Donnellan et al. (2006); Buttner et al. (2013): Rook and Fisher (1995)

The results in Table 6.8 show the final five factor solution for the Big-five personality traits with all the items loading significantly onto their respective factors. The KMO value has been found to be 0.75, with the communalities ranging between 0.58 and 0.76. The overall variance explained has been 62.4 per cent. The factor loadings range between 0.66 and 0.86. The Cronbach alpha values for different constructs i.e. extraversion, agreeableness, conscientiousness, neuroticism and intellect have been 0.81, 0.79, 0.80, 0.82 and 0.74 respectively.

6.2.1.3 Chronic Shopping Orientation Scale:

For determining one's attitude towards the shopping activity, the chronic shopping orientation scale developed by Buttner et al. (2013) has been used. It contains seven items representing both experiential shopping aspects as well as utilitarian aspects. Buttner et al. (2013) used the term 'Chronic' with shopping orientation to indicate that it is a stable consumer disposition. In their study, shopping orientation had been found to be stable over time and across different retail domains. Accordingly, for the purpose of the present research, the terms shopping orientation and chronic shopping orientation have been used to mean one and the same thing.

In order to check for the dimensionality of all the shopping orientation scale items in the present study, EFA has been used. Before doing that, three negatively worded items have been reverse coded in SPSS 19.0. The analysis has led to formation of single factor, as suggested by Buttner et al. (2013). However, one item i.e. SO-5-'When shopping, I mainly carry out what I have planned' had to be removed because of very low loading value of 0.21. The final results have been shown in Table 6.8, according to which the KMO value has been found to be 0.81, communalities range between 0.58 and 0.78, variance explained is 52.8%, factor loadings range between 0.61 and 0.78 and the Cronbach's Alpha value has been found to be 0.86. All these values have been found to be within the threshold limits suggested by Hair et al. (2010).

6.2.1.4 Impulse Buying Tendency Scale:

For determining the impulse buying tendency, the scale developed by Rook and Fisher (1995) has been used. It is a nine items scale representing the tendency of a person to indulge in impulse buying. Based on the exploratory factor analysis run on this scale, one item i.e. IB-8- 'I carefully plan most of my purchases' having a very low factor loading of 0.23 with the communality of 0.12, has been removed and the EFA has been re-run. The final results have been- KMO (0.92), communalities (ranging between 0.51 and 0.66), total variance explained (58.8%), factor loadings (ranging between 0.71 and 0.80), Cronbach's Alpha value (0.89) (refer Table 6.8). All the values have been found to be within the threshold limits suggested by Hair et al. (2010).

6.2.2   RESULTS OF CONFIRMATORY FACTOR ANALYSIS (CFA)

Confirmatory factor analysis (CFA) has been used to confirm the factor structure established by the exploratory factor analysis for all the variables under study. Before doing this, firstly, the second-order construct of 'Retail Therapy Behavior', has been formed to represent all the four dimensions of retail therapy (i.e. 'Therapeutic Shopping Motivation', 'Therapeutic Shopping Value: Positive Reinforcement', 'Therapeutic Shopping Value: Negative Mood Reduction', and 'Therapeutic Shopping Outcomes'). This has been done based on the suggestions of Kang (2009) to use all the four constructs together while analyzing one's retail therapy behavior, rather than using any of the constructs separately.

The results for the second-order CFA model have been found to be within the acceptable range with the normed chi-square value of 4.46; CFI being 0.935; TLI being 0.926; RMSEA being 0.07 and SRMR being .043. Further, the standardized factor loadings for the constructs have been- Therapeutic Shopping Motivation (0.891), Therapeutic Shopping Value: Positive Reinforcement (0.744), Therapeutic Shopping Value: Negative Mood Reduction (0.879) and Therapeutic Shopping Outcomes (0.856) respectively.

Following this, the overall measurement model with all the variables including- Big-Five Personality Traits, Chronic Shopping Orientation, Impulse Buying Tendency and Retail Therapy, has been tested for model fitness and validity. The results have been shown in Table 6.9.

Table 6.9: Parameter Estimates, Standard Errors, Critical Ratios, and Squared Multiple Correlations (SMC) for the Measurement Model Items

FACTOR	STATEMENTS	Standardized Factor Loadings	Unstandardized Factor Loadings	Standard Error	Critical Ratios (T-values)	SMC
	RETAIL THERAPY BEHAVIOR					
TSM	Therapeutic Shopping Motivation	.89	1.30	.08	16.07	.79
TSV-P	Therapeutic Shopping Value: Positive Reinforcement	.76	1.00	a	a	.58
TSV-N	Therapeutic Shopping Value: Negative Mood Reduction	.87	1.20	.07	16.26	.76
TSO	Therapeutic Shopping Outcomes	.85	1.09	.06	16.35	.72
	CHRONIC SHOPPING ORIENTATION					
SO1	When shopping, I often have fun.	.76	.964	.05	18.44	.58
SO4	When shopping, I am usually looking for entertainment.	.74	.988	.05	18.07	.55
SO6	I like to kill time (pass free time) by shopping.	.65	.893	.05	16.06	.42
SO7	When shopping, I like to browse around.	.72	1.00	a	a	.52
SO2	When shopping, I try to get it over with as soon as possible (i.e. finish shopping as soon as possible).	.71	1.07	.06	17.08	.50
SO3	When shopping, I act as deliberately and goal-focused as possible	.69	1.04	.06	16.94	.48
	IMPULSE BUYING TENDENCY					
IB1	I often buy things spontaneously.	.75	1.00	a	a	.56
IB2	"Just do it" describes the way I buy things.	.74	.968	.04	22.25	.56
IB3	I often buy things without thinking.	.73	.895	.04	18.94	.53
IB4	"I see it, I buy it" describes me.	.72	1.02	.05	18.81	.52
IB5	"Buy now, think about it later" describes me.	.74	.981	.05	19.27	.55
IB6	Sometimes I feel like buying things on the spur of the moment.	.75	.919	.04	19.48	.56
IB7	I buy things according to how I feel at the moment.	.67	.818	.04	17.27	.45
IB9	Sometimes, I am bit reckless/careless about what I buy.	.71	.891	.05	18.00	.50

FACTOR	STATEMENTS	Standardized Factor Loadings	Unstandardized Factor Loadings	Standard Error	Critical Ratios (T-values)	SMC
	EXTRAVERSION					
P1	I am life of the party	.68	.931	.05	16.31	.46
P2	I don't talk a lot.	.82	1.23	.06	18.75	.68
P3	I talk to a lot of different people at parties.	.71	.985	.05	16.76	.50
P4	I keep in the background.	.73	1.00	a	a	.54
	AGREEABLENESS					
P5	I sympathize with others' feelings	.81	1.00	a	a	.66
P6	I am not interested in other people's problems.	.68	.972	.05	16.38	.48
P7	I feel others' emotions.	.65	.836	.05	15.74	.42
P8	I am not really interested in others.	.69	.983	.06	16.49	.48
	CONSCIENTIOUSNESS					
P9	I get chores done right away.	.66	.769	.04	15.84	.44
P10	I often forget to put things back in their proper place	.72	.954	.05	16.94	.51
P11	I like order.	.65	.825	.05	15.59	.42
P12	I make a mess of things.	.80	1.00	a	a	.64
	NEUROTICISM					
P14	I am relaxed most of the time.	.89	1.38	.08	17.26	.80
P15	I get upset easily.	.73	1.16	.06	17.05	.54
P16	I seldom feel blue.	.71	1.00	a	a	.50
	INTELLECT					
P18	I am not interested in abstract ideas.	.83	1.00	a	a	.69
P19	I have difficulty understanding abstract ideas.	.64	.792	.06	12.83	.41
P20	I do not have a good imagination.	.66	.863	.06	12.92	.44

Source: Authors elaboration based on own survey data.
: Scales used- Kang & Johnson (2011)/ Kang (2009); Buttner et al. (2013): Rook and Fisher (1995); Donnellan et al. (2006)
Note 1: 'a' indicates a parameter fixed at 1.0 in the original solution

As per the results shown in Table 6.9, all the standardized factor loadings have been found to range between 0.64 and 0.89, with all the p-values being significant at 0.001 level. The squared multiple correlation values (SMC) have been found to range between 0.41 and 0.80. Ideally, SMCs need to be more than 0.5 for a good model. However, Hair et al. (2010) quoted that the values below this may also be accepted in cases where the sample size exceeds 300, which is so in this case. Thus, all the items with the SMC values below 0.5 have also been retained in the model for further analysis. The pictorial presentation of the CFA model has also been shown in figure 6.1.

6.2.2.1 Model Fit:

As per the CFA results for the measurement model, the normed chi square ($\chi2/df$) has been found to be 2.53, which shows an acceptable fit (Hair et al., 2010). The Tucker-Lewis Index (TLI) is 0.91, which is above the minimum required value of 0.90, while the comparative fit index (CFI) is 0.92, which is again above the threshold value of 0.90 (Hair et al., 2010). The root mean square error of approximation (RMSEA) has been found to be 0.047, which is below the maximum threshold value of 0.08 (Hair et al., 2010). Further, the value of standardized root mean residual (SRMR) has been found to be 0.044, which is again within the maximum limit of 0.08 (Hair et al., 2010). The summarized results have been shown in Table 6.10.

Table 6.10: Model Fit Indices of the Measurement Model

Indices	Criteria (Hair et al., 2010)	Final Model Fit
Normed $\chi2$ or $\chi2/df$	<2= very good; Up to 5= acceptable	2.53**
TLI	> 0.90	0.91
CFI	> 0.90	0.92
RMSEA	< 0.08	0.047
SRMR	< 0.08	0.044

Source: Authors elaboration based on own survey data.

** Significant at 0.01 level (2-tailed)

Note: $\chi2/df$– Chi-square divided by degrees of freedom; TLI- Tucker Lewis Index; CFI- Comparative Fit Index; RMSEA- Root Mean Squared Error of Approximation; SRMR- Standardized Root Mean Residual.

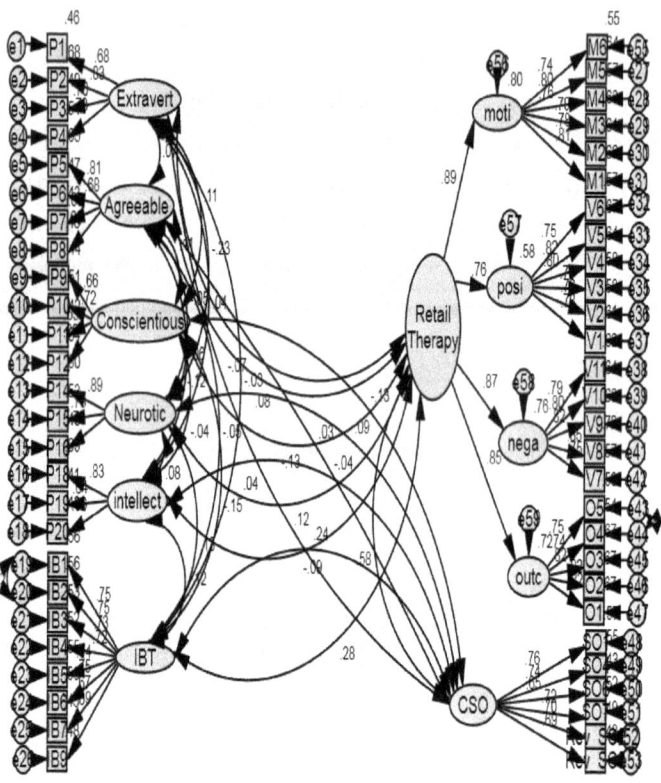

Figure 6.1: Standardized Factor Loadings for Measurement Model (CFA)

Source: Authors elaboration based on own survey data.

6.2.2.2 Validity Measures

For the present study, two types of construct validity measures i.e. convergent validity and discriminant validity have been calculated. The convergent validity has been checked based on the standardized factor loadings, average variance extracted (AVE) and composite reliability. As shown in Table 6.9, the standardized factor loadings for all the items in different constructs have been found to be more than the threshold value of 0.5. The values are also significant at 5 percent level of significance.

Further, the AVE values have also been found to range between 0.504 and 0.715, thereby being greater than the minimum threshold value of 0.5 (refer Table 6.11). Similarly, the composite reliability scores have been found to range between 0.754 and 0.909, again exceeding the minimum threshold value of 0.7 (Hair et al., 2010) (refer Table 6.11). All these above results are indicative of convergent validity.

In addition to this, the discriminant validity for the constructs has also been established by comparing the values of average variance extracted (AVE) with that of the maximum shared variance (MSV) and average shared variance (ASV). According to Fornell and Larcker (1981), in order to prove discriminant validity, the values of AVE must exceed the values of both MSV and ASV. The results shown in Table 6.11 are thus a proof of the discriminant validity, where values of AVE for all the constructs are greater than the values of MSV and ASV.

Table 6.11: Convergent and Discriminant Validity Analysis

	CR	AVE	MSV	ASV
Retail Therapy Behavior	0.909	0.715	0.341	0.067
Extraversion	0.826	0.544	0.053	0.011
Conscientiousness	0.801	0.504	0.023	0.014
Neuroticism	0.820	0.605	0.053	0.016
Agreeableness	0.803	0.506	0.013	0.005
Intellect	0.754	0.508	0.015	0.005
IBT	0.899	0.527	0.076	0.027
CSO	0.859	0.505	0.341	0.061

Source: Authors elaboration based on own survey data.

Note: CR- Composite Reliability, AVE- Average Variance Extracted, MSV- Maximum Shared Variance, ASV- Average Shared Variance, IBT- Impulse Buying Tendency, CSO- Chronic Shopping Orientation.

6.3   HYPOTHESES TESTING - ESTIMATING THE PATH MODEL

Based on previous literature (refer chapter-2), the following relationships are expected between different personality variables and retail therapy behavior:

H₅: Extraversion positively influences Retail Therapy Behavior.

H₆: Agreeableness negatively influences Retail Therapy Behavior.

H₇: Conscientiousness negatively influences Retail Therapy Behavior.

H_8: Neuroticism positively influences Retail Therapy Behavior.

H_9: Intellect positively influences Retail Therapy Behavior.

H_{10}: Chronic Shopping Orientation positively influences Retail Therapy Behavior.

H_{11}: Impulse Buying Tendency positively influences Retail Therapy Behavior.

In order to test the hypotheses, Path Analysis has been used. This technique helps in ascertaining the cause and effect relationship between the given constructs. Results for the study have been analyzed based on the regression weights for different paths from the independent variables i.e. the Big-Five, Chronic Shopping Orientation and Impulse Buying Tendency, to the dependent variable i.e. Retail Therapy Behavior. In addition, two demographics characteristics, i.e. age and employment status, that had been earlier found to have a significant relation with retail therapy, have also been taken as the control variables in the model.

The proposed model and the results of the path analysis have been presented in Figure 6.2.

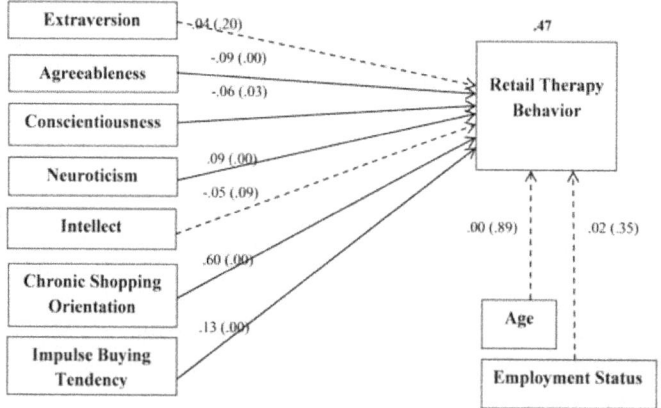

Figure 6.2: Path Model (effect of Big-Five, Chronic Shopping Orientation and Impulse Buying Tendency on Retail Therapy, with Age and Employment Status as Control Variables)

Source: Authors elaboration based on own survey data.
Note: 1. Values shown on the paths represent the standardized regression weights
2. Values in the brackets represent the p-values
3. Dark lines represent the significant paths
4. Dotted lines represent the non-significant paths

Figure 6.2 shows that, out of the total seven hypothesized relationships, five have been confirmed (represented by dark lines). In addition, the dotted lines from the demographics indicate that their effect is weak and they do not confound the relationship of other personal factors with that of retail therapy. The hypotheses testing results have also been shown in Table 6.12.

Table 6.12: Conceptual Model- Regression Weights

	Standardized Regression Weights	Unstandardized Regression Weights	S.E.	C.R.	P	Hypotheses Results
Retail Therapy <-- Extrovert	.038	.035	.028	1.281	.200	*Not Supported*
Retail Therapy <-- Agreeable	-.091	-.076	.025	-3.074	.002**	*Supported*
Retail Therapy <-- Conscientious	-.062	-.049	.022	-2.167	.030*	*Supported*
Retail Therapy <-- Neurotic	.089	.095	.030	3.173	.002**	*Supported*
Retail Therapy <-- Intellect	-.049	-.037	.022	-1.673	.094	*Not Supported*
Retail Therapy <-- CSO	.604	.510	.025	20.703	.000***	*Supported*
Retail Therapy <-- IBT	.125	.093	.022	4.246	.000***	*Supported*

Source: Authors elaboration based on own survey data.

*** Significant at 0.001 level (2-tailed)

** Significant at 0.01 level (2-tailed)

* Significant at 0.05 level (2-tailed)

Note: CSO- Chronic Shopping Orientation, IBT- Impulse Buying Tendency, S.E- Standard Error, C.R.- Critical Ratios, P- Significance Value.

All the hypotheses testing results shown in Table 6.12 have been explained one-by-one as under:

Hypothesis 5 states that 'Extraversion positively influences Retail Therapy Behavior'. The study results do not support this hypothesis (β= .038, p>0.05), which implies that being an extrovert or introvert does not make a difference in whether or not a person chooses shopping for therapeutic reasons.

Hypothesis 6 states that 'Agreeableness negatively influences Retail Therapy Behavior'. The results support this hypothesized relationship (with $\beta= -.091$, $p<0.01$). Previous research has shown that people who are low on agreeableness are comparatively less able to neutralize their thoughts and also lack social adaptability (Costa, Jr & McCrae, 1992; Pervin, 2006). Carver and Smith (2010) had observed a negative relation of agreeableness with disengagement coping which is basically emotion-based coping. Since, shopping is also one of the emotion-based coping strategies only; thus the results of the present study are in line with the previous literature. Finally, it can be concluded that women, who are low on social skills and lack trust and sympathy, are more likely to indulge in retail therapy.

Hypothesis 7 states that 'Conscientiousness negatively influences Retail Therapy Behavior'. As per the results of path analysis, this has been found to be true (with $\beta= -.062$, $p<.05$). This depicts that women who are less disciplined and who do not plan things in advance are more likely to indulge in therapeutic shopping behavior. It might be because of the reason that due to lack of planning and discipline, they might not be able to handle a negative situation tactically and thus might try to get rid of it through any possible way instantly coming to their mind. In this regard, the shopping activity might be helping them out in reducing anxiety created by the unforeseen negative situation. These results are also in consonance with the existing literature that states that conscientious individuals plan for stressors in advance (Vollrath, 2001) and engage less in compensatory behaviors (John & Srivastava, 1999).

Hypothesis 8 states that 'Neuroticism positively influences Retail Therapy Behavior'. The study results support this hypothesized relationship (with $\beta=.089$, $p<.01$). Previous research shows that the neurotic individuals take events and things more negatively and do not easily express their emotions (Penley & Tomaka 2002, Suls & Martin 2005; Sadr, 2016). A positive relation of this trait with retail therapy indicates that the women who are weak in stress handling are more likely to show a positive attitude towards retail therapy and they also use shopping for therapeutic reasons. A probable reason might be that shopping for something new might be helping them to regain some control over the negative situation and deal with their hidden emotions.

Hypothesis 9 states that 'Intellect positively influences Retail Therapy Behavior'. The present research has not been able to verify this hypothesis; rather the relationship between intellect and retail therapy has been found to be negative (although not statistically significant). Though, no clear answer could be found for the same, however, it might be due to the reason that such women might be using more of the problem-focused strategies or some other type of emotion-focused strategies that lead to more positive experiences.

Hypothesis 10 states that 'Chronic Shopping Orientation positively influences Retail Therapy Behavior'. The hypothesized relationship has been found to be true for the present study (with $\beta=.604$, $p<.001$). This finding is in line with the previous research results also, which state that the individuals who love the shopping activity, experience fun in it and like to browse around in shops, are more likely to have a positive attitude towards therapy shopping also (Kang & Johnson, 2010). This indicates that shopping lovers not only believe in the positive experiences of shopping, they also believe in the therapeutic powers of shopping in mood-alleviation. They not only go for shopping when happy, but also choose it for dealing with their negative emotions.

Hypothesis 11 states that 'Impulse Buying Tendency positively influences Retail Therapy Behavior'. The results of path analysis also showed this relationship to be true (with $\beta=.125$, $p<.001$). This indicates that women, who are less able to control their impulses during shopping and find excitement in buying for unplanned products, are more likely to choose shopping activity for mood-alleviative reasons also. The results are also in consonance with the existing literature e.g. Baumeister (2002), Son and Chang (2016) etc.

CONCLUSION

Based on the results from this chapter, it can be concluded that personal factors do play a significant role in retail therapy behavior. Although, there have been certain studies that have explained the relationship of shopping orientation and impulse buying with retail therapy, however, the impact of the basic personality traits had altogether been ignored by the previous researchers. Thus, the proposed relationship between the Big-Five and retail therapy had been framed based on hints from related shopping behaviors and also from psychology research.

The personality traits have been found to play an important role in one's life. Even the way people react to stress and the type of strategies they use to deal with it, have been found to be affected by their personality. In the present study, three of the elementary personality traits i.e. Agreeableness, Conscientiousness and Neuroticism have been found to significantly affect the retail therapy behavior of women. In addition, both the shopping-related personality traits i.e. Chronic Shopping Orientation and Impulse Buying Tendency have also been found to significantly predict one's retail therapy behavior. Amongst the demographic variables, age and employment status have been found to have a significant relationship with retail therapy.

REFERENCES

1. Baumeister, R. F. (2002). Yielding to temptation: Self-control failure, impulsive purchasing, and consumer behavior. *Journal of Consumer Research,* 28(4), 670-676.

2. Buttner, O., Florack, A. & Goritz, A. S. (2013). Shopping orientation as a stable consumer disposition and its influence on consumers' evaluations of retailer communication. *European Journal of Marketing,* 48(5/6), 1026-1045.

3. Carver, C. S. & Smith, J. C. (2010). Personality and coping. *Annual Review of Psychology*, 61, 679–704.

4. Costa, P. T. & McCrae, R. R. (1992). NEO personality inventory professional manual. Odessa, FL: *Psychological Assessment Resources.*

5. Donnellan, M. B., Oswald, F. L., Baird, B. M. & Lucas, R. E. (2006). The Mini-IPIP Scales: Tiny-yet-effective measures of the big five factors of personality. *Psychological Assessment,* 18, 192-203.

6. Fornell, C. & Larcker, D. F. (1981). Evaluating structural equation models with un-observable variables and measurement error. *Journal of Marketing Research*, 18(1), 39–50.

7. Hair, Jr. J. F., Black, W. C., Babin, B. J. & Anderson, R. E. (2010). *Multivariate data analysis.* Pearson Education Inc., New Delhi, India.

8. Huddleston, P. & Minahan (2011). *Consumer behavior: Women and shopping.* Business Expert Press.

9. John, O. & Srivastava, S. (1999). The big five trait taxonomy: History, measurement, and theoretical perspectives. In L. Pervin & O. P. John (Eds.), *Handbook of Personality: Theory and Research.* New York, NY: Guildford.

10. Kang, M. (2009). *Retail therapy: A qualitative investigation and scale development.* Doctoral dissertation, University of Minnesota.

11. Kang, M. & Johnson, K. K. P. (2010). Let's shop! Exploring the experiences of therapy shoppers. *Journal of Global Fashion Marketing*, 1(2), 71-79.

12. Kang, M. & Johnson, K. K. P. (2011). Retail therapy: Scale development. *Clothing and Textiles Research Journal,* 29(1), 3-19.

13. Penley, J., Tomaka, J. & Wiebe, J. (2002). The association of coping to physical and psychological health outcomes: A meta-analytic review. *Journal of Behavioral Medicine,* 25(6), 551-603.

14. Pervin, L. A. (2006). *The science of personality.* (3rd ed.), New York: Oxford University Press.

15. Rook, D. W. & Fisher, R. J. (1995). Trait and normative aspects of impulsive buying behavior. *Journal of Consumer Research*, 22 (3), 305-13.

16. Sadr, M. M. (2016). The role of personality traits predicting emotion regulation strategies. *International Academic Journal of Humanities*, 3(4), 13-24.

17. Son, J. & Chang, H. J. (2016). Retail therapy: What makes you feel relieved and happy? *2016, International Textile and Apparel Association, Inc. ITAA Proceedings, #73 – http://itaaonline.org*

18. Suls, J. & Martin R. (2005). The daily life of the garden-variety neurotic: Reactivity, stressor exposure, mood spillover, and maladaptive coping. *Journal of Personality.* 73, 1485–509.

19. Tiwari, R. K. & Abraham, A. (2010). Understanding the consumer behavior towards shopping malls in Raipur city. *International Journal of Management and Strategy.* 1(1).

20. Vollrath, M. (2001). Personality and stress. *Scandavian Journal of Psychology.* 42, 335–47.

THERAPY SHOPPING TRIP BEHAVIOR OF RETAIL THERAPY SHOPPERS

CHAPTER – 7

THERAPY SHOPPING TRIP BEHAVIOR OF RETAIL THERAPY SHOPPERS

The previous chapter (Chapter-6) dealt with digging out the role of personal characteristics in retail therapy behavior of Indian women. It shows as to what personality and demographic variables may help in predicting whether one indulges in therapeutic shopping or not. This chapter further contributes to the literature by analyzing the shopping behavior of the therapy shoppers when they go for a retail therapy trip. This can help the retailers and marketers in better understanding of their likes and dislikes and thus focusing on the particular areas which can contribute more towards mood alleviation and also motivate these shoppers to buy more.

As observed from the existing literature, shoppers usually behave somewhat differently during a retail therapy trip, as compared to what they do during any other normal shopping trip. A summary of the major observations has been given below:

1. Most of the therapy shoppers prefer to shop alone when feeling sad or depressed. This gives them a chance to take decisions on their own without anyone's interference (Woodruffe, 2001; Kang, 2009; Huddleston & Minahan, 2011; D'Souza, 2012).

2. Consumers who shop for stress relief engage more in self-gifting i.e. they like to buy something for themselves (Mick and De Moss, 1990; Luomala, 2002; Atalay & Meloy, 2011; Mortimer et al., 2015).

3. During a retail therapy trip, the products are mostly bought on impulse, which adds to the excitement related to their purchase (Tice et al., 2001; Baumeister, 2002; Sneath et al., 2009; Atalay & Meloy, 2011).

4. The mode of payment used by therapy shoppers is mostly credit card. This is because when card payment is made, the pain of losing money is lesser, as compared to when paying through cash (Woodruffe, 2001).

170

5.   Therapy shoppers spend more than usual time and money during a retail therapy trip as compared to any other normal shopping trips (Kim et al., 2005; Kang, 2009).

6.   Therapy shoppers mostly like to purchase appearance related products like fashionable clothing, accessories, jewelry etc. However, sometimes they even buy certain non-appearance related products such as kitchenware items, household items, electronics, hardware, books, bicycle items etc. (Kang, 2009). Some of the shoppers even purchase items which they might not ordinarily purchase, such as high-priced items or fashionable and trendy items. This is because their attention and focus is entirely shifted towards mood-alleviation (Atalay & Meloy, 2011).

7.   Male and female therapy shoppers differ in their choice for products they buy. Whereas, women mainly prefer to buy apparels, accessories, jewelry etc., men mostly purchase food, electronics, movies and games (Surendran & Vardhan, 2014; D'souza, 2012).

8.   Although, most of the shoppers feel happy only after buying something, the role of other elements in the shopping process cannot be undermined. Research has shown that sometimes, even the shopping experience and the sensory stimulation may itself be therapeutic (Luomala, 2002; Woodruffe, 2001). For some people, even a thought about going for shopping can cheer them up (Kang, 2009), while some may feel a high from bargaining (Lee, 2013; Surendran & Vardhan, 2014).

9.   Therapy shoppers mainly like to shop at brick and mortar stores, rather than online or other means. This is because, interacting with fellow shoppers and like-minded people, generates good feelings (Kim et al., 2005; Gray et al., 2011; Borges et al., 2010).

All these above mentioned observations have been established by the researchers in the context of shoppers from western countries. Thus, through this study, it has been analyzed whether the same things hold true for the Indian shoppers also.

METHODOLOGY

Since, this part of the research deals specifically with the therapy shoppers' behavior, the respondents had been asked, during survey, to answer the questions for this section, only if they actually shopped for mood-alleviation and considered themselves as therapy shoppers. Out of the total 800 women approached, 413 had identified themselves as therapy shoppers. Accordingly, they form the sample base for this objective. Amongst these 413 respondents, about 60 percent of the women are married; 56 percent are post graduates while 32 percent are graduates; 60 percent have monthly discretionary income of less than Rs. 10,000, while about 25 percent have between Rs. 10,000 to Rs. 20,000, 7 percent having between Rs. 20,000 to Rs. 30,000 and remaining 8 percent with above Rs. 30,000. 51 percent of the respondents belong to the working class, while remaining 49 percent belong to the non-working class. Mean age of respondents is 30 years.

The respondents had been asked to answer different shopping behavior questions like- the products they like to buy for mood-alleviation, the shopping formats they like to visit, the payment mode they like to use, frequency of buying impulsively, time and money spend, the role that shopping environment plays in uplifting their mood etc. The data analysis results for all these questions have been shown in Section 7.1. Further, Section 7.2 presents a general discussion and conclusion for the chapter.

7.1   DATA ANALYSIS

The findings related to the shopping behavior of Indian women retail therapy shoppers have been explained in the form of answers to the following questions-

7.1.1   Whom they like to accompany them during therapy shopping trip?

The first question relates to the person that the therapy shoppers like to take along when they shop for mood-alleviation. It has been found that, out of the total 413 respondents, nearly half i.e. 48 percent, prefer to shop with someone from their family, followed by those who like to go for shopping with their friends (43%) when feeling sad/depressed/bored/lonely (for details refer Table 7.1).

172

As a total contrast to the findings of the previous studies (Huddleston & Minahan, 2011; Kang & Johnson, 2010) where the researchers had observed that retail therapy shoppers tend to shop alone, this study shows that only about 9 percent of the respondents like to shop alone during a therapy shopping trip (refer Table 7.1).

7.1.2   For whom the products are purchased?

Although, most of the respondents have been found seeking someone's company for therapy shopping; interestingly, 55 percent of the respondents have agreed that during such a shopping trip, they mostly like to buy something for themselves. At the same time, about 40 percent of them have also said that they buy something for their family. This indicates that these shoppers do not necessarily feel good by buying for themselves, rather gifting to others also carries therapeutic value for them. The details have been shown in Table 7.1.

7.1.3   How they Pay?

Paying for products through credit cards has been found to be less painful than using cash because of reduced transparency and little realization of the money outflow (see Lee, 2013). As such, therapy shoppers have also been found to make more use of the credit mode for payments during a mood-alleviative trip (Woodruffe, 2001). However, in this study, out of the total 413 therapy shoppers, about 82 percent have said that they prefer to make cash payment for the products purchased during a retail therapy trip, while only 18 percent of them like to make use of credit or debit card (refer Table 7.1).

7.1.4   Do they make impulse purchases?

Researchers have found that therapy shoppers usually indulge in unplanned buying. Since their brain becomes busy in managing mood, their ability to control their impulse is reduced. Thus, they are not able to rationally decide what is required and what not (Atalay & Meloy, 2011). Sometimes even they intentionally buy impulsively, just to gift something to themselves as a compensation for something lost in their life or something not in their hands (Mortimer et al., 2015). In this study, about 40 percent of the respondents have said that they sometimes buy impulsively during retail therapy trip, followed by those (approx. 25%) who rarely do so. Further 19 percent have said

173

that they never buy anything unplanned. There are only about 12 percent of the respondents who have agreed that they 'often' and just 5 percent who have said that they 'always' buy impulsively during retail therapy shopping (refer Table 7.1).

Table 7.1: Descriptive Data for Therapy Shopping Trip Behavior Elements

Variables	Therapy shoppers (N=413)	
	Frequency	%age
Company:		
Friends	179	43.3
Family	198	47.9
Alone	36	8.7
For:		
Myself	228	55.2
Family	164	39.7
Friends/others	21	5.1
Mode:		
Cash	338	81.8
Credit/debit card/others	75	18.2
Impulse buying:		
Never	79	19.1
Rarely	101	24.5
Sometimes	163	39.5
Often	49	11.9
Always	21	5.1
Time:		
Yes	223	54.0
No	190	46.0
Money:		
Yes	162	39.2
No	251	60.8

Source: Authors elaboration based on own survey data.

7.1.5 How much time they spend?

It is said that when people go for shopping to alleviate negative mood, they tend to spend more than usual time in shopping (Kang, 2009). They like to spend time browsing in the stores, trying on items, searching for offers, seeking social connection, talking to the sales associates or fellow shoppers etc. (Kim et al., 2005; Atalay & Meloy, 2011). All these activities may consume more time. The same thing has been observed in this study also where overall 54 percent of the respondents have admitted that when they go for therapy shopping, they spend more time as compared to the time spend during any other shopping trip (refer Table 7.1).

7.1.6 How much money they spend?

In the study by Kang and Johnson (2010), it had been found that majority of the therapy shoppers tend to spend more money and buy expensive items during retail therapy trip. In addition, they also tend to buy more number of items than they usually buy during any other normal shopping trip. In this study, about 40 percent of the therapy shoppers have agreed that they spend more than usual money during therapy shopping, whereas, majority i.e. 60 percent have disagreed to this (refer Table 7.1).

7.1.7 Which products are bought during therapy shopping?

The respondents had been given a list of five categories of products, identified on the basis of previous literature, including: clothing, accessories, shoes, home furnishing and cosmetics. Out of these, they had to select those products whose purchase makes them feel more relaxed and happy during therapy shopping and to rank them in order of their importance in up-lifting of mood. Rank 'I' for a product meant that it was the top most choice, followed by other ranks respectively.

In order to know the comparative preference for the products, weights have been assigned to the ranks in reverse order and their sum has been calculated. A weight of 5 has been given to the first rank and similarly 4 to the second and so on. During the survey, respondents had the freedom to choose any number of products out of the given five and no forced choice or ranking had been required. Thus, while analyzing the results, the number of respondents who did not chose a particular product in their list

175

(i.e. non-responses) have also been taken into account. A weight of zero has been given for such non-responses (https://help.surveygizmo.com/help/limit-ranked-items).

The relative importance of products has been judged based on the weighted mean ranks calculated as shown below:

Weighted Mean Rank = <u>Total of Weighted Ranks</u>
Total Number of Respondents
(Including non-responses)

Based on weighted mean ranks, clothing has been found to be the most preferred product category (weighted mean rank= 4.04), followed by accessories (2.09), shoes (1.94), cosmetics (1.58) and home furnishing (1.25). Table 7.2 shows the number of respondents choosing a particular product in their list, frequency of different ranks assigned to them along with weighted ranks, weighted mean rank, and finally showing the number of respondents who did not choose that particular product in their list.

Table 7.2: Frequency, Ranks and Weighted Ranks for Products Purchased During Therapy Shopping

Product/ Rank	Frequency of rank and weighted rank	I	II	III	IV	V	Total (in list)	Weighted mean rank	Not in list
Clothing	Frequency	282	48	17	6	2	**355**		58
	Weighted rank	1410	192	51	12	2	**1667**	4.04	
Accessories	Frequency	38	91	68	46	14	**257**		156
	Weighted rank	190	364	204	92	14	**864**	2.09	
Shoes	Frequency	36	77	67	45	24	**249**		164
	Weighted rank	180	308	201	90	24	**803**	1.94	
Home Furnishing	Frequency	28	28	26	40	105	**227**		186
	Weighted rank	140	112	78	80	105	**515**	1.25	
Cosmetics	Frequency	30	37	59	68	43	**237**		176
	Weighted rank	150	148	177	136	43	**654**	1.58	

Source: Authors elaboration based on own survey data.

7.1.8 Which retail formats they prefer?

Five options for retail formats had been given to the respondents, out of which they had to select and rank those formats that they prefer to shop from for retail therapy. For the purpose of analyzing this data, all the calculations for weighted ranks and weighted mean ranks have been made in the similar manner as that done for analyzing the product preferences. It has been found that the therapy shoppers prefer malls the most (weighted mean rank= 2.79), followed by multi-brand stores (1.92), traditional shops (1.84) and hypermarkets (1.72) along with single-brand store (1.04) at the last position (refer Table 7.3).

Table 7.3: Frequency, Ranks and Weighted Ranks for Retail Formats Visited During Therapy Shopping

Retail format/ Rank		I	II	III	IV	V	Total (in list)	Weighted rank	Not in list
Mall	Frequency	173	41	22	22	15	273		140
	Weighted rank	865	164	66	44	15	1154	2.79	
Super/Hyper market	Frequency	60	52	40	33	17	202		211
	Weighted rank	300	208	120	66	17	711	1.72	
Multi-brand stores	Frequency	67	58	57	25	5	212		201
	Weighted rank	335	232	171	50	5	793	1.92	
Single-brand stores	Frequency	20	32	30	33	46	161		252
	Weighted rank	100	128	90	66	46	430	1.04	
Traditional shops	Frequency	91	36	18	27	52	224		189
	Weighted rank	455	144	54	54	52	759	1.84	

Source: Authors elaboration based on own survey data.

7.1.9 What is the role of shopping process elements?

The respondents had been given a list of ten different elements present in a typical shopping trip and they were required to choose and rank them according to their importance in mood-alleviation. For the purpose of analyzing this data, all the calculations for weighted ranks and weighted mean ranks have been made in the similar manner as that done for analyzing the product preferences. Based on the results, as shown in Table 7.4, 'Getting knowledge of new trends' (weighted mean rank= 2.33) has been found to be the most important element in mood-alleviation, followed by retail attributes like 'visual display' (2.09) and 'shopping place ambience' (2.01). 'Actual purchase' (1.75) of a product has been placed at the fourth position. Many shoppers have even agreed that a simple 'thought of going for shopping' (1.54) also leads to happiness. The other elements include- 'trying on items' (1.21), 'using the product purchased' (1.20), 'bargaining' (1.15), 'personnel behavior' (1.13), and 'watching other shoppers' (0.68) at shopping place (being at the last position).

Table 7.4: Frequency, Ranks and Weighted Ranks for Role of Shopping Process Elements during Therapy Shopping

Shopping process elements/ Rank		I	II	III	IV	V	Total (in list)	Weighted rank	Not in list
Thought of shopping	Frequency	65	33	28	25	20	**171**	1.54	242
	Weighted rank	325	132	84	50	20	**638**		
Ambience	Frequency	78	55	33	43	36	**245**	2.01	168
	Weighted rank	390	220	99	86	36	**831**		
Visual display	Frequency	55	73	59	35	49	**271**	2.09	142
	Weighted rank	275	292	177	70	49	**863**		
Personnel behavior	Frequency	11	41	46	39	33	**170**	1.13	243
	Weighted rank	55	164	138	78	33	**468**		
Watching other shoppers	Frequency	6	12	33	37	31	**119**	0.68	294
	Weighted rank	30	48	99	74	31	**282**		
Knowledge of trends	Frequency	73	55	67	67	44	**306**	2.33	107
	Weighted rank	365	220	201	134	44	**964**		
Trying on items	Frequency	8	42	46	59	35	**190**	1.21	223
	Weighted rank	40	168	138	118	35	**499**		

Shopping process elements/ Rank		I	II	III	IV	V	Total (in list)	Weighted rank	Not in list
Bargaining	Frequency	33	33	25	35	33	**159**		254
	Weighted rank	165	132	75	70	33	**475**	1.15	
Actual purchase	Frequency	55	41	42	45	69	**252**		161
	Weighted rank	275	164	126	90	69	**724**	1.75	
Use of the item purchased	Frequency	27	34	34	27	69	**191**		222
	Weighted rank	135	136	102	54	69	**496**	1.20	

Source: Authors elaboration based on own survey data.

7.2   DISCUSSION AND CONCLUSION

The overall results have led to an understanding that, for some of the aspects, Indian women shoppers also exhibit similar kind of therapy shopping behavior, as that found in the context of shoppers from the western countries e.g. buying self-gifts, spending more than usual time and money, buying more appearance related products, preferring to buy from malls etc. Many of them have agreed that they buy impulsively during retail therapy trip. They also find the role of retail attributes as important in mood-alleviation. Buying of a product is also important for them. Even a thought of going for shopping can bring a smile on their face.

Apart from this, certain unique behavioral elements, specific to the Indian women shoppers, have also been observed. Whereas, the previous studies had shown that retail therapy shoppers tend to shop alone (Woodruffe, 2001; Luomala, 2002; Kang, 2009; Huddleston & Minahan, 2011; D'Souza, 2012), the same has not been found to be true for the Indian shoppers. Majority of them seek company of others when they want to shop for mood-alleviative reasons. Secondly, Indian women not only like to buy for themselves, rather, buying for others also gives them a therapeutic feeling. Most of them prefer to make cash payment during therapy shopping trip.

Although Indian women find malls and hypermarkets to be better places for therapy shopping; many of them also feel happy while shopping at traditional stores. Table 7.5 shows this comparison in a summarized form.

Table 7.5: Summarized Comparison of Results of Present Study with Previous Studies

Shopping behavior elements	Previous studies	Present study
Company	Prefer to shop alone (Woodruffe, 2001; Kang, 2009; Huddleston & Minahan, 2011; D'Souza, 2012)	Seek company
Self-gifting	Indulge more in self-gifting (Mick and De Moss, 1990; Luomala, 2002; Atalay and Meloy, 2011; Mortimer et al., 2015)	Indulge more in self-gifting, but also like to buy for family
Mode of payment	Mostly prefer card payment (Woodruffe, 2001)	Prefer cash payment
Impulse buying	Indulge more in impulse buying (Baumeister, 2002; Atalay and Meloy, 2011)	Similar findings as that of previous studies
Time	Spend more than usual time (Kim et al., 2005; Kang, 2009)	Similar findings as that of previous studies
Money	Spend more than usual money (Kim et al., 2005; Kang, 2009)	About 40 per cent agreed
Products	Buy more appearance related products like clothing and accessories etc. (Kang, 2009; D'souza, 2012; Surendran and Vardhan, 2014)	Similar findings as that of previous studies
Retail format	Mostly prefer malls and other brick and mortar stores (Kim et al., 2005; Gray et al., 2011; Borges et al., 2010)	Prefer malls, but also prefer traditional stores
Shopping process elements	Retail ambience, personnel behavior, purchase, updated knowledge, bargaining, thought of shopping, using the products etc. (Woodruffe, 2001; Luomala, 2002; Kang, 2009; Lee, 2013; Surendran & Vardhan, 2014)	Similar findings as that of previous studies

Source: Authors elaboration.

Based on the findings and discussion, it can be finally concluded that, although, like in other countries, Indian women might also be commonly indulging in retail therapy; however, their style and behavioral attitude is quite distinct. The effects of collectivistic cultural values like caring for others by taking them along or gifting to others etc. are also well reflected in their shopping behavior. These findings have important implications for retailers as well as academicians.

REFERENCES

1. Atalay, A. S. & Meloy, M. G. (2011). When the going gets tough, the tough go shopping- An examination of self-gifting behaviour. *Advances in Consumer Research,* 33, 259-260.

2. Baumeister, R. F. (2002). Yielding to temptation: Self-control failure, impulsive purchasing, and consumer behaviour. *Journal of Consumer Research,* 28(4), 670-676.

3. Borges, A., Chebat, J. C. & Babin, B. J. (2010). Does a companion always enhance the shopping experience? *Journal of Retailing and Consumer Services,* 17 (4), 294–299.

4. D'Souza, D. (2012). *Retail therapy: A study in the Indian context to understand compensatory consumption and its implications on consumer's psyche,* Dissertation in partial fulfillment of the requirements for the Post Graduate Programme for Communications Management Diploma.

5. Gray, H. M., Ishii, K. & Ambady, N. (2011). Misery loves company: When sadness increases the desire for social connectedness. *Personality and Social Psychology Bulletin,* 37(11), 1438–1448.

6. https://help.surveygizmo.com/help/limit-ranked-items

7. Huddleston & Minahan (2011). *Consumer behaviour: Women and shopping.* Business Expert Press.

8. Kang, M. & Johnson, K. K. P. (2010). Let's shop! Exploring the experiences of therapy shoppers. *Journal of Global Fashion Marketing,* 1(2), 71-79.

9. Kang, M. (2009). *Retail therapy: A qualitative investigation and scale development.* Doctoral dissertation, University of Minnesota.

10. Kim, Y. K., Kang, J. & Kim, M. (2005). The Relationship among family and social interaction, loneliness, mall shopping motivation and mall spending of older consumers. *Psychology and Marketing,* 22(12), 995-1015.

11. Lee, L. (2013). The emotional shopper: Assessing the effectiveness of retail therapy. *Foundations and Trends in Marketing,* 8(2), 69-145.

12. Luomala, H. T. (2002). An empirical analysis of the practices and therapeutic power of mood-alleviative consumption in Finland. *Psychology & Marketing,* 19(10), 813-836.

13. Mick, D. G. & DeMoss, M. (1990). Self-gifts: Phenomenological insights from four contexts. *Journal of Consumer Research*, 17(3), 322-32.

14. Mortimer, G., Bougoure, U. S. & Fazal-E-Hasan, S. (2015). Development and validation of the self-gifting consumer behaviour scale. *Journal of Consumer Behaviour*, 14, 165-179.

15. Sneath, J., Lacey, R. & Kennett-Hensel, P. (2009). Coping with a natural disaster: Losses, emotions, and impulsive and compulsive buying. *Marketing Letters.* 20, 45-60.

16. Surendran, J. & Vardhan, R. (2014). Retail therapy: Understanding the phenomenon to improve customer experience, available at *http://tejas.iimb.ac.in/articles/Tejas_December%20Edition_Article%204.pdf.*

17. Tice, D. M., Bratslavsky, E. & Baumeister, R. F. (2001). Emotional distress regulation takes precedence over impulse control: If you feel bad, do it! *Journal of Personality and Social Psychology*, 80, 53-67.

18. Woodruffe, H. (2001). *Retail therapy: An investigation of compensatory consumption and shopping behaviour.* Thesis submitted to Lancaster University for the Degree of Doctor of Philosophy (Phd).

SUMMARY, IMPLICATIONS AND FUTURE RESEARCH DIRECTIONS

CHAPTER-8

SUMMARY, IMPLICATIONS AND FUTURE RESEARCH DIRECTIONS

8.1   INTRODUCTION

'Retail Therapy' refers to the act of going on a shopping spree to alleviate negative mood (Kang, 2009). It is a consumption behavior that is engaged in to cope with stress or depression, caused by some negative event that a person is either unwilling to or unable to tackle directly (Woodruffe, 2001). Consequently, she (/he) uses shopping or buying as an indirect means to reduce the tension and feel relaxed (Woodruffe, 2001). Shopping activity works as a coping mechanism that generates happiness in short-run (Hama, 2001; Kang, 2009; Atalay & Meloy, 2011), and enhances psychological well-being in the long-run (Kang & Johnson, 2011). Different types of therapeutic benefits offered by shopping include- distraction, escape, indulgence, relaxation, sensory stimulation, social connection etc. (Luomala, 2002; Lee, 2013).

The act of retail therapy works on dynamic mood theory in which, people are not focused on 'present' emotions, but on 'outcome' emotions i.e. emotions following an act (Andrade, 2005). They indulge in shopping expecting that their current negative mood would change and they would feel better. As such, lonely individuals seek social connection through shopping; bored shoppers seek sensory stimulation; stressed out shoppers seek distraction through shopping etc. (Luomala, 2002; D'Souza, 2012; Lee, 2013). Sometimes, shoppers even unconsciously behave in a particular way, unknowing that their mood is driving them to do so e.g. making unplanned purchases followed by a bad mood (Atalay & Meloy, 2011).

The following sections give a brief-up of the concept of retail therapy, its prevalence and its importance for the shoppers as well as retailers and marketers. Further, the research gaps, rationale of the study, objectives, methodology, and the summarized data analysis results have been given. This is followed by implications for the different stakeholders and the future research directions.

183

8.1.1 Concept of Retail Therapy:

Within the existing literature, the concept of retail therapy has mainly been explained through two approaches- the 'Compensatory Consumption Approach' and 'Mood-Alleviative Approach'. As compensatory consumption, retail therapy refers to the use of shopping as compensation for some 'lack' or 'psychological deficiency' in life, that cannot be satisfied with primary fulfillment. Accordingly, shopping is used as a substitute to that 'lack' (Woodruffe, 2001; Yurchisin et al., 2006; Yurchisin et al. 2008). From the mood-alleviative perspective, on the other hand, retail therapy is the "consumption behavior, including shopping and buying, that individuals engage in to improve their negative mood" (Kang, 2009). Earlier, the terms compensatory consumption and retail therapy had been used interchangeably. However, Kang (2009) highlighted that both are different and in fact, retail therapy (as a mood-alleviative shopping) is a part of compensatory consumption behavior, which is a wider term.

8.1.2 Prevalence of Retail Therapy:

The tendency of using shopping for therapeutic reasons is more common in western countries. The concept mainly originated from U.S. The Chicago Tribune mentioned the term in 1980's, stating that people go to stores to improve their mood (Reyhle, Jan. 8, 2014). In 2013, Ebates.com carried out a survey of 1000 people in U.S., in which it was found that more than half of them indulged in shopping for mood-alleviative reasons (64 percent among them being women). A survey by Yarrow (2013), in Times Magazine, also showed that about 52 percent of the Americans indulged in retail therapy, where more than 62 percent shopped for cheering themselves up. In a later survey of 2000 Americans, by Paul (2017), it was found that, in a year, more than one fifth of the products were purchased by Americans for therapy reasons.

Apart from U.S., retail therapy is also common in other countries e.g. the Greenpeace study (2016) about the shopping behavior of people in China, Hong Kong, Taiwan, Italy and Germany, found that 31 percent of the Chinese and 14 percent of the Germans shop when they are feeling bored or lonely. Similarly, a survey by dendyneville.co.uk (Jan, 16, 2018) found that about four-tenth of the people in U.K. use shopping activity for cheering themselves up. In Britain also, retail therapy has become the most pleasurable leisure activity. The reason is mainly attributed to the modernization of the retailing sector, which has offered beautiful and attractive shopping options to the shoppers (McVeigh, 2000).

As far as the usage of retail therapy in India is concerned, the term 'therapy' is, now days, quite commonly used in magazine articles or promotional advertisements etc., e.g. in 2019, lifestyleasia.com published an article listing out seven best stores in India where people can enjoy both retail therapy and food. Similarly, in an article in the retail section of 'The Economic Times' newspaper (dated October, 13, 2019), described as how online and offline stores in India are promoting retail therapy by building up experiential zones in their stores. An article in Hindustan Times (dated September 2, 2019) criticized retail therapy. It mentioned that, although, retail therapy can help in alleviating a sad mood, but it can also lead to negative consequences in the form of reduced savings and increased financial debt. To sum up, the usage of the term retail therapy is becoming common in India and it seems people are adopting this practice.

8.1.3   Role of Retail Therapy in Women's Lives:

Previous research has highlighted that women are more inclined towards the emotional features of shopping. They engage in shopping not only for utilitarian reasons; rather also to get a break from their overscheduled lives or to deal with boredom or loneliness (Woodruffe, 1996; Underhill, 1999; Luomala, 2002; Arnold & Reynolds, 2003). Shopping gives them energy and a feeling of control (Woodruffe, 1997). The studies like 'Why women go shopping when they're fed up and other stories' (Woodruffe, 1997); 'Consumer shopping behaviour and the role of women in shopping- A literature review' (Kumaravel, 2017); 'Enhancing older females' psychological well-being through social shopping.......' (Kang & Ahn, 2014); 'Indian women and compensatory consumption......' (Singh, 2017) etc. are all the examples where the emotional role played by shopping in women's lives has been clearly stated. It is not that men do not go for therapy shopping, but the therapeutic values derived from shopping have been found to be more strong and effective in case of women (Dittmar & Drury, 2000; Noble, 2006).

185

8.1.4 Importance of Retail Therapy from Retailers' and Marketers' View-point:

The act of therapy shopping is not only beneficial for the shoppers; rather it also carries special importance for the retailers and marketers as well (Lee, 2013). This is mainly because of the unique behavioral characteristics exhibited by the therapy shoppers e.g. frequently visiting shopping places; making more impulse purchases when in sad mood; buying more self-gifts; spending more time in browsing and trying on different items etc. (Kang, 2009; D'Souza, 2012). Also, it has been found that, many of the therapy shoppers are store loyal. They like to visit the same retail stores every time they are in a down mood (Kang, 2009). Thus, if retailers can exactly know as to what makes these shoppers happy; they can work on those issues and increase the chances of retaining therapy shoppers in the long-run. In this regard, previous literature has highlighted that some of the retail elements can be emphasized upon to help therapy shoppers in mood-alleviation e.g. courteous behavior of the employees, attractive displays, offers and discounts, store ambience etc. (D'Souza, 2012; Lee, 2013; Surendran & Vardhan, 2014).

8.2   RESEARCH GAPS AND RATIONALE OF THE STUDY

On the basis of the review of previous studies on retail therapy, the following research gaps have been observed based on which the rationale of the study has been designed.

8.2.1 Problem with Regard to Conceptualization of Retail Therapy:

The concept of retail therapy has been, many a times, confused with other related types of emotional shopping behaviors. Firstly, the terms retail therapy and compensatory consumption have been used interchangeably in a number of studies. At the same time, the concept has also been found to share a close bond with other shopping behaviors like impulse buying, compulsive buying, self-gifting, hedonic shopping etc. This has led to a confusion regarding conceptualization of retail therapy.

The present research has attempted to theoretically clarify these behaviors and present the similarities and dissimilarities that they all share with retail therapy. This has, however, been done only theoretically (in chapter 1) and no empirical data has been analyzed for the same.

8.2.2   Most of the Research Work is Concentrated in Western Countries:

As explained in Chapter 1 also, retail therapy has been found to be a commonly adopted mood-alleviative activity in western countries, especially U.S. and U.K. Accordingly, major portion of the research work in this field is also concentrated in these countries only. Although, the term retail therapy is now being used in India too, however, the research work in this field is just at a nascent stage. Only few of the researchers have worked on exploring the concept and understanding its usage e.g. Nair (2004); D'Souza (2012); Surendran and Vardhan (2014); Rai et al. (2018) etc. Further, most of these studies are either interview-based or review-based and there is a lack of empirical work on this topic in India. Thus, whether and to what extent people in India shop for therapeutic reasons and what kind of shopping behavior they exhibit during such a shopping trip is not much known.

To fill in this gap, the present research has been carried out in the Indian context. The study is particularly focused on women shoppers. It is expected that carrying out research in a country like India where the retail scenario as well as the lifestyle of people (especially women) is much different than that of the western countries, can offer new insights in research on retail therapy.

8.2.3   Lack of Recognition of Shopping as a Coping Strategy:

Although, consumer behavior literature contains a number of studies that have highlighted the usage and importance of retail therapy in mood-alleviation and well-being; shopping activity has still not got a recognizable place amongst the list of coping strategies. It has been found that most of the studies on coping have made use of some standardized coping scales (adopted from psychology literature) that rarely mention shopping activity as any of the items. As a result, these studies have not been able to throw much light on whether or not people recognize shopping as a coping strategy.

The present study has dealt with this issue by particularly asking the women respondents about the different types of strategies and activities that they use to cope with negative mood situations. It has been tried to find out whether shopping is also one of these activities.

187

8.2.4 Lack of Empirical Work:

Most of the existing studies on retail therapy have either been based on in-depth interviews or experiments or are review-based e.g. Woodruffe (1997/98/2001); Luomala (1998/2001/02); Nair (2004); Garg & Lerner (2006); Kang & Johnson (2010); Kim & Rucker (2012); D'Souza (2012); Garg & Lerner (2013); Lee (2013); Kim & Gal (2013); Rick et al. (2014); Surendran & Vardhan (2014); Mortimer (2015); Urkmez & Wagner (2016); Lee & Bottger (2017), Mandel et al. (2017); Cifci & Ekinci (2018); Irwin (2018) etc. These theoretical and experimental studies have contributed a lot towards the basic understanding of retail therapy behavior and also about its positive role in mood-alleviation and well-being. However, the extent to which people practically make use of shopping for therapeutic reasons; the outcomes they experience; the role of personal or situational factors that lead to retail therapy etc. can be better assessed by taking up of a larger chunk of respondents. As such carrying out a public survey can solve the matter and help in understanding the attitude and behavior of respondents in a better way (The SAGE Encyclopedia of Communication Research Methods). This can also help in authenticating the results of the previous experimental studies while making the research more competent (ukdissertations.in). To fill this gap, data has been collected from Indian women using survey method, to assess their retail therapy behavior.

8.2.5 Role of Personal Factors has been ignored:

Consumer shopping behavior has been found to be highly influenced by the personal characteristics of the shoppers. It has been found that people not only consume products for the mere sake of consumption, rather, the products they consume also reflect their personality and image in the society (Solomon et al., 2010). Many of them prefer to buy those products which they perceive to be similar to their own identity i.e. who they are (Dalton, 2009). Emphasizing on the importance of the personal factors in shopping behavior, Badgaiyan and Verma (2014) suggested that, though, marketers can do nothing about customers' personality, but having knowledge about the same can, at least, help them in devising better policies.

As far as coping with or managing of mood is concerned, research has shown that personal characteristics of individuals affect the way they deal with stress and the type of strategies they use to overcome it (Andrade, 2005). However, despite their importance, very few studies have attempted to determine the role of such personal factors in retail therapy behavior. Some of the factors covered in the previous literature include- regulatory focus, distress tolerance, shopping orientation etc. The factors that have been mostly ignored by the previous researchers include- basic human characteristics (e.g. personality traits, demographics etc.) that might be predictive of engaging in retail therapy.

The present research has attempted to fill this gap by analyzing the influential impact of some of the selected personal factors on retail therapy. These include- the basic/elementary personality traits i.e. The 'Big-five traits'; two shopping-related personality variables i.e. 'Chronic shopping orientation' and 'Impulse buying tendency' and the 'Demographic characteristics' of respondents.

8.3 RELEVANCE OF STUDYING RETAIL THERAPY IN INDIAN CONTEXT

Carrying out a research on retail therapy in Indian context has been found to be relevant mainly because of two reasons i.e. uniqueness of the Indian retail market as compared to the western countries and different lifestyle and culture of Indian women. These reasons have been explained in the following sub-sections:

8.3.1 The Indian Retail Market:

According to the previous literature, establishment of modern retail formats offering huge variety and discounts to the shoppers, has been regarded as one of the major reasons for adoption and popularity of retail therapy in western countries (Gillan, 2019; Lee, 2013). As such, the Indian retail market has also undergone some major transformations over past few years. Earlier, there used to be only unorganized market with small shops being managed single-handedly by their owners. However, with time, the market developed a lot and witnessed tremendous changes in its structure and functioning (Kaur & Kaur, 2013; India Brand Equity Foundation's retail report, 2017). Especially, after the economic reforms for liberalization and globalization, the Indian retail sector has been left open for the entry of private players, corporate players and international players (Bansal & Yadav, 2008). Today's Indian retail market comprises of departmental stores, specialty stores, hypermarkets, supermarkets, malls and so on (Sinha

189

& Uniyal, 2005; Tanwar et al., 2011). Indian consumers have also shown overwhelming acceptance to these formats (Kaur, 2013). Further, entry of foreign players has created an altogether new kind of retail environment while offering huge discounts, faster billing system, creative loyalty programs, and an added entertainment element to shopping (Ghosh et al., 2010; Srivastava et al., 2012). This, however, also posed some challenges to the existing Indian retailers and reminded them of focusing on the 7 P's of marketing for their successful survival (Kaur, 2014). Such up-gradation has led to a sea change in the shopping style and behavior of the shoppers too. They are now not only concerned with fulfilling their product needs; rather they have also started seeking more entertainment and emotional value (Kaur & Kaur, 2013; Kiran & Jhamb, 2011).

The uniqueness of the Indian retail market lies in the fact that, despite all the developments, the traditional market still dominates over the modern organized market (India Brand Equity Foundation's retail report, 2017). Many people still choose to go to local bazaars for shopping. Apart from this, in India, shopping is more of a familial activity. A large proportion of people like to shop with families and visit malls to spend their family leisure time and feel relaxed (D'Souza, 2012). These features of Indian retail market make it quite different from that of the western countries, where the retail markets are much modern and developed. Accordingly, it seems to be meaningful to study the adoption of retail therapy in context of shoppers from the Indian market.

8.3.2   The Culture, Lifestyle and Status of Indian Women:

The lifestyle and status of women in India is much different from that of women in western countries. Comparatively, Indian women enjoy less independence. Although, country laws might support them; they usually lack support from their families and society (Srinivasan, 2013). Even when large number of Indian women are earning on their own, many of them still depend upon others for their life decisions (whether financial or non-financial). Further, the condition has been found to be more disadvantageous for housewives, who get very less financial independence and also bear more societal pressures and restrictions (Solanki et al., 2019). They mostly get less time for themselves and devote more time to their families (D'Souza, 2012). Primarily, they are responsible for managing the house, but enjoy very less freedom to move out or take major decisions related to their personal requirements e.g. decisions related to their health care, visiting parents, buying expensive items like jewelry, going to market without permission etc. (Kishor & Gupta, 2004).

In most of the middle class families, men usually give only limited money to their wives, while at the same time, expecting them to rationally manage the monthly household expenses (Bains, 2010, 'The Tribune'). Due to all these factors, many of the Indian women go through depression and anxiety disorders. Over and above, they (especially housewives) also get very few coping options to deal with their problems. They love to shop, but they lack independence in that also. Even there are many of the women in India who feel that they have to justify their purchases to other family members (Sheth & Vittal, 2007).

It follows from the above discussion that, as compared to the modern western women; Indian women might be enjoying less independence in making use of shopping for mood-alleviative reasons. Further, if they do so, their lifestyle and culture is most likely to be reflected in their shopping behavior.

Taking into consideration the above mentioned points, it is expected that some new insights can be found by carrying out retail therapy research in India. Some of the research questions that the present study has tried to answer, include- How Indian women handle stress or deal with negative mood situations? What type of coping/mood-alleviative activities they use? Whether and to what extent they use shopping for mood-alleviation? What is their belief about shopping as a therapeutic activity? What outcomes they experience after shopping for therapeutic reasons? How they behave during a typical retail therapy trip etc.

8.4   OBJECTIVES OF THE RESEARCH STUDY

The objectives of the present research have been:

1.   To explore different types of coping strategies/activities adopted by Indian women to overcome negative mood (with special focus on determining the usage of shopping for coping).

2.   To analyze the retail therapy behavior of women in India. Within that, to analyze the-

191

> ➢ Therapeutic shopping motivations

> ➢ Therapeutic shopping values, and

> ➢ Therapeutic shopping outcomes.

3. To assess the influential impact of personal characteristics on retail therapy behavior of women in India. Within that, to assess the impact of-

> ➢ Demographic characteristics

> ➢ Big-five personality traits

> ➢ Chronic shopping orientation, and

> ➢ Impulse buying tendency.

4. To analyze the retail therapy trip behavior of women therapy shoppers in India. Within that, to analyze-

> ➢ The shopping decisions undertaken by Indian women during a retail therapy trip (e.g. decisions relating to retail format, products, payment mode, person accompanying, time and money etc.), and

> ➢ The role of shopping process elements in mood-alleviation (including the role of retail attributes).

8.5 SCOPE OF THE STUDY

The scope of the present research has been explained in the following sub-sections:

8.5.1 Concept-wise Scope:

Concept-wise, the scope of this study is limited to the 'Mood-alleviative' perspective of retail therapy, which is also more commonly accepted by the previous researchers like Atalay & Meloy (2011); Kang & Johnson (2010), Rick et al. (2014), Luomala (2002) etc. Accordingly, for this research, the term retail therapy has been used to mean use of shopping to overcome negative mood caused by temporary negative situations like an argument with someone, a bad day at work, feeling bored or lonely etc.

Apart from this, following Kang (2009), the term 'retail therapy' includes both buying as well as shopping without buying (i.e. window shopping) and is also limited to shopping for non-perishable products only e.g. clothing, accessories etc. Thus, it shall not include grocery shopping, eating or consumption of services.

8.5.2 Gender-wise Scope:

Since, based on the review of existing literature, retail therapy has been found to be more commonly prevalent among women as compared to men; the present study has been focused on women only.

8.5.3 Variables-wise Scope:

The variables studied in the present research include- 'Retail Therapy Behavior', 'Big-Five Personality Traits' (extraversion, agreeableness, conscientiousness, neuroticism and intellect), 'Chronic Shopping Orientation', 'Impulse Buying Tendency', 'Demographics' and 'Shopping Trip Behavior Elements'.

8.5.4 Geographical Area-wise Scope:

Area-wise, scope of the study has been limited to some of the major cities of Punjab (Northern India). The state of Punjab has been one of the most prosperous states in India (Tata Strategic Management Group, 2013) and has witnessed tremendous transformations in the retailing sector over the past one and a half decade. Some of the major cities that have seen the maximum retail development include the capital city Chandigarh, Ludhiana, Amritsar, SAS Nagar (Mohali) and Jalandhar (India Retail Report, 2013; Jhamb & Kiran, 2011; Sharma et al., 2011; Valsan & Bhola, 2014). Due to the retail modernization, it is expected that people in these cities might be using shopping for reasons over and above the utilitarian reasons. Accordingly, women from these cities have been chosen to form the target population of the study.

8.6 RESEARCH METHODOLOGY

The research methodology for the present study has been presented as under:

8.6.1 Preliminary Study:

To get an initial insight about what Indian women do to cope with stress and whether shopping activity is used by them as a coping strategy, a preliminary study had

193

been carried out with twenty five women respondents selected on convenience basis from a University in Amritsar (Punjab). In total three questions had been asked:

1. Frequency of experiencing negative mood (e.g. irritation/ stress/ depression) in a month, on an average.

2. Activities indulged in to cope with negative mood.

3. Frequency of using shopping for dealing with negative mood.

8.6.2 Pilot Study:

Following the preliminary study, a survey instrument had been designed and got evaluated from academicians (researcher's own supervisor and two others) and industry experts (retail managers of two different multi-brand retail stores in Jalandhar city). Based on their suggestions, some explanations and examples had been added up to certain statements to make them more understandable to the respondents e.g. meaning of certain terms like 'seldom feel blue', 'vivid imagination', 'abstract ideas' etc. had been explained in brackets along with the statements. Similarly, examples explaining different types of retail formats had also been added.

Using the designed survey questionnaire, a pilot study with 169 respondents from five cities of Punjab i.e. Chandigarh, Mohali, Ludhiana, Amritsar and Jalandhar, had been carried out. The results had been found to be satisfactory, with all the research scales being reliable. The respondents, at this stage, found layout of the questionnaire to be appealing and most of them filled in the information with enthusiasm. On an average, they took around 15-20 minutes to complete the questionnaire.

8.6.3 Final Study:

The sampling and data collection details of the final survey have been as under:

➤ *Universe of the study*

All the women within the Punjab state (Northern India), whether working or non-working and who are above the age of 21 years, form the universe of this study.

➤ *Sampling design and sample*

Based on the requirements of minimum desired sample size as suggested by Hair et al. (2010) and also by Krejcie & Morgan (1970), 800 questionnaires had been distributed among women in the selected cities. Out of these, 703 (87.9% response rate) had been found to be complete and consistent in all respects. For the purpose of data collection, different sampling techniques had been used, including- purposive/ judgemental sampling, quota sampling technique, convenience sampling, snowball sampling etc. Firstly, using purposive sampling, it was decided to select only those cities within Punjab that have witnessed retail developments over past few years so that women therein at least have opportunity to go for therapeutic kind of shopping. Further, since the size and population of these cities is quite different, it was decided to select sample from each city in proportion to the women population of that city, just like it is done in stratified sampling.

Following this, quota sampling had been used to evenly distribute the questionnaires in the selected cities to fairly represent both working and non-working women segments. Again, using judgement, it had been decided to take up working women from some common occupations where women could be easily found. These occupations included- teaching, banking and insurance and other occupations (including some other government and private office employees). At individual level, data from these working women had been collected at their convenience during their free time or break time, after getting a verbal permission from their branch/staff head.

The non-working class, on the other hand, included college/university students and housewives. It was purposely decided to collect data only from post-graduate students with the expectation that they could better understand the questionnaire than junior students. Data had been collected from them during their free lectures, so that they could comfortably answer to the survey questions. Housewives, on the other hand, had been approached through snowball sampling. For this, references had first been taken from working women and then from other housewives. Data had been collected from them either at their home by employing door to door survey or meeting them at some get-togethers like kitty parties.

➢   *Sampling period*

The pilot study had been carried out in year 2017 during the months of January-February, while the final data collection had been done during the period July, 2017-April, 2018.

> ➤ *Demographic profile of the respondents*

The final usable sample of 703 women comprises of 372 (53%) working women, out of whom 50 percent are teachers, 23 percent are from banking/insurance line and remaining 27 percent from other occupations. Amongst the non-working category, 70 percent are the students, while 30 percent are housewives. The mean age of the respondents has been found to be 30 years and more than half of the study respondents have been found to be post-graduates. As far as the marital status is concerned, about 60 percent of the respondents have been found to be unmarried. Further, since, the study included both working and non-working women, thus, to maintain parity for comparison of income available with both the groups, their monthly discretionary income (i.e. what they had in their hands after deducting for the necessary expenses like grocery, bills etc.) out of the monthly family income, was asked for. As per the given data, discretionary income with most of the respondents (i.e. 61%) was found to be less than Rs. 10,000.

8.6.4 Survey Instrument:

The survey instrument used for the data collection has been organized into five different sections explained as under:

Section A: This section covers questions related to frequency of experiencing negative mood, the coping strategies used to deal with negative mood and frequency of using shopping for mood-alleviation. Respondents had to mention any three activities that they indulged in to up-lift their mood.

Section B: The second section (Section B) includes different scales related to the shopping behavior of the respondents including- 'Retail Therapy' scale (by Kang & Johnson, 2011/ Kang, 2009); the 'Impulse Buying Tendency' scale (by Rook & Fisher, 1995) and the 'Chronic Shopping Orientation' scale (by Buttner et al., 2013). All the statements in these scales have been measured on a seven-point Likert scale ranging from '1= strongly disagree' and '7= strongly agree'.

Section C: The third section (i.e. Section C) relates to the 'Big-Five Personality Variables'. For this, the twenty items Mini-IPIP Scale developed by Donnellan et al.

196

(2006) has been used. This scale is a short-form of the 50-item 'International Personality Item Pool' developed by Goldberg (1999). It comprises of five sub-scales measuring different personality traits i.e. 'Extraversion', 'Agreeableness', 'Conscientiousness', 'Neuroticism' and 'Intellect'. All the scale items have been measured on a seven-point Likert scale ranging from '1= strongly disagree' and '7= strongly agree'.

Section D: Section D contains various questions related to the therapy shopping trip behavior of the retail therapy shoppers, including- the retail formats they like to visit for therapy shopping, the person they like to accompany them, the products that help them in getting rid of sad mood, extent of unplanned buying, time and money spend, mode of payment, etc. Since, these questions were related to a therapy shopping trip; they could be answered only by retail therapy shoppers. Accordingly, a note had been given in the beginning of this section, asking the respondents to answer it only if they actually went for retail therapy shopping. In other words, the section had been filled in only by self-identified therapy shoppers.

Section E: The last section (Section E) in the survey instrument consists of the general questions related to the demographics of the respondents including their age, marital status, education level, occupation, monthly family income and monthly discretionary income (after deducting all necessary expenses like grocery, bills etc.).

8.6.5 Statistical Software and Techniques Used:

Depending upon the objectives of this research, different types of statistical techniques have been applied using the SPSS 19 and AMOS 19 software. The techniques include- Descriptive Analysis (including mean, standard deviation, frequencies and percentage); Exploratory Factor Analysis (EFA), Confirmatory Factor Analysis (CFA), Correlation Analysis, Independent Sample T-test, One-way Anova and Path Analysis.

8.7 DATA ANALYSIS AND FINDINGS

The objective-wise data analysis results and the major findings of the research have been presented in the following sub-sections.

8.7.1 Coping Strategies and Use of Shopping for Mood Regulation:

For fulfilling the first objective of the research, respondents had been asked about their frequency of experiencing negative mood in a month; any three activities used by them for coping with the negative mood and the frequency of using shopping for mood-alleviation in a month. The results have been as under:

1. Approximately, 57 percent of the respondents have mentioned that they experience negative mood only sometimes. This has been followed by 23 percent who rarely experience negative mood and approximately 16 percent who have said that they frequently experience negative mood. There have also been sixteen such women (2.3%) who have said that they always experience negative mood.

2. Ranking-wise list of coping strategies used includes the activities such as- talking on phone to someone in the family or friends, using social media, meeting friends, listening to music, shopping, watching television, comfort eating, remaining quiet and stop talking to anyone or at least to the person concerned, sleeping, actively and directly handling the stressful situation, cleaning or doing household work, religious practice/meditation, indulging in hobbies, reading/studying, cooking, crying, doing nothing and accepting the situation as such, going out for a movie/ dining out, exercise/dance, and others including spending time with kids, walking, singing, writing etc.

3. Approximately 37 percent of females have said that they sometimes go for shopping when they are stressed out or experiencing any other kind of negative mood. At the same time, nearly 28 percent have said that they rarely go for shopping for mood-alleviation, followed by nearly 19 percent who never go for mood-alleviative shopping. Further, there are 91 (12.9%) females who have said that they frequently make use of shopping when they are upset or stressed out. It is only 3.4 percent of women who have said that they always go for shopping for mood-alleviation.

4. Correlation between frequency of experiencing negative mood and frequency of going for therapeutic shopping has not been found to be significant. Thus, it is not necessary that people who are more frequently upset always go for shopping

198

for mood-alleviation. Nor does it mean that people, who experience negative mood less frequently, do not go for mood-alleviative shopping.

Conclusion: Based on the results, it can be concluded that most of the women in India make use of emotion-focused coping strategies to deal with negative mood and only few of them try to tackle the problem directly. Out of the different emotion-focused strategies, shopping is also one. About one-fourth of the women mentioned shopping to be amongst the top three activities that they do to manage negative mood. Further, when specifically asked about their frequency of using shopping as a coping strategy, in total, more than half of the respondents agreed that they sometimes/frequently/always do so. It is, however, not necessary that they choose to go for shopping with the same frequency as they experience negative mood. One may experience negative mood only occasionally, but may always go for shopping to overcome it and vice-versa.

8.7.2 Retail Therapy Motivations, Therapeutic Shopping Values and Outcomes:

In order to analyze the underlying motivations of retail therapy, the therapeutic shopping values and outcomes of retail therapy as experienced by the Indian women, the retail therapy scale by Kang & Johnson (2011)/ Kang (2009) has been used. The scale has been first tested for its dimensionality, reliability and validity in the Indian context. This has been followed by analyzing the mean scores on individual scale items, along with determining the number and percentage of women agreeing or disagreeing to each of the items. The results have been as under-

1.   ***Exploratory Factor Analysis (EFA):*** Exploratory factor analysis led to the formation of the four factor structure as in the original scale by Kang & Johnson (2011)/ Kang (2009), explaining the total variance of 70.32%. The KMO measure of sampling adequacy has been found to be 0.95. The communalities for all the items range between 0.633 and 0.778 i.e. greater than the minimum standardized value of 0.5 (Hair et al., 2010). The factor loadings range between 0.533 and 0.925, again above the minimum threshold of 0.5 (Hair et al., 2010). The factor naming has remained the same as in the original scale i.e. 'Therapeutic Shopping Motivation', 'Therapeutic Shopping Value: Positive Reinforcement', 'Therapeutic Shopping Value: Negative Mood Reduction', and 'Therapeutic Shopping Outcomes'.

2. ***Confirmatory Factor Analysis (CFA):*** After checking the dimensionality through exploratory factor analysis, the four factor confirmatory model has been estimated based on the maximum likelihood procedure using AMOS 19 software. As per the results, all the standardized factor loadings have been found to range between 0.74 and 0.85 i.e. above the minimum threshold value of 0.5 and also the ideal value of 0.7, suggested by Hair et al. (2010). Further, the squared multiple correlation values have been found to range between 0.54 and 0.72 i.e. above the minimum threshold value of 0.5 (Hair et al., 2010).

    While checking the model fitness, all the values of the goodness and badness of fit indices and normed chi-square have been found to be within the threshold limits suggested by Hair et al. (2010) (i.e. $\chi2/df = 5.00$; TLI = 0.914; CFI = 0.924; RMSEA = 0.07; and SRMR = 0.048). Further, convergent validity has been examined through several measures including- factor loadings (ranged between 0.73 and 0.85), average variance extracted (AVE) (ranging between .606 and .644) and composite reliability (CR) (ranging between .897 and .904). Discriminant validity has been established by comparing the values of Average Variance Extracted (AVE) with that of the Maximum Shared Variance (MSV) and Average Shared Variance (ASV). All the values for AVE have been found to be greater than MSV and ASV.

3. **Descriptive Analysis of Retail Therapy Scale Items:** Based on the mean values and number of women agreeing or disagreeing towards each of the scale items, the following results have been observed.

➢   The most resorted mood situations for which retail therapy is used by Indian women includes- feeling good about oneself, followed by cheering up, and feeling better and relaxed. The remaining two items in the therapeutic motivations construct i.e. shopping for stress relief and shopping to compensate for a bad day, have been agreed to by comparatively lesser number of women.

➢   Majority of the women believe in the positive mood reinforcement values of shopping and mention that shopping helps them in getting knowledge about new fashion trends, offers a pleasant environment, gives them sensory stimulation and a sense of achievement.

➤ For the negative mood alleviation values also, nearly 50 percent of the women have agreed that shopping distracts them from stress in one or the other way. It also helps them in filling an empty feeling, or dealing with loneliness etc.

➤ It has been found that at least half of the women find a retail therapy trip to be successful. Shopping generates good feelings in them and these feelings are also retained for a sufficiently long time. About 51 percent of the respondents had mentioned that when they use the products bought during a retail therapy trip, they remember the good shopping experience and do not carry a guilt feeling afterwards.

Conclusion: This objective has two major findings- firstly, the results of EFA and CFA lead to conclusion that the retail therapy scale by Kang & Johnson (2011)/ Kang (2009) is valid and reliable for use in Indian context; secondly, at least more than half of the respondents have been found to have a positive attitude towards retail therapy. They shop for managing their mood, believe in the therapeutic powers of shopping and also feel good after a retail therapy trip.

8.7.3 Impact of Personal Characteristics on Retail Therapy Behavior:

As mentioned earlier in scope and research gaps sections, the present study has analyzed the impact of four types of personal characteristics on retail therapy behavior, including- (i) Demographic characteristics, (ii) 'Big-Five' personality traits, and two shopping related personality traits i.e. (iii) Shopping orientation (chronic) and (iv) Impulse buying tendency. Based on the existing literature, the following hypotheses have been framed and tested:

H_1: *Age negatively relates to Retail Therapy Behavior, such that youngsters are more inclined towards therapy shopping.*

H_2: *Marital Status negatively relates to Retail Therapy Behavior, such that unmarried women are more inclined towards therapy shopping.*

H_3: *Employment Status negatively relates to Retail Therapy Behavior, such that non-working women are more inclined towards therapy shopping.*

H_4: *Discretionary Income positively relates to Retail Therapy Behavior, such that women with more discretionary income are more inclined towards therapy shopping.*

H_5: Extraversion positively influences Retail Therapy Behavior.

H_6: Agreeableness negatively influences Retail Therapy Behavior.

H_7: Conscientiousness negatively influences Retail Therapy Behavior.

H_8: Neuroticism positively influences Retail Therapy Behavior.

H_9: Intellect positively influences Retail Therapy Behavior.

H_{10}: Chronic Shopping Orientation positively influences Retail Therapy Behavior.

H_{11}: Impulse Buying Tendency positively influences Retail Therapy Behavior.

The major results have been highlighted as under-

1. **Role of Demographics in Retail Therapy Behavior:** The relation of different demographics with retail therapy behavior has been observed to be as under:

➤   **Age:** Based on the results of correlation analysis, age has been found to have a significant negative relation with 'Therapeutic shopping motivation' at 1 percent level of significance; and with 'Therapeutic shopping values- positive mood reinforcement' and 'Therapeutic shopping outcomes' at 5 percent level of significance. At the same time, the relation between age and 'Therapeutic shopping values- negative mood reduction' has been found to be significant only at 10 per cent level of significance. The results indicate that, as women get older, their inclination towards retail therapy gets reduced.

➤   **Marital status:** As per the results of Independent sample T-test and the factor-wise mean values for the retail therapy scale, it has been found that, both married and unmarried women have a positive response towards all the constructs of retail therapy and their responses are not statistically significantly different from each other.

➤   **Employment status:** Employment status has been found to have a significant negative relation with all the constructs of retail therapy, in the way that those who are not working, indulge more in retail therapy and those women who are working, indulge comparatively less in retail therapy (tested using Independent sample T-test).

➢   **Discretionary income:** Discretionary income does not have a significant effect on retail therapy behavior. In other words, the amount of discretionary income available with the women does not affect their perception and usage of retail therapy.

2.   **Impact of Big-five Personality Traits, Shopping Orientation and Impulse Buying Tendency:** After analyzing the relationship between demographics and retail therapy, the study proceeds with analyzing as to what extent the personality factors affect retail therapy behavior. Here, two types of personality variables have been taken up- the basic personality factors (i.e. the big-five traits) and the shopping-related personality factors (i.e. shopping orientation and impulse buying tendency). The data for the same has been analyzed using SPSS 19.0 and AMOS 19.0 software. Before proceeding with the hypotheses testing, all the scales used for the analysis have been tested through exploratory and confirmatory factor analysis and their reliability and validity has been checked for. The summarized results have been presented as under:

➢   **Exploratory Factor Analysis (EFA):** Based on the results, one item from the chronic shopping orientation scale i.e. SO-5- 'When shopping, I mainly carry out what I have planned'; one from the impulse buying tendency scale i.e. IB-8- 'I carefully plan most of my purchases' and two items from the Big-five personality scale i.e. 'I have frequent mood swings-P13' and 'I have a vivid imagination-P17' have been removed because of low factor loadings and cross loading issues. For all the remaining items, the factor loadings have been found to range between 0.61 and 0.86 and the communalities have been found to range between 0.51 and 0.78. The Cronbach alpha values have been found to be- Extraversion (0.81), Agreeableness (0.79), Conscientiousness (0.80), Neuroticism (0.82), Intellect (0.74), Chronic Shopping Orientation (0.86) and Impulse Buying Tendency (0.89).

➢   **Confirmatory Factor Analysis (CFA):** Following the exploratory factor analysis, confirmatory factor analysis has also been run. In that, firstly, a second-order construct of retail therapy has first been formed. The results for the second-order CFA model have been found to be within the acceptable range with the normed chi-square value of 4.46; CFI being 0.935; TLI being 0.926; RMSEA being 0.07 and SRMR being .043. Further, the standardized factor loadings for the constructs have been- Therapeutic Shopping Motivation (0.891), Therapeutic Shopping Value: Positive Reinforcement (0.744), Therapeutic Shopping Value: Negative Mood Reduction (0.879) and Therapeutic Shopping Outcomes (0.856) respectively.

Following this, the overall measurement model with all the variables including-Big-Five Personality Traits, Chronic Shopping Orientation, Impulse Buying Tendency and Retail Therapy, has been tested for model fitness and validity. As per the results, all the standardized factor loadings have been found to range between 0.64 and 0.89, with all the p-values being significant at 0.001 level. The squared multiple correlation values (SMC) have been found to range between 0.41 and 0.80. Further, the model-fitness results have been- normed chi square ($\chi2/df$) has been found to be 2.53, TLI is 0.91, CFI is 0.92, RMSEA has been found to be 0.047, and SRMR has been found to be 0.044. Apart from this, the average variance extracted i.e. AVE for the constructs have been found to be ranging between 0.504 and 0.715. Composite reliabilities have been found to be between 0.754 and 0.909. Further, all the values of AVE have been found to exceed that of the MSV and ASV, thereby proving discriminant validity.

➢ **Hypotheses Testing:** In order to test the hypotheses, SEM has been used. In the model, the effects of different types of personality variables have been tested. Further, the demographics (age and employment status) have been taken as the control variables to test if they confound the proposed relationship between the personality variables and retail therapy behavior. The results have been explained as under:

o As per the results, 'Extraversion' has not been found to significantly affect 'Retail Therapy Behavior' (β= .038, p>0.05). This implies that being an extrovert or introvert does not make a difference in whether or not a person chooses shopping for therapeutic reasons.

204

o   'Agreeableness' has been found to negatively influence 'Retail Therapy Behavior' (with β= -.091, p<0.01). Previous research has shown that people who are low on agreeableness are comparatively less able to neutralize their thoughts and also lack social adaptability (Costa, Jr & McCrae, 1992; Pervin, 2006). Carver and Smith (2010) had observed a negative relation of agreeableness with disengagement coping which is basically emotion-based coping. Since, shopping is also one of the emotion-based coping strategies only; thus the results of the present study are in line with the previous literature. Finally, it can be concluded that women, who are low on social skills and lack trust and sympathy, are more likely to indulge in retail therapy.

o   'Conscientiousness' has been found to negatively influence 'Retail Therapy Behavior' (with β= -.062, p<.05). This depicts that women who are less disciplined and who do not plan things in advance are more likely to indulge in therapeutic shopping behavior. It might be on account of lack of planning and discipline, they might not be able to handle a negative situation tactically and thus, might try to get rid of it through any possible way instantly coming to their mind. In this regard, the shopping activity might be helping them out in reducing anxiety created by the unforeseen negative situation. These results are also in consonance with the existing literature that states that conscientious individuals plan for stressors in advance (Vollrath, 2001) and engage less in compensatory behaviors (John & Srivastava, 1999).

o   'Neuroticism' has been found to positively influence 'Retail Therapy Behavior' (with β=.089, p<.01). Previous research shows that the neurotic individuals take events and things more negatively and do not easily express their emotions (Penley & Tomaka 2002, Suls & Martin 2005; Sadr, 2016). A positive relation of this trait with retail therapy indicates that the women who are weak in stress handling are more likely to show a positive attitude towards retail therapy and they also use shopping for therapeutic reasons. A probable reason might be that shopping for something new might be helping them to regain some control over the negative situation and deal with their hidden emotions.

205

o   'Intellect' has not been found to have any significant relation to 'Retail Therapy Behavior'. It had been hypothesized that intellect would positively predict retail therapy. The results, however, show a negative relation (although not statistically significant). Though, no clear answer could be found for the same, however, it might be due to the reason that such women might be using more of the problem-focused strategies or some other type of emotion-focused strategies that lead to more positive experiences.

o   'Chronic Shopping Orientation' has been found to positively influence 'Retail Therapy Behavior' (with β=.604, p<.001). This finding is in line with the previous research results also, which state that the individuals who love the shopping activity, experience fun in it and like to browse around in shops, are more likely to have a positive attitude towards therapy shopping also (Kang & Johnson, 2010).

o   'Impulse Buying Tendency' positively influences 'Retail Therapy Behavior' (with β= .125, p<.001). Thus, women, who are less able to control their impulses during shopping and find excitement in buying for unplanned products, are more likely to choose shopping activity for mood-alleviative reasons also. These results are also in consonance with the existing literature e.g. Baumeister (2002), Son and Chang (2016) etc.

o   'Demographic Characteristics' did not have any significant effect on the relationship between different personality factors and retail therapy behavior.

Conclusion: Based on the results, it can be concluded that personal factors do play a significant role in retail therapy behavior. Overall, shopping orientation, impulse buying tendency and neuroticism have been found to positively influence retail therapy, whereas, conscientiousness and agreeableness have been found to negatively affect one's indulgence in retail therapy. Demographics, including age and employment status can also help predicting retail therapy behavior. Within that, youngsters and non-working women have been found to go more for therapy shopping. To conclude, most of the findings of this study have been observed to be in consonance with the findings of the previous studies.

8.7.4   Therapy Shopping Trip Behavior of Retail Therapy Shoppers:

The last objective of the present research has been to analyze the shopping behavior of the women shoppers when they are out for a retail therapy trip. Since, this part of the questionnaire could be answered only by those women who actually go for therapy shopping, it had been filled in by the self-identified therapy shoppers i.e. who believed themselves to be retail therapy shoppers. As such, during the survey, 413 women identified themselves as therapy shoppers. The major findings of data analysis for these shoppers have been listed below:

1.   48% of women have said that they like someone from their family to accompany them during a retail therapy trip, followed by 43% who like the company of some friend(s). Only 9% have said that they like to go alone for therapy shopping.

2.   55% women like to buy something for themselves during a retail therapy trip, whereas about 40% like to buy for some family members and only 5% who feel good when they buy something for some friend.

3.   Most of the Indian women (i.e. 82%) usually make cash payments for the products purchased during mood-alleviative shopping, whereas only remaining 18% make use of any other options.

4.   40% women have said that they 'sometimes' buy impulsively during retail therapy trip, followed by about 25% who 'rarely' do so, 19% who 'never' buy anything unplanned, approximately 12% who often buy impulsively during therapy shopping and just 5% who have said that they 'always' buy impulsively.

5.   54% women have agreed that they spend more than usual time when shopping for therapeutic reasons.

6.   About 40% respondents agreed that they spend more than usual money for therapy reasons.

7.   Amongst the product categories, it has been found that the most preferred product category is clothing, followed by accessories, shoes, cosmetics and then home furnishing.

8.   Amongst the choice for different retail formats, it has been found that women in India prefer malls the most, followed by multi-brand stores, traditional shops and hypermarkets, along with single-brand stores being at the last position.

9.   For the final question relating to the role of different shopping process elements in mood-alleviation, 'Getting knowledge of new trends' has been found to be the most important element, followed by retail attributes like 'visual display' and 'shopping place ambience'. 'Actual purchase' of a product has been placed at the fourth position. Many shoppers have even agreed that a simple 'thought of going for shopping' also leads to happiness. The other elements include- 'trying on items', 'using the product purchased', 'bargaining', 'personnel behavior', and 'watching other shoppers' at shopping place (being at the last position).

Conclusion: The results for the therapy shopping behavior of Indian women have been compared to what had been found in the previous studies in respect of shoppers in western countries. It has been found that the results match on certain aspects like spending more than usual time, buying apparels, buying on impulse, self-gifting, preferring to buy from malls etc. Similar to the findings of previous studies, purchasing a product is also not necessary for Indian women to feel good. Their mood can also be alleviated by getting updated of the fashion trends, or display and ambience at the stores, or even by imagining consumption.

At the same time, certain unique behavioral elements, specific to the Indian women shoppers, have also been observed e.g. previous studies showed that therapy shoppers tend to shop alone, but the present study reflects that Indian women mostly seek company of family or friends for a retail therapy trip. Similarly, they not only like to buy for themselves, but also for their family members. Most of them do not spend more than usual money on a retail therapy trip and further, many of them also like to shop at local bazaars when they are upset.

The above generates the distinct contributions of the present research study for different stakeholders. These contributions and implications have been given in the implications section below.

8.8   IMPLICATIONS OF THE STUDY

The present study has brought out important implications for consumer behavior research, for retailers/marketers and for consumers. These have been presented in the following sub-sections:

8.8.1   Implications for the Consumer Behavior Research:

The main purpose of the present research has been to assess the retail therapy behavior of women in India. Some of the major implications for consumer behavior research include:

➢   The primary contribution of the study has been regarding extending the retail therapy research to the emerging economy of India. Since, the major portion of the research work on therapy shopping had only been limited to western countries; extending it to the lesser explored market of India has helped in bringing forward certain unique behavioral aspects of therapy shopping among Indian shoppers. Especially, the findings for the retail therapy trip behavior have been quite different from what had been observed in the previous studies. As an example, Indian women like someone to accompany them during a retail therapy trip, whereas previous research had mentioned that therapy shoppers like to shop alone (Woodruffe, 2001; Kang, 2009). Similarly, other differences have also been observed.

➢   The study has also methodologically contributed to the research field by carrying out extensive survey of the women population with diverse demographic characteristics. Most of the earlier studies, on the other hand, had been based on experimental designs, in-depth interviews or review-based work. Even in survey-based studies, the sample had mostly been limited to university students. The present study, however, includes both working as well as non-working women and also women belonging to different age groups.

➢   To the best of our knowledge, this is first study that has validated the existing retail therapy scale (by Kang & Johnson, 2011/ Kang, 2009) in the Indian context. The results have been an indication that the scale can effectively be used to determine the retail therapy behavior of Indian women shoppers.

209

➢ Another contribution of the study has been with regard to the assessment of the impact of personal characteristics in retail therapy behavior. As mentioned in the research gaps section also, previous studies on retail therapy have mainly ignored the probable role of basic human personality variables and even the effect of demographic variables. The contribution of this study lies in the fact that it has analyzed the impact of a variety of personal factors on retail therapy behavior. These factors include- demographics characteristics, Big-five personality traits, shopping orientation (chronic) and impulse buying tendency.

➢ The present study also has implications for the psychology research. As explained in the research gaps section, shopping activity has not yet got a recognizable place in the coping strategies scales. Looking at the importance of therapy shopping as given by the previous literature and also based on the results of the present study regarding the number of women using shopping for therapeutic reasons and also experiencing positive outcomes from it; it is highly recommended for the inclusion of the shopping activity also within the existing coping scales.

8.8.2   Implications for the Retailers and Marketers:

Understanding the mood-alleviative needs of therapy shoppers and the importance of different retail elements in meeting these needs can help the retailers and marketers in devising better strategies for attracting and retaining these shoppers. The findings of the present study have major implications for the retailers and marketers. Some of these have been given below:

➢ As per the results, most of the study respondents have been found to agree that shopping keeps them up-dated about the new fashion trends. They feel overjoyed with the visual stimulation that shopping provides and are also delighted by the courteous behavior of employees. More than half of the respondents agreed that shopping helps them in escaping from the negative situation and feeling in control. Following this, retailers are recommended to work for these shoppers on those elements in the retail environment that have more distractive power e.g. ambient factors, visual display etc. They can keep on updating their window display frequently with the latest stock to attract this segment.

➢ Further, since shoppers have a direct interface with the retail personnel, training may also be given to them to recognize those shoppers, who seem to be sad or lethargic and an extra effort may be put in to make them feel more comfortable in the store. A nice and friendly gesture of the store personnel may help the sad or stressed out shoppers to feel relaxed and can also help in building up strong customer relations. For this, firstly the employees themselves need to be happy and relaxed. This, therefore, generates the need of effective employee relationship management (ERM) for maintaining efficient customer relationship management (CRM) (Kaur, 2010).

➢ Retailers may even work on specifically identifying those customers who frequently shop for therapy reasons. This can be done using the validated retail therapy scale. Identifying this segment separately can help in understanding their shopping behavior in a better way and offering customized services to them. This may help in creating an emotional connectedness and instill loyalty.

➢ According to the survey results, more than half of the self-identified therapy shoppers mentioned that when they go for a retail therapy trip, they like to buy something for themselves. Further, many of them also indulge in impulse buying. They spend more than usual time and mostly prefer to buy apparels and accessories. Retailers can take advantage of these behavioral aspects and can encourage impulse buys and self-gifts. For this, they may add up some special discount offers and lucrative deals to boost their sales. Further, self-gifting may be promoted by advertising slogans such as 'From me! To me' or 'Shopping is cheaper than therapy' etc.

➢ More than forty percent of the respondents had also mentioned that they like to buy something for others when they shop for therapeutic motives. Thus, sales in the form of gifting to others may also be promoted by advertising such as 'Feel good! Buy for your loved ones' etc.

➤ Although, most of the respondents had said that they like to shop at modern formats for mood-alleviative reasons, many of them had also agreed that they choose to go to traditional stores. Local bazaars can take advantage of this and offer such services to satisfy these shoppers, which the modern formats might fail to provide, e.g. facilitating personalized services, offering bargaining option, credit facility etc.

➤ Some of the demographic differences in retail therapy behavior of Indian women have also been observed in this study. It has been found that youngsters and non-working females go more for retail therapy. Retailers can focus on these segments and can advertise the products suitable for such shoppers e.g. sales among housewives can be promoted by conveying promotional messages appreciating them to shop for themselves as an escape from their mundane life or as a self-gift for the efforts they put in to run the family. Similarly, some cool and trendy items may be displayed to attract the younger segment, so that they feel fascinated by the store.

8.8.3 Implications for the Consumers:

Based on the findings of the present research, some of the implications for the consumers include:

➤ In the present research, more than half of the women respondents have agreed that they go for retail therapy to feel good, cheer themselves up and to feel better and relaxed. Further, they also agreed that their therapy shopping trips are successful and they feel good even after a time lag. The products purchased during retail therapy also do not go waste. Rather, they remind the shoppers of the pleasurable shopping experience. It, thus, follows that retail therapy may help in enhancing happiness among Indian women and may play a positive role in the lives.

➤ A negative finding, however, of the study has been that some of the personality traits, that have been found to be significantly affecting retail therapy, seem to be somewhat problematic. These include- being high on neuroticism, low on conscientiousness, low on agreeableness, having a tendency to buy on impulse

212

etc. According to the previous research, all these traits have also been observed to be predictors of compulsive buying (Balabanis, 2001; Otero-López & Villardefrancos, 2013) and have been found to lead to low life satisfaction and negative affect in long-run (Carver & Smith, 2010). Thus, it is suggested to such women that they use retail therapy only in a controlled way, so that they do not become addicted to it or experience any ill consequences in long-run.

8.9   LIMITING FACTORS AND DIRECTIONS FOR FUTURE RESEARCH

The limiting factors in this research and the future research directions based on them have been given as under:

➤   The present research has covered only the women shoppers (this has resulted in getting a better knowledge about this segment exclusively). Men also go for therapy shopping, though they might be doing so less frequently than women and might be exhibiting somewhat different kind of shopping behavior. A future research may be carried out with male shoppers while replicating the variables covered under this study, or data may be collected simultaneously from both males and females and their therapy shopping behavior may be compared. This can have additional implications for the retailers as well as research field.

➤   The second limiting factor has been regarding the personal characteristics covered under the study. The present study analyzes the impact of variables including- demographic characteristics, the Big-five traits, shopping orientation and impulse buying tendency, on retail therapy behavior. Previous research has shown that the basic personality variables i.e. the Big-five traits significantly affect one's orientation towards shopping and also impulse buying tendency. Further, shopping orientation also affects impulse buying tendency. The inter-relationship between these variables can be studied to check for any negative or positive effects on the predictive value of any of these variables on retail therapy. Apart from this, the variable base can even be further expanded in future to cover additional variables like regulatory focus, type of coping strategies used, level of loneliness etc., and even the role of cultural factors can also be studied in future.

213

➢ In this study, the discussion of the results for the therapy shopping behavior of Indian women has primarily been based on their comparison to the western shoppers. But these discussions points are only based on previous studies and not the current data. Thus, a future research may be carried out in which data from different types of countries may be collected, analyzed and compared.

➢ In the present study, the data has been collected from women in Punjab and its capital city Chandigarh. The geographical scope can be expanded further to cover some more different types of cities e.g. the metro cities to have more diversity in the sample and to make the results more generalizable.

➢ Data for the study has been collected based on recall of a therapy shopping trip. Since, moods are just temporary feelings; responses at the time of data collection might not be exactly the same as what the shoppers would have actually experienced during shopping. This might have affected their response to the questionnaire items. A solution to this can be to carry out an intercept survey covering both the pre and post shopping mood experiences and then analyzing their actual shopping behavior in the real-time.

➢ The scope of the study has also been limited to brick-and-mortar or physical stores, malls and local bazaars. However, in today's time, internet shopping has become very popular. Many people, who lack time and want to shop at their convenience, are preferring online shopping over going out to physical stores. The trend of e-tail therapy is continuously gaining popularity. Accordingly, the retail therapy research can be further extended to cover online retail therapy also in its scope.

➢ The present study has primarily worked on validating the existing retail therapy scale (by Kang & Johnson, 2011/ Kang, 2009) and understanding the therapeutic shopping behavior of women in India. The results have indicated that most of the women have a positive attitude towards retail therapy. However, at the same time, there are also a considerable number of women who have disagreed to most of the items in the retail therapy scale. Further, the mean scores for the items in the 'positive reinforcement values' construct have been much higher than that of the other constructs. These variations in the results probably indicate about the presence of different segments of shoppers e.g. those who do not like going for shopping at all; or those who like shopping otherwise, but might not choose it for therapeutic purposes and those who be actually going for therapy shopping. A future research can work on using the retail therapy scale to identify these probable segments and understand their characteristics and shopping behavior more intensely.

➤ The importance of different retail attributes has been studied in this research, only as a part of the overall shopping process. Since, retail attributes can create a first-hand impression on the shoppers; it is recommended to carry out a study exclusively focused on studying the role of these attributes in mood-alleviation. For that the pre and post-shopping moods can also be analyzed. In addition, the ultimate effect of the relation between retail attributes and therapy shopping behavior, on shopping outcomes like sales, revisit, loyalty etc. can further be determined.

REFERENCES

1.   Agarwal, M. (2019). *Retail therapy: A little good, lot of bad.* Hindustan Times (September 2, 2019), available at https://www.hindustantimes.com/business-news/ retail-therapy-a-little-good-lot-of-bad/story-YmsDQOhrhJSdOKq1KFWFjL.html.

2.   Andrade, E. B. (2005). Behavioral consequences of affect: Combining evaluative and regulatory mechanisms. *Journal of Consumer Research*, 32(3), 355-362.

3.   Arnold, M. J. & Reynolds, K. E. (2003). Hedonic shopping motivations. *Journal of Retailing,* 79(2), 77-95.

4.   Atalay, A. S. & Meloy, M. G. (2011). When the going gets tough, the tough go shopping- An examination of self-gifting behaviour. *Advances in Consumer Research,* 33, 259-260.

5.   Badgaiyan, A. J. & Verma, A. (2014). Intrinsic factors affecting impulsive buying behaviour—Evidence from India. *Journal of Retailing and Consumer Services*, 21(4), 537–549.

6.   Bains, H. K. (2010). *Cost of living quite high in Ludhiana* (April 17, 2010). Available at https://www.tribuneindia.com/2010/20100417/edit.htm.

7.   Balabanis, G. (2001). The relationship between lottery ticket and scratch-card buying behaviour, personality and other compulsive behaviors. *Journal of Consumer Behavior*, 2(1), 7-22.

8.   Bansal & Yadav (2008). An analytical study on mall shopping- Attitude and perception among young adults. *Synthesis*, 5(2).

9.   Baumeister, R. F. (2002). Yielding to temptation: Self-control failure, impulsive purchasing, and consumer behavior. *Journal of Consumer Research*, 28(4), 670–676.

10.   Buttner, O., Florack, A. & Goritz, A. S. (2013). Shopping orientation as a stable consumer disposition and its influence on consumers' evaluations of retailer communication. *European Journal of Marketing,* 48(5/6), 1026-1045.

216

11. Carver, C. S. & Smith, J. C. (2010). Personality and coping. *Annual Review of Psychology*, 61, 679–704.

12. Census (2011). Available at https://www.census2011.co.in/

13. Cifci, S. & Ekinci, Y. (2018). *Undesirable effects of retail therapy on consumer emotions and consumer-based brand equity (CBBE).* Paper presented at the Management International Conference, Bled, Slovenia, 30 May- 2 June, 2018, 169-176.

14. Costa, P. T. & McCrae, R. R. (1992). NEO personality inventory professional manual. Odessa, FL: Psychological Assessment Resources.

15. D'Souza, D. (2012). *Retail therapy: A study in the Indian context to understand compensatory consumption and its implications on consumer's psyche*, Dissertation in partial fulfillment of the requirements for the Post Graduate Programme for Communications Management Diploma.

16. Dalton, A. (2009). Look on the bright side: Self-expressive consumption and consumer self-worth. *ACR North American Advances*, 36, 131-134.

17. dendyneville.co.uk (2018). UK consumers spending significant amounts on 'impulse buys', survey reveals (January 16, 2018), available at https://www.dendyneville.co.uk/news/business-news/archive/article/2018/January/uk-consumers-spending-significant-amounts-on-impulse-buys-survey-reveals.

18. Dittmar, H. & Drury, J. (2000). Self-image – is it in the bag? A qualitative comparison between "ordinary" and "excessive" consumers. *Journal of Economic Psychology*, 21(2), 109–142.

19. Donnellan, M. B., Oswald, F. L., Baird, B. M & Lucas, R. E. (2006). The Mini-IPIP scales: Tiny-yet-effective measures of the Big Five factors of personality. *Psychological Assessment,* 18, 192-203.

20. Duttagupta, I. (2019). *Online and offline brands offering retail therapy now have a new category: Experiential zones.* The Economic Times, October13, 2019.

21. Ebates.com (2013). Available at http://www.businesswire.com/news/home/ 20130402005600/en/Ebates-Survey-51.8-Americans-Engage-Retail-Therapy% E2%80%94.

22. Garg, N. & Lerner, J. S. (2013). Sadness and consumption. *Journal of Consumer Psychology*, 23(1), 106-113.

23. Ghosh, P., Tripathi, V. & Kumar, A. (2010). Customer expectations of store attributes: A study of organized retail outlets in India. *Journal of Retail & Leisure Property*, 9(1), 75-87.

24. Gillan, J. (2019). *The changing psychology of shopping: three trends set to shape retail.* The Drum (January 23, 2019). Available at https://www.thedrum. com/opinion/ 2019/01/23/the-changing-psychology-shopping-three-trends-set-shape-retail.

25. Goldberg, L. R. (1990). An alternative 'description of personality': The Big-five factor structure. *Journal of Personality and Social Psychology,* 59(6), 1216-1229.

26. Greenpeace (2016). Available at https://theculturetrip.com/asia/china/articles/ are-chinese-shoppers-using-retail-therapy-as-an-antidepressant/.

27. Hair, Jr. J. F., Black, W. C., Babin, B. J. & Anderson, R. E. (2010). *Multivariate data analysis.* Pearson Education Inc., New Delhi, India.

28. Hama, Y. (2001). Shopping as a coping behavior for stress. *Japanese Psychological Research, Special Issue- Consumer Behavior,* 43(4), 218-224.

29. https://www.census2011.co.in/

30. India Brand Equity Foundation Retail Report (2017). Available at https://www.ibef.org/ archives/industry/indian-retail-industry-analysis-reports/ indian-retail-industry-analysis-january-2017.

31. *India's next 100 retail markets.* India Retail Report (2013), http://www. asipac.com/uploaded/pdfFiles/1366786671full_IRR_Indias_Next_ 100_Retail__ Markets_2013.pdf, retrieved on 12.08.2017.

32.   Irwin, C. (2018). Emotional outlet malls: Exploring retail therapy. *BU Well*, 3(1), 8.

33.   Jhamb, D. & Kiran, R. (2011). Organized retail in India- Drivers facilitator and SWOT analysis. *Asian Journal of Management Research*, 2(1), 264-273.

34.   John, O. P. & Srivastava, S. (1999). *The Big-five trait taxonomy: History, measurement, and theoretical perspectives.* In L. A. Pervin & O. P. John (Eds.), Handbook of personality: Theory.

35.   Kang, J. & Ahn, M. (2014). Enhancing older females' psychological well-being through social shopping, social coping, and informal social activities. *Family and Consumer Sciences Research Journal*, 42(4), 341-357.

36.   Kang, M. (2009). *Retail therapy: A qualitative investigation and scale development.* Doctoral dissertation, University of Minnesota.

37.   Kang, M. & Johnson, K. K. P. (2010). Let's shop! Exploring the experiences of therapy shoppers. *Journal of Global Fashion Marketing*, 1(2), 71-79.

38.   Kang, M. & Johnson, K. K. P. (2011). Retail therapy: Scale development. *Clothing and Textiles Research Journal,* 29 (1), 3-19.

39.   Kaur, J. & Kaur, C. (2013). *The Indian retailing sector- Recent trends and future prospects.* Seminar proceedings "Building Competitiveness in Indian Manufacturing Sector", GNA Institute of Management and Technology, Phagwara, Punjab, India, ISBN: 978-81-921766-2-8, 185-191.

40.   Kaur, J. (2014). Role of FDI in restructuring retailing sector in India: Is it a blessing or curse- Opinion---retailers and customers. *International Conference on Management −"Changing Face of Modern Retail: The New Economic Order", GDGU-ICON, 2014*, 128-139. GD Goenka University, Gurgaon & Excel India Publishers, New Delhi.

41.   Kaur, J. (2013). Customers perception towards global retailers influencing the Indian organized retailing. *The Indian Journal of Commerce*, Quarterly publication of the Indian Commerce Association, 66(3), 41-50.

42. Kaur, J. (2010). *Customer relationship management: A study of selected banks in India.* (Ph.D. thesis). Department of Commerce and Business Management, Guru Nanak Dev University, Amritsar.

43. Kim, S. & Rucker, D. (2012). Bracing for the psychological storm: Proactive versus reactive compensatory consumption. *Journal of Consumer Research*, 39, 815-830.

44. Kim, S. & Gal, D. (2014). From compensatory consumption to adaptive consumption: The role of self-acceptance in resolving self-deficits. *Journal of Consumer Research*, 41, 526–542.

45. Kiran, R. & Jhamb, D. (2011). A strategic framework for consumer preferences towards emerging retail formats. *Journal of Emerging Knowledge on Emerging Markets,* 3(1), 437-453.

46. Kishor, S. & Gupta, K. (2004). *Women's empowerment in India and its states: Evidence from the NFHS.* Economic and Political Weekly. 39. 694-712.

47. Krejcie, R. V. & Morgan, D. W. (1970). Determining sample size for research activities. *Educational and Psychological Measurement*, 30, 607-610.

48. Kumaravel, R. (2017). Consumer shopping behaviour and the role of women in shopping- A literature review. *Research journal of social science and management.* 7, 50.

49. Lee, L. (2013). The emotional shopper: Assessing the effectiveness of retail therapy. *Foundations and Trends in Marketing,* 8(2), 69-145.

50. Lee, L. & Bottger, T. M. (2017). The therapeutic utility of shopping: Retail therapy, emotion regulation, and well-being. *The Routledge Companion to Consumer Behavior.*

51. lifestyleasia.com (2019). *Eat, shop, love: 7 beautiful store where you can indulge in both retail therapy & food.* Lifetsyle Asia (April 30, 2019). Available at https://www. lifestyleasia.com/ind/culture/architecture/the-most-beautiful-stores-in-indian-to-shop-and-eat-at/.

52. Luomala, H. (1998). Self-regulation of negative moods in a consumption context. Irritation-, stress-, and dejection-alleviative self-gift behaviours in focus. *Vaasa: Universitas Wasaensis,*

53. Luomala, H. T. (1998). A mood-alleviative perspective on self-gift behaviors: Stimulating consumer behavior theory development. *Journal of Marketing Management*, 14, 109–132.

54. Luomala, H. T. (2001). Consumption as therapy: A phenomenological inquiry into mood-alleviative consumer behaviors. *Asia-Pacific Advances in Consumer Research,* 4.

55. Luomala, H. T. (2002). An empirical analysis of the practices and therapeutic power of mood-alleviative consumption in Finland. *Psychology & Marketing,* 19(10), 813-836.

56. Mandel, N., Rucker, D. D., Levav, J. & Galinsky, A. D. (2017). The compensatory consumer behaviour model: How self-discrepancies drive consumer behaviour. *Journal of Consumer Psychology*, 27(1), 133-146.

57. Mortimer, G., Bougoure, U. S. & Fazal-E-Hasan, S. (2015). Development and validation of the self-gifting consumer behaviour scale: The self-gifting consumer behaviour scale. *Journal of Consumer Behaviour*, 14(3), 165–179.

58. Nair, K. (2004). *Compensatory consumption among modern Indian women: A phenomenological exploration*, Submitted in partial fulfillment of post-graduate diploma in communications, Mudra Institute of Communications, Ahmedabad.

59. Noble, S., Griffith, D. & Adjei, M. (2006) Drivers of local merchant loyalty: Understanding the influence of gender on shopping motives. *Journal of Retailing*, 82, 177–188.

60. Otero-López, J. M. & Villardefrancos, E. (2013). Compulsive buying and the five factor model of personality: A facet analysis. *Personality and Individual Differences,* 55, 585-590.

61. Paul, S. (2017). Americans spend $1,652 per year on retail therapy (December 6, 2017), available at https://nypost.com/2017/12/06/americans-spend-1652-per-year-on-retail-therapy/.

62. Penley, J., Tomaka, J. & Wiebe, J. (2002). The association of coping to physical and psychological health outcomes: A meta-analytic review. *Journal of Behavioral Medicine,* 25(6), 551-603.

63. Pervin, L. A. (2006). *The science of personality.* (3rd ed.), New York: Oxford University Press.

64. Rai, K. A., Joseph, A. S. & Mayya, S. (2018). Shopping is a serious affair: Alleviating negative emotions through retail therapy. *IOSR Journal of Business and Management (IOSR-JBM),* 1-7.

65. Reyhle, N. (2014). *The history of retail shopping: A millennium of change.* Retail Minded.com (January, 2014).

66. Rick, S. I., Pereira, B. & Burson, K. A. (2014). The benefits of retail therapy: Making purchase decisions reduces residual sadness. *Journal of Consumer Psychology*, 24(3), 373-380.

67. Rook, D. W. & Fisher, R. J. (1995). Trait and normative aspects of impulsive buying behavior. *Journal of Consumer Research*, 22 (3), 305-13.

68. Ruchika (2014). Burdens and benefits of empirical research. UK Dissertations. Available at http://www.ukdissertations.in/blog/burdens-and-benefits-of-empirical-research/

69. Sadr, M. M. (2016). The role of personality traits predicting emotion regulation strategies. *International Academic Journal of Humanities*, 3(4), 13-24.

70. Sharma, G., Mahendru, M. & Singh, S. (2011). Impact of organized retail on the economy of Punjab. *Global Journal of Management and Business Research*, 11(2), 94-102.

71. Sheth, K. K. & Vital, l. (2007). *India: Shopping with the family.* The McKinsey Quarterly, 74-5.

72.   Singh, S. (2017). Indian women and compensatory consumption: A confirmatory factor analysis approach. *International Journal of Engineering Technology Science and Research (IJETSR)*, 4(9), 19-31.

73.   Sinha, P. K. & Uniyal, D. P. (2005). Using observational research for behavioral segmentation of shoppers. *Journal of Retailing and Consumer Services*, 12(1), 35-48.

74.   Solanki, H. K., Kaur, A., Das, M., Awasthi, S. & Jain, S. (2019). Coping mechanism used by homemakers in Kumaon region (Uttarakhand, India) to deal with stress in their day-to-day life. *Journal of Family Medicine and Primary Care*, 1138-1144.

75.   Solomon, M. R. (2011). *Consumer behavior: Buying, having, and being.* Global Edition. Pearson, 14(2), 116-124.

76.   Son, J. & Chang, H. J. J. (2016). Retail therapy: What makes you feel relieved and happy? In the *Blending Cultures, International Textile and Apparel Association (ITAA) Annual Conference Proceedings*, 2016.

77.   Srinivasan, M. (2013). *Differences on women rights and choice between the US, India and the-Middle-East,* available at https://www.esamskriti.com/e/National-Affairs/Current-Affairs/Differences-on-women-colon-s-rights-and-choice-between-the-US,-India-and-the-Middle-East-1.aspx.

78.   Srivastava, C., Sternquist, B. & Mahi, H. (2012). Organized retailing in India-Upstream channel structure and management. *Journal of Business and Industrial Marketing*, 27(3), 176-195.

79.   Suls, J. & Martin, R. (2005). The daily life of the garden-variety neurotic: Reactivity, stressor exposure, mood spillover, and maladaptive coping. *Journal of Personality,* 73, 1485–509.

80.   Surendran, J. & Vardhan, R. (2014). Retail therapy: Understanding the phenomenon to improve customer experience. Available at http://tejas.iimb.ac.in/articles/Tejas_ December%20Edition_Article%204.pdf

81.   *Surveys, advantages and disadvantages of,* The SAGE Encyclopedia of Communication Research Methods, (Ed.) Allen, Mike. Sage Publications. DOI-https://dx.doi.org/ 10.4135/9781483381411.n616.

82. Tanwar, S., Kaushik, N. & Kaushik, V. K. (2011). Retail malls: New mantra for success. *Sri Krishna International Research & Educational Consortium*, 2, 103-113.

83. Tata Strategic Management group (2013). *Well-being and female security indices.*

84. Underhill, P. (1999). *Why we buy: The science of shopping.* New York: Simon & Shuster.

85. Urkmez, T. & Wagner, R. (2016). Retail therapy: A European perspective on buying luxury items. *Paper presented in the Marketing Trends Conference, Venice*, January 2012-13.

86. Valsan, S. & Bhola, S. (2014). *Retail reality in India: Evolution and potential. A comparison and contrast with the emerging cities of Asia.* Retailers association of India. Published by Jones Lang LaSalle.

87. Vollrath, M. (2001). Personality and stress. *Scandavian Journal of Psychology*, 42, 335–47

88. Woodruffe, H. (1996). Methodological issues in consumer research: Towards a feminist perspective. *Marketing Intelligence & Planning*, 14, 13-18.

89. Woodruffe, H. (1997). Compensatory consumption: Why women go shopping when they're fed up and other stories. *Marketing Intelligence & Planning*, 15(7), 325-334.

90. Woodruffe, H. (1998). Private desires, public display: Consumption, postmodernism and fashion's "New Man". *International Journal of Retail & Distribution Management,* 26(8), 301-310.

91. Woodruffe, H. (2001). *Retail therapy: An investigation of compensatory consumption and shopping behavior*, Thesis submitted to Lancaster University for the Degree of Doctor of Philosophy (Phd).

92. Yarrow, K. (2013). *Is retail therapy for real? 5 ways shopping is actually good for you.* Business.time.com (April 16, 2013).

93.   Yurchisin, J., Yan, R. N., Watchravesringkan, K. & Chen, C. (2006). Why retail therapy? A preliminary investigation of the role of liminality, self-esteem, negative emotions, and proximity of clothing to self in the compensatory consumption of apparel products. *Psychology*, 60(6), 895-910.

94.   Yurchisin, J., Yan, R., Watchravesringkan, K. & Chen, C. (2008). Investigating the role of life status changes and negative emotions in compensatory consumption among college students. *College Student Journal*, 42(3), 860-868.

POSTFACE-
Retail Therapy and the Covid-19 Era

Postface

POSTFACE

RETAIL THERAPY AND THE COVID-19 ERA

The present research study has brought forward the popularity of retail therapy, as a shopping behavior, among Indian women and has furthered the research in this field by analyzing its relationship with the personality variables, shopping orientation and also impulse buying tendency. Some of the unique therapeutic shopping behavior aspects of Indian women have also been highlighted, which retailers and marketers are expected to take care of while trying to target them. The study has been limited to therapy shopping in physical retail spaces. Even though, in today's time, online shopping is also catching much attention of therapy shoppers; it has, nevertheless, been decided to be covered in a separate research study in future.

The analysis clearly highlights as to how most of the Indian women therapy shoppers prefer to go to malls and even traditional bazaars for meeting their therapeutic needs. Like women in western countries, they also like to go out to different stores, explore items, try them on, buy self-gifts, and shop on impulse when they are in a down mood. Based on the findings, some important implications for different stakeholders including researchers, retailers/marketers and consumers have also been indicated, while summarizing this thesis. However, given the present situation (The Covid-19 Era) that has occurred just at the brink of submission of this thesis, it has been felt extremely obligatory to add few words as to how this is expected to affect the retail industry, mall culture and the consumer behavior scenario in the post COVID-19 epoch.

As a matter of fact, the Corona pandemic has not left any sector or section of world to be unaffected. The whole economic system has been traumatized. Many people have lost their jobs and many others are at the verge of it (Sharma, 2020- CMIE Report). With the fear of catching the disease or being affected by it, people are confining themselves to the four walls of their homes only. They are moving out only for urgent work and that too under extreme fear and anxiety. Buying is also happening, but only for the essentials. Industry Experts are predicting a good long time for the normal life to happen (Retailers Association of India, 2020).

226

Given this scenario, it is anticipated that, at least, therapeutic kind of shopping might not happen for a while. People might not choose to go out for buying non-essential items and rather prioritize their needs and buy accordingly (Rajesh, 2020- thehindubusinessline.com). Malls and retail stores are anticipating much reduced footfalls, at least, for six months post Covid-19. A recent survey report by the Retailers Association of India (2020) has highlighted that most of the non-food retailers have huge piled up stocks and their revenue has fallen down to almost nothing. In order to re-establish their business, retailers may take some actions in the form of restricting to short-term plans, reallocating budget, going for Omni channel presence etc. (Forum Gandhi, 2020- thehindubusinessline.com).

Within this negative set-up, a ray of hope is that, given the human nature of 'moving on', it is expected that once people get freed from the corona fear, they will certainly rush towards these stores again (Rajesh, 2020- thehindubusinessline.com). Their shopping behavior is bound to change in the post pandemic time; however, this is never likely to lead to an end to experiential shopping. People are certain to come out, visit stores and seek therapy. They might increase their buying on internet, but for experiential satisfaction, they shall undoubtedly prefer brick-and-mortar over online shopping. This would also, at the same time, increase responsibility of these stores to serve their customers with much safer yet pleasing environment (Rajesh, 2020- thehindubusinessline.com; Andrew, 2020- Forbes.com).

The whole retail scene is, in fact, expected to change with the onset of new procedures including contact-free payment system, checkout-free retail and adoption of BOPIS (buy online pickup in stores) etc. (Walton, 2020- Forbes.com). In addition, with focus on improved services; employee engagement is expected to be the bottom-line of every retail business. With adaption to this 'New Normal', the industry is anticipated to find an 'oasis' in the mighty 'desert' engendered by COVID-19 (Amritsar Tribune, May 20, 2020).

REFERENCES

1. Amritsar Tribune (2020). *Webinar on new normal in travel, tourism industries,* dated May 21, 2020.

2. Andrew, B. (2020). *How can retail survive in the post coronavirus era? Five practical steps.* Forbes.com, dated May 10, 2020.

3. Forum Gandhi (2020). *Taking stock: How retailers are preparing for post Covid-19 era.* Business line, dated April 20, 2020, available at thehindubusiness line.com.

4. *Managing the sandstorm of Covid-19 over 'THAR' Desert (2020).* Webinar 2.0 organized by University Business School,. Guru Nanak Dev University, Amritsar, on May 20, 2020.

5. Rajesh, V. (2020). *The retail sector outlook post Covid-19.* Business Line, dated May 11, 2020, available at thehindubusinessline.com.

6. Retailers association of India (2020). *Survey on impact of COVID-19 on Indian retail.*

7. Sharma, Y. S. (2020). *27 million youth in age group of 20-30 years lost jobs in April: CMIE,* dated May 13, 2020, economictimes.com.

8. Walton, C. (2020). *The domino effect: 5 ways coronavirus will forever change retail,* dared April 1, 2020, Forbes.com.

BIBLIOGRAPHY

BIBLIOGRAPHY

1. Burnett, M. S. & Lunsford, D. A. (1994). Conceptualizing guilt in the consumer decision-making process. *Journal of Consumer Marketing*, 11(3), 33-43.

2. Chen, T. & Lee, M. C. (2015). Personality antecedents of online buying impulsiveness. *Journal of Economics, Business and Management*, 3(4), 425-429.

3. Cryder, C. E., Lerner, J. S., Gross, J. J. & Dahl, R. E. (2008). Misery is not miserly: Sad and self-focused individuals spend more. *Psychological Science*, 19(6), 525–530.

4. Han, S., Lerner, J. S. & Keltner, D. (2007). Feelings and consumer decision making: The appraisal-tendency framework. *Journal of Consumer Psychology*, 17(3), 158–168.

5. Isen, A. M. (2000). Some perspectives on positive affect and self-regulation. *Psychological Inquiry*, 11, 184-187.

6. Kaur, J. & Kaur, C. (2013). Customers' perception towards service quality delivery in retail malls in the Punjab. *Envision- International Journal of Commerce and Management* (An annual journal of Apeejay College of Fine Arts, Jalandhar), 7, ISSN: 0973-5976.

7. Kaur, J. & Kaur, C. (2013). FDI in Indian retailing sector-Boon or bane (retails marketers & retails customers' perspective). Presented at National Seminar on Indian Economy in the Post Reform Era, April, 2013, by National Institute of Technology, Kurukshetra.

8. Kaur, J. & Kaur, C. (2013). *The reality show of modern competitive retail mall culture.* Paper presented in 66th All India Commerce Conference, held on December 5-7, 2013, at Bangalore University, Bangalore.

9. Kaur, J. & Kaur, C. (2016). Customer mall shopping behavior: A bibliometric analysis. *Indore Management Journal*, 8(1), January- June 2016 (ISSN 0975-1653).

10. Kaur, J. & Kaur, C. (2017). *Retail therapy shoppers: Exploring the differences in the personality, shopping orientation and impulse buying tendency.* Presented at IIM Indore- NASMEI Summer Marketing Conference, July, 2017.

11. Kaur, J. & Kaur, C. (2017). *Individual differences among therapy and non-therapy women shoppers: A segmentation approach.* Presented at 7th IIMA conference on Marketing in Emerging Economics, January, 2017.

12. Larsen, R. J. (2000). Toward a science of mood regulation. *Psychological Inquiry*, 11(3), 129 – 141.

13. Luomala, H. T., Kumar, R., Worm, V. & Singh, J. D. (2004). Cross-cultural differences in mood regulation: An empirical comparison of individualistic and collectivistic cultures. *Journal of International Consumer Marketing*, 16(4), 39-62.

14. Pelau, C., Serban, D. & Chinie, A. C. (2018). The influence of personality types on the impulsive buying behavior of a consumer, *Proceedings of the 12th International Conference on Business Excellence*, 751-759.

15. Plastow, M. (2012).Retail therapy- The enjoyment of the consumer. *British Journal of Psychotherapy*, 28(2), 204–220.

16. Raghunattan, R. & Pham, M. T. (1999). All negative moods are not equal: Motivational influences of anxiety, and sadness on decision making. *Organizational Behaviour and Human Decision Processes*, 79(1), 56 – 77.

17. Rajnish, J. & Shilpa, B. (2011). Music and consumption experience: A review. *International Journal of Retail and Distribution Management*, 39(4), 289-302.

18. Rook, D. W. & Gardner, M. P. (1993). In the mood: Impulse buying's affective antecedents. *Research in Consumer Behaviour*, In Costa, J. A., & Belk, R. W., (Eds.), Greenwich, Jal Press, 6, 1-28.

19. Wertheim, E. H. & Schwarz, J. C. (1983). Depression, guilt, self management of pleasant and unpleasant events. *Journal of Personality and Social Psychology*, 45(4), 884-889.

ANNEXURES

SHOPPING BEHAVIOR SURVEY

CONSENT FORM

Greetings! You are invited to participate in this shopping behavior survey. This research is being conducted by CHANDANDEEP KAUR, a doctoral student in the University Business School (UBS) of Guru Nanak Dev University, Amritsar. By participating in this survey, you are providing your consent for the inclusion of your data in this research study.

General Information:

1. The purpose of this research is to get an insight about the shopping behavior of women in India (in general and at the times when they use it for mood-alleviation).

2. It would take about 15 minutes to fill the questionnaire.

3. Any information shared by you will be kept completely confidential and used only for academic purposes.

4. There are no risks or benefits attached with your participation in this research.

5. Your participation in the survey is completely voluntary and you are free to withdraw at any time.

INSTRUCTIONS:

For the purpose of this survey,

Shopping shall *include* shopping for non-perishable consumer products e.g. clothing, accessories (*like handbags, belt, jewelry etc.*), shoes, cosmetics, home furnishings etc.

Shopping shall *exclude* grocery shopping or dining out and consuming any services *e.g. salon and spa, movies etc.*

Shopping may also *include* window shopping (i.e. browsing without buying).

SECTION A: MOOD AND SHOPPING

1. In a month, on an average, how often do you experience a negative mood (e.g. irritation/stress/depression etc.)?

   Never ☐   Rarely ☐   Sometimes ☐   Frequently ☐   Always ☐

2. Name any three activities you usually indulge in to cope with your negative mood state?
   1. _____
   2. _____
   3. _____

3. How often do you choose to go for shopping to up-lift your mood?

   Never ☐   Rarely ☐   Sometimes ☐   Frequently ☐   Always ☐

SECTION B: SHOPPING MOTIVATIONS AND BEHAVIOR

4. The following statements are related to your shopping motivations and your experiences during and after shopping. Please **circle** the number that most accurately indicates your level of agreement or disagreement with the given statement, where:

1	2	3	4	5	6	7
Strongly Disagree	Disagree	Somewhat Disagree	Neutral	Somewhat Agree	Agree	Strongly Agree

	Statements	Strongly Disagree			Neutral			Strongly Agree
1	I shop to relieve my stress.	1	2	3	4	5	6	7
2	I shop to cheer myself up.	1	2	3	4	5	6	7

	Statements	Strongly Disagree			Neutral		Strongly Agree	
3	I shop to make myself feel better.	1	2	3	4	5	6	7
4	I shop to compensate for a bad day.	1	2	3	4	5	6	7
5	I shop to feel relaxed.	1	2	3	4	5	6	7
6	I shop to feel good about myself.	1	2	3	4	5	6	7
7	Shopping is a positive distraction.	1	2	3	4	5	6	7
8	Shopping gives me a sense of achievement.	1	2	3	4	5	6	7
9	I like the visual stimulation shopping provides.	1	2	3	4	5	6	7
10	Shopping provides me with knowledge of new styles.	1	2	3	4	5	6	7
11	I enjoy being in a pleasant environment that shopping provides.	1	2	3	4	5	6	7
12	Finding a great deal reinforces positive feelings about myself.	1	2	3	4	5	6	7
13	Shopping is an escape from loneliness.	1	2	3	4	5	6	7
14	Shopping is a way to remove myself from stressful environment.	1	2	3	4	5	6	7
15	Shopping is a way to take my mind off things that are bothering me.	1	2	3	4	5	6	7
16	Shopping for something new fills an empty feeling.	1	2	3	4	5	6	7
17	Shopping is a way to control things when other things seem out of control.	1	2	3	4	5	6	7
18	My shopping trip to relieve my bad mood is successful.	1	2	3	4	5	6	7
19	After a shopping trip to make myself feel better, the good feelings generated last at least for the rest of the day.	1	2	3	4	5	6	7
20	I feel good immediately after my shopping trip to relieve a bad mood.	1	2	3	4	5	6	7
21	I use items I bought during my shopping to relieve a bad mood.	1	2	3	4	5	6	7
22	When I use items I bought during my shopping to relieve my bad mood, I remember the shopping experience.	1	2	3	4	5	6	7

5. The following set of statements is related to your general orientation/attitude towards shopping. Think about each statement and <u>circle</u> the number that most accurately indicates your level of agreement or disagreement with the given statement, where:

1	2	3	4	5	6	7
Strongly Disagree	Disagree	Somewhat Disagree	Neutral	Somewhat Agree	Agree	Strongly Agree

	Statements	Strongly Disagree		Neutral		Strongly Agree		
1	When shopping, I often have fun.	1	2	3	4	5	6	7
2	When shopping, I try to get it over with as soon as possible (i.e. finish shopping as soon as possible).	1	2	3	4	5	6	7
3	When shopping, I act as deliberately and goal-focused as possible.	1	2	3	4	5	6	7
4	When shopping, I am usually looking for entertainment.	1	2	3	4	5	6	7
5	When shopping, I mainly carry out what I have planned.	1	2	3	4	5	6	7
6	I like to kill time (pass free time) by shopping.	1	2	3	4	5	6	7
7	When shopping, I like to browse around.	1	2	3	4	5	6	7

6. The following set of statements is related to your buying behavior. Think about each statement and <u>circle</u> the number that most accurately indicates your level of agreement or disagreement with the given statement, where:

1	2	3	4	5	6	7
Strongly Disagree	Disagree	Somewhat Disagree	Neutral	Somewhat Agree	Agree	Strongly Agree

	Statements	Strongly Disagree		Neutral		Strongly Agree		
1	I often buy things spontaneously.	1	2	3	4	5	6	7
2	"Just do it" describes the way I buy things.	1	2	3	4	5	6	7
3	I often buy things without thinking.	1	2	3	4	5	6	7
4	"I see it, I buy it" describes me.	1	2	3	4	5	6	7
5	"Buy now, think about it later" describes me.	1	2	3	4	5	6	7
6	Sometimes I feel like buying things on the spur of the moment.	1	2	3	4	5	6	7

	Statements	Strongly Disagree			Neutral			Strongly Agree
7	I buy things according to how I feel at the moment.	1	2	3	4	5	6	7
8	I carefully plan most of my purchases.	1	2	3	4	5	6	7
9	Sometimes, I am bit reckless/careless about what I buy.	1	2	3	4	5	6	7

SECTION C: PERSONALITY TRAITS

7. The following set of statements is related to your personality. Think about each statement and <u>circle</u> the number that most accurately indicates your level of agreement or disagreement with the given statement, where:

1	2	3	4	5	6	7
Strongly Disagree	Disagree	Somewhat Disagree	Neutral	Somewhat Agree	Agree	Strongly Agree

	Statements	Strongly Disagree			Neutral			Strongly Agree
1	I am the life of the party (/ center of attraction at any social gathering)	1	2	3	4	5	6	7
2	I sympathize with others' feelings (/ understand their sentiments)	1	2	3	4	5	6	7
3	I get chores done right away.	1	2	3	4	5	6	7
4	I have frequent mood swings.	1	2	3	4	5	6	7
5	I have a vivid imagination (/able to imagine clear ideas and images).	1	2	3	4	5	6	7
6	I don't talk a lot.	1	2	3	4	5	6	7
7	I am not interested in other people's problems.	1	2	3	4	5	6	7
8	I often forget to put things back in their proper place.	1	2	3	4	5	6	7
9	I am relaxed most of the time.	1	2	3	4	5	6	7
10	I am not interested in abstract ideas (i.e. things that are visualized and not physically present e.g. an emotion, hypothesis, culture etc.).	1	2	3	4	5	6	7
11	I talk to a lot of different people at parties.	1	2	3	4	5	6	7
12	I feel others' emotions.	1	2	3	4	5	6	7

	Statements	Strongly Disagree			Neutral			Strongly Agree
13	I like order (Organization and discipline).	1	2	3	4	5	6	7
14	I get upset easily.	1	2	3	4	5	6	7
15	I have difficulty understanding abstract ideas.	1	2	3	4	5	6	7
16	I keep in the background.	1	2	3	4	5	6	7
17	I am not really interested in others.	1	2	3	4	5	6	7
18	I make a mess of things.	1	2	3	4	5	6	7
19	I seldom feel blue (/rarely feel depressed)	1	2	3	4	5	6	7
20	I do not have a good imagination.	1	2	3	4	5	6	7

SECTION D: THERAPY SHOPPING TRIP BEHAVIOR

INSTRUCTIONS   **(Please read first and then proceed)**

For answering to this section, think about any shopping trip/trips when you go for shopping *to uplift a sad or depressed mood, or to cheer yourself up when feeling bored or lonely.*

Note: If you never choose shopping to alleviate your negative mood, kindly leave this section and proceed to the last section (i.e. Demographics).

8. a) **During any such shopping trip to cheer yourself up, whom do you like to accompany you? Please tick in the appropriate box.**

Friends ☐   Family ☐   No one (I like to shop alone) ☐

b) **Which products usually help you to get rid of sad mood and make you happy? Rank in case of multiple options, where rank 1 shall mean "most preferred".**

Items	Rank
Clothing	
Accessories (e.g. handbags, belt, watch, jewelry etc.)	
Shoes	
Home Furnishing	
Cosmetics	

(If any other, please specify) _____.

c) For whom do you mostly like to purchase during such shopping trip?

Myself ☐   Family ☐   Friends/Others ☐

d) What mode of payment do you often use for your purchases?

Cash ☐   Credit/Debit Cards/Others ☐

If any other, please specify_____.

e) How often do you make unplanned buying during your trip for mood-alleviation?

Never ☐   Rarely ☐   Sometimes ☐   Often ☐   Always ☐

f) Do you agree that you spend more than usual 'time' during a shopping trip to up-lift your mood?

Yes ☐   No ☐

g) Do you agree that you spend more than usual 'money' during a shopping trip to up-lift your mood?

Yes ☐   No ☐

h) Where do you mostly like to go for shopping when feeling sad/lonely/bored. Select and rank in case of multiple options, where rank 1 shall mean "most preferred".

Rank

	Rank
☐ Mall	
☐ Super/Hypermarket *(e.g. Big Bazaar, Hypercity, Vishal Mega Mart)*	
☐ Multi-brand retail stores *(e.g. Reliance Trends, Shoppers Stop, Lifestyle, etc.)*	
☐ Single-brand retail stores *(e.g. Adidas, Puma, Reebok, etc.)*	
☐ Traditional retail shops (/local bazaars)	

i) Throughout the whole process of shopping, what makes you feel most happy and relaxed? Select and rank in case of multiple options, where, rank 1= makes you most happy and relaxed.

S. no.	Items	Rank
1.	Thought of going for shopping	
2.	Store ambience (Music, Lighting, fragrance etc.)	
3.	Attractive visual display	

S. no.	Items	Rank
4.	Treatment and behavior of sales personnel	
5.	Crowd at the shopping place (/Watching other shoppers)	
6.	Getting knowledge of new fashion trends	
7.	Trying on items	
8.	Bargaining	
9.	Making an actual purchase	
10.	Using the items purchased	

SECTION E: DEMOGRAPHIC DETAILS

Name: _____

Age: _____

City: _____

E-mail ID: _____

Marital Status: Married ☐   Unmarried/Single/Divorced ☐

Education: Under-graduate ☐   Graduate ☐   Post-graduate ☐   Other ☐

Employment Status: Working ☐   Non-working/ Retired ☐

Occupation: Teacher ☐   Student ☐   Housewife ☐   Bank/Insurance ☐   Others ☐

Monthly Family Income: Less than INR 20,000 ☐   20,001-40,000 ☐   40,001-60,000 ☐

60,001-80,000 ☐   More than INR 80,000 ☐

Monthly Discretionary Income (free cash in your hand, after deducting all your necessary expenses like grocery, bills and other necessities etc.)

Less than INR 10,000 ☐   10,001-20,000 ☐   20,001-30,000 ☐   More than INR 30,000 ☐

Coding of Scale Items in SPSS 19.0 Software

I) Retail Therapy Scale:

	Statements	Coding
1	I shop to relieve my stress.	M1
2	I shop to cheer myself up.	M2
3	I shop to make myself feel better.	M3
4	I shop to compensate for a bad day.	M4
5	I shop to feel relaxed.	M5
6	I shop to feel good about myself.	M6
7	Shopping is a positive distraction.	V1
8	Shopping gives me a sense of achievement.	V2
9	I like the visual stimulation shopping provides.	V3
10	Shopping provides me with knowledge of new styles.	V4
11	I enjoy being in a pleasant environment that shopping provides.	V5
12	Finding a great deal reinforces positive feelings about myself.	V6
13	Shopping is an escape from loneliness.	V7
14	Shopping is a way to remove myself from stressful environment.	V8
15	Shopping is a way to take my mind off things that are bothering me.	V9
16	Shopping for something new fills an empty feeling.	V10
17	Shopping is a way to control things when other things seem out of control.	V11
18	My shopping trip to relieve my bad mood is successful.	O1
19	After a shopping trip to make myself feel better, the good feelings generated last at least for the rest of the day.	O2
20	I feel good immediately after my shopping trip to relieve a bad mood.	O3
21	I use items I bought during my shopping to relieve a bad mood.	O4
22	When I use items I bought during my shopping to relieve my bad mood, I remember the shopping experience.	O5

B) Chronic Shopping Orientation Scale:

	Statements	Coding
1	When shopping, I often have fun.	SO1
2	When shopping, I try to get it over with as soon as possible (i.e. finish shopping as soon as possible).	SO2
3	When shopping, I act as deliberately and goal-focused as possible.	SO3
4	When shopping, I am usually looking for entertainment.	SO4
5	When shopping, I mainly carry out what I have planned.	SO5
6	I like to kill time (pass free time) by shopping.	SO6
7	When shopping, I like to browse around.	SO7

C) Impulse Buying Tendency Scale:

	Statements	Coding
1	I often buy things spontaneously.	IB1
2	"Just do it" describes the way I buy things.	IB2
3	I often buy things without thinking.	IB3
4	"I see it, I buy it" describes me.	IB4
5	"Buy now, think about it later" describes me.	IB5
6	Sometimes I feel like buying things on the spur of the moment.	IB6
7	I buy things according to how I feel at the moment.	IB7
8	I carefully plan most of my purchases.	IB8
9	Sometimes, I am bit reckless/careless about what I buy.	IB9

D) Big-Five Personality Traits Scale:

	Statements	Coding
1	I am the life of the party.	P1
2	I sympathize with others' feelings.	P5
3	I get chores done right away.	P9
4	I have frequent mood swings.	P13
5	I have a vivid imagination.	P17
6	I don't talk a lot.	P2
7	I am not interested in other people's problems.	P6
8	I often forget to put things back in their proper place.	P10
9	I am relaxed most of the time.	P14
10	I am not interested in abstract ideas.	P18
11	I talk to a lot of different people at parties.	P3
12	I feel others' emotions.	P7
13	I like order.	P11
14	I get upset easily.	P15
15	I have difficulty understanding abstract ideas.	P19
16	I keep in the background.	P4
17	I am not really interested in others.	P8
18	I make a mess of things.	P12
19	I seldom feel blue.	P16
20	I do not have a good imagination.	P20

CPSIA information can be obtained
at www.ICGtesting.com
Printed in the USA
BVHW041538140423
662364BV00008B/526